Praise for *Attach*

"Trust me. This is the only baby book y
warming, and completely user-friendly. Just add your heart!"

—**Christiane Northrup, MD,** author of *Mother-Daughter Wisdom,
The Wisdom of Menopause,* and *Women's Bodies, Women's Wisdom*

"Attachment parenting has worked so well for our family, and I'm thrilled that more and more people are becoming familiar with the idea. *Attached at the Heart* will help acquaint parents with principles to ensure connected, confident children and provide them with tools they can use in every rela-tionship or endeavor in their adult lives. I have seen the benefits with my own children, and I hope you will find some words of wisdom and useful techniques in this wonderful book."

—**Melora Hardin,** actress,
plays Jan in the hit NBC show *The Office*

"No two babies are born the same—they come with no instructions and no guarantee, and yet parents are expected to raise perfect children every time! Parents have to rely on their instincts, but human instincts are intensely colored by our own childhood experiences of being raised—for better or for worse. . . . This thought-provoking anthology has been intelligently organized into eight principles that guide readers on a journey of discovery—sometimes reassuring and sometimes a reality check! The authors have managed to make a précis of academic research findings with a light touch and merge them with years of personal experience and of helping count-less parents through Attachment Parenting International (API). The depth of knowledge presented in Attached at the Heart allows readers to draw their own conclusions about how best to apply the information to their own personal circumstances. Attachment parenting is in many ways the practical application of my father's theory."

—**Sir Richard Bowlby, Bt,** son of Dr. John Bowlby, MD

"This is a wise and nurturing book for parents, helping them nurture their children according to their emotional and developmental need'
A much-needed guide to attuned parenting. I highly recommend it."

—**Harville Hendrix, PhD,** coauthor with Helen LaKelly Hunt,
Giving the Love That Heals: A Guide for Parents

"*Attached at the Heart* is the first book to present attachment theory in an accessible and contemporary way. Its eight principles are critical guideposts by which parents can light their way to a healthy relationship with their children."

—**Peggy O'Mara**, editor and publisher of
Mothering magazine

"*Attached at the Heart* is a breathtaking wake-up call for parents and children everywhere. With stunning acuity, scientific insight, and a rare passion, authors Barbara Nicholson and Lysa Parker unlock the keys to creating compassionate, connected families. The result is that there is truly no other parenting book that covers as much crucial ground as deeply, accessibly, and comprehensively as this one. The gift is that they have succeeded in writing a revolutionary book that offers a shining light for parents, and a huge impetus for positive, lasting change."

—**Lu Hanessian**, author of acclaimed memoir
Let the Baby Drive: Navigating the Road of New Motherhood
former NBC anchor/syndicated columnist and parent educator

"Here's the book that not only answers your questions about attachment parenting but includes the research that backs it up. *Attached at the Heart* is a gift for all of us looking for practical information on how to strengthen the emotional connections in our families, a powerful and undeniable influence toward achieving a compassionate world."

—**Marian Tompson**, cofounder of La Leche League International
Founder and president of Another Look at Breastfeeding and HIV/AIDS

"This is really quite a remarkable book. It's a veritable encyclopedia of attachment parenting. Hard to think of any area not covered, and hard to find any reference that's missing. The style is clear and from beginning to end suffused with the warmth and gentleness of the authors. *Attached at the Heart* will serve as a comprehensive reference resource for attachment-parenting parents who want to support their choices with the wide-ranging research that's out there, but hard to find in one place."

—**Elliott Barker, MD**, Forensic psychiatrist and founder of
the Canadian Society for the Prevention of Cruelty to Children (CSPCC)

"*Attached at the Heart* communicates an enormous spectrum of information that is valuable and inspirational to parents and professionals. It defines attachment parenting in the most comprehensive and profound way. *Attached at the Heart* is an indispensable primer for any new parent."

—Isabelle Fox, PhD,
Being There: The Benefits of a Stay-at-Home Parent

"Sometimes, we parents lose sight of just how important we are. *Attached at the Heart* is a loving reminder of how crucial mothers and fathers are to children—and to the human story. Nicholson and Parker have put together an accessible, to-the-point, and inspiring manual that offers practical ways to foster a sense of the sacred in the work of raising children."

—Enola Aird, director of the Motherhood Project,
former visiting scholar, Judge Baker Children's Center, Boston, MA

"*Attached at the Heart* is a marvelous guide to raising children. Everyone should read it, even those who are not parents. The book greatly surpasses the typical advice parents receive and offers insights to both new and experienced parents. It is filled with thoughtful recommendations for caregivers that help them understand and provide what babies need. I highly recommend it!"

—Darcia Narvaez, PhD, Department of Psychology professor at
University of Notre Dame, assistant provost of Faculty Affairs,
and editor of the *Journal of Moral Education*

"Just as the breastfeeding world changed its message from benefits of breastfeeding to the harm of not breastfeeding, the second edition of *Attached at the Heart* offers parents insight into the damage done to our children, our families, and our society by normative abusive parenting. Parents will read this book and understand how abusive parenting has been passed down for generations. Parents will get the help they need to break the cycle and create peaceful, loving families."

—Barbara A. Hotelling, MSN, WHNP-BC, LCCE, CD (DONA), IBCLC
Women's health nurse-practitioner and former chairwoman of the
Coalition for Improving Maternity Services (CIMS)

"In my mind, no two people anywhere on the planet have worked and sacrificed more than Barbara and Lysa to promote healthy and happy attachment relationships between mothers, fathers, and their infants. Their book provides careful and accurate if not cautious recommendations about infants and their caregivers that closely follow more balanced scientific findings—and not simply those that support their own personal philosophies or political agendas—a description accurately applied to more traditional medical authoritative associations.

I recommend their book without hesitation and with much enthusiasm."

—**James J. McKenna, PhD,** Edmund P. Joyce C.S.C. Chair in Anthropology, and Director, Mother-Baby Behavioral Sleep Laboratory, University of Notre Dame

Attached
at the
Heart

Attached
at the
Heart

Eight Proven Parenting Principles for Raising Connected *and* Compassionate Children

(From Preconception to Age 5)

REVISED and UPDATED

Barbara Nicholson & Lysa Parker

Praeclarus
Press

PraeclarusPress.com

www.PraeclarusPress.com

Praeclarus Press, LLC
2504 Sweetgum Lane
Amarillo, Texas 79124 USA
806-367-9950

www.PraeclarusPress.com

DISCLAIMER
The information contained in this publication is advisory only and is not intended to replace sound clinical judgment or individualized patient care. The author disclaims all warranties, whether expressed or implied, including any warranty as the quality, accuracy, safety, or suitability of this information for any particular purpose.

ISBN: 9781946665454

We dedicate this book to
our beloved husbands and children,
for the encouragement and sacrifices they made
to help make API and this book possible:

Gary Nicholson and Jim Parker

Nathan, Travis, Adam, and Luke Nicholson

Jesse and Jamison Parker

You taught us the power of love.

ಬಜ

In loving memory of
Max Ellendorff and Betty Pearce Lowery

"We need to give birth to a new vision of parenting. This vision would be based on what we know about the special bond between parent and child, through which even ordinary communication is a sacrament. It would be based on reverence for what our children can bring to us, as well as what we can bring to them. By their light, we see what is hurt and hidden in ourselves, and we open creatively to new ways of responding to problems. Through them, we understand that parenting is a spiritual process in which we get back tenfold the love we give."

—**Harville Hendrix, PhD,** and **Helen Hunt, PhD,**
Giving the Love That Heals: A Guide for Parents

Contents

Foreword

Why has attachment parenting, the most time-honored and widespread parenting style in the world, recently been portrayed as "extreme" and "guilt-producing," according to *Time* magazine (May 21, 2012)? *Attachment parenting* is a term we coined in the mid-1980s, after years of observing families in our pediatric practice. This natural, intuitive style of child care is as old as birth itself. Yet, like many methods of child rearing, it has been the subject of confusion and misinterpretation by some psychologists and even a few pediatricians. Perhaps the simplest way to explain attachment parenting is to imagine that Mom and Dad are in a remote part of the world and birthing their first baby. There would be no advisors around, such as baby books, well-meaning friends and family, pediatricians, or psychologists. They would have only their own personal resources to care for that baby. Attachment parenting is what they would do instinctively. For instance, the baby would be breastfed, comforted when crying, and kept close to the parents for protection.

As parents of eight and with a long-standing medical practice, we believe that the Western style of parenting—a more detached style—is the extreme and unusual. Our society is sick, emotionally and physically, and at all ages. So-called adult onset diseases, those illnesses that used to occur only in older adults, are now occurring in youngsters. We have an epidemic of "D's" among our school-age children: OCD, BPD, ASD, ADD, and the big "D"—diabetes. Another "D" that concerns me as a doctor who cares about the future of our children is that more children are being drugged for more illnesses than at any other time in history. Isn't it about time we rethink the nutritional and emotional start we give our infants? In our books, *The Attachment Parenting Book* and *The Baby Book*, we coined the term *attachment parenting* to describe a high-touch style of baby care using what we call the "Seven Baby B's" to bring out the best in parents and their children. It was also an attempt to help parents rediscover the importance of their own intuitive knowledge and the empathetic care of infants after decades of detachment advice.

One of the most devastating pieces of detachment advice is from the "let 'em cry it out" crowd, which encourages new parents to let their baby cry so he or she won't get spoiled and will learn to "self-soothe." Experiments that were performed decades ago showed that when a mother was hooked up to measuring devices in a laboratory and she heard her baby cry, the blood flow to her breasts increased and she had a biological urge to comfort her baby in response. However, teaching a mother to let her baby cry it out desensitizes a mother precisely when an increase in mutual sensitivity between a mother-infant pair is most desired. This is why, in our teachings on attachment parenting, we say the only person in the whole world who knows if and how long to let her baby cry is the one who shared an umbilical cord with the baby—the mother.

The biggest difference we have noticed over the last forty years with the children in our practice is the quality of empathy. Attachment parenting raises connected kids, kids who care—the cornerstone of a more compassionate society. Attachment-parenting mothers and fathers learn to develop their ability to empathize with the baby and ask themselves, "If I were my baby, how would I want my mother or father to react?" Moreover, they nearly always get it right. For example, a baby wakes up crying at 3:00 AM. An attuned mother naturally imagines, "If I were my baby, would I want to be left alone to cry myself back to sleep? Or would I want to be consoled and helped to go back to sleep by someone I trust?" Gradually, the mother (or father) learns whether to respond quickly or to wait just a bit, assessing the baby's age and temperament accordingly. When parents understand the starter tools of attachment parenting, they will develop sensitivity toward their baby about how to nurture and discipline. This attunement comes from on-the-job training, not from outside experts.

How do we reverse the perception that attachment parenting is extreme and guilt-producing? *Attached at the Heart* takes a giant step in moving this discussion forward by painting the big picture, asking the tough questions, and getting the research into the hands of parents so they can make the best decisions for themselves, their babies, and their young children. Parents need principles for optimum child development. Eight such principles are offered in this book with numerous scientific studies to support them.

These principles, which were influenced by the "Baby B's" of attachment parenting from our previously mentioned books, are intended to guide parents. The principles are designed to build trust in the baby and trust in the mother so that her responses will fit her baby's needs. They are tools, not rules. Each mother-baby pair will work out the details as the relationship develops and as Mom and Dad grow into their roles as parents. Along with providing the Eight Principles of Parenting, *Attached at the Heart* gives you the understanding of why raising empathetic human beings is the most important job in the world.

—Dr. William and Martha Sears, January 2013

Preface

If we are to reach real peace in this world
and if we are to carry on a real war against war, we shall
have to begin with children; and if they will grow up in their natural
innocence, we won't have to struggle; we won't have to pass
fruitless idle resolutions, but we shall go from love to love and
peace to peace, until at last all the corners of the world are
covered with that peace and love for which consciously or
unconsciously the whole world is hungering.

—Mahatma Gandhi

More than fifteen years ago, we hatched our idea to "save the world." We were and remain hopelessly optimistic (with occasional bouts of despair) that we, as individuals, can effect change in our society. Both of us are parents—with six sons between us—and we were both teachers with experience on the front lines, which gave us the perspective, determination, and passion to begin a grassroots nonprofit organization called Attachment Parenting International (API).

Why did we do it? When we were new mothers, we felt insecure about our abilities. We didn't feel knowledgeable or prepared, even though we read just about every book we could get our hands on. We both lived far from other family members, so when we became friends, we held on to each other for support. We also found support and education from our local La Leche League, a group that teaches new mothers how to breastfeed.

Our experience with La Leche League prepared us in so many ways and provided us with opportunities to learn from other, more experienced mothers. These experiences gave us much-needed confidence and skills. At these monthly meetings, we first learned about attachment parenting and read books by husband-and-wife team William Sears, MD, and Martha Sears, RN. Their books were like a buoy in the ocean—guiding our way and helping us keep our sanity by reassuring us that we were doing the right thing. In time, we learned to trust our own innate wisdom and mothering instincts, which allowed us to connect with our children in ways that we would never have thought possible. Of course, we made a lot of mistakes along the way—just ask our sons. But the fact is that we are better for the experience, and our children are better for it, too.

In the early 1990s, we began to read about kids killing kids and kids killing their parents. What in the world was happening to these children that would cause them to commit such heinous crimes? Then we read a book called *High Risk: Children Without a Conscience* by Ken Magid and Carol McKelvey. This was the first time we learned about Dr. John Bowlby and *attachment theory*, which hypothesized that the lack of emotional connection created all kinds of emotional and social problems, including violence.

The work of Alice Miller awakened our awareness of the influences of culture on the treatment of children. Until we come to terms with how we were treated as children, we will continue to perpetuate the same attitudes and treatment with our own children. The culture in which we live has tremendous power over us, and it takes consistent and conscious efforts to go upstream against the current of popular opinion. Dr. Miller made it her mission to abolish corporal punishment in every country because she believed that is the only way we can begin to move forward in eliminating violence toward children.

Given all this information and from our own experiences, we knew in our heart of hearts that attachment parenting was the key to creating emotional connections and making families stronger. We believe that if parents are given good information about why it is so important to nurture children, the tools to do so, and parent groups that support them in their choices, then we will have more empowered mothers and fathers and a lot less violence and dysfunction in the world. Renowned anthropologist Margaret Mead once said, "Never doubt that a small group of thoughtful, committed people can change the world. Indeed, it is the only thing that ever has." We see evidence that parents are beginning to create a paradigm shift in child rearing.

We began going to the library (this was before the Internet was widely used) and spending hours researching and reading articles, books, and magazines from as far back as the 1940s. Days soon turned into months and months into years. We called anyone we thought would give us advice or information, and many were more than happy to talk to us. They shared their wisdom and encouraged us along the way. *Attached at the Heart* is the culmination of more than fifteen years of information gathering, investigative research, and practice. We believe that it is critical for parents to have this information to make informed decisions for their children in our increasingly complex society. Until recently, we have heavily relied on and trusted others to know what is best for our children. We can no longer rely on others; we have to educate ourselves and rely on our own knowledge of our children.

Since the early 1990s, the world seems to have become worse, not better —even more violent and chaotic. People are looking for answers, for something they can do to change this direction, because we can no longer rely on politics and governments. Many realize that it has to begin with each individual and within each family.

The intent of our book is to give you practical answers to everyday problems and to raise your awareness in the hope that you might be more conscious and purposeful in interactions with your children. Unless we understand why we do what we do, we will undoubtedly continue the same practices, whether they make sense or not. We will be vulnerable to the advice of others who may say things with authority but without any basis for backing up their advice. This book will give you the evidence you need to feel confident in your decisions.

Attachment parenting is an idea whose time has come, supported by a worldwide organization of education, support, advocacy, and research.

What began at the kitchen table as a simple idea to support parents in this new way of parenting has grown into a worldwide network of parent support groups, a comprehensive support-group leadership training program, and a new curriculum. It also serves as a national clearinghouse of research and information for parents and professionals. A nonprofit organization founded in 1994, API offers parents information, education, and support to help them in their parenting journeys from preconception through the teen years and to strengthen their relationships with their children. The basic principles of attachment parenting are a blueprint for change and are discussed in *Attached at the Heart*. Rooted in sound science and common sense, these principles provide a framework of an overarching belief—*listen to your baby and trust your instincts!*

We have learned that every family is unique with unique circumstances and that there is no such thing as perfect parents. We always carry with us the legacy of the generations before us. The way we were parented and the wounds that we carry inevitably work their way into our interactions with our children, which is why it's so important to consciously work on those issues. As you read our book, please know that the principles are not intended to be standards of perfection but rather to be used as guidelines to help you feel informed, validated, supported, and confident in your child-rearing decisions. It's so important to base your daily decisions on what will strengthen your attachment with your baby (or child), given the current circumstances. Ask yourself, *Will this strengthen my connection with my baby?*

When you're faced with a situation that is not ideal but necessary, ask yourself what you can do to minimize the impact of the situation on your baby and what you can do to reconnect with your baby or young child. Enjoy your baby, knowing that the love you give will come back to you in more ways than you can imagine for generations to come.

Acknowledgments

The principles described in this book are based on the Sears's Baby B's, reworked and clearly defined with the collective effort of many parents actively involved with API—support group leaders, many of whom are professionals in social work, psychology, or child development; lactation consultants; childbirth educators; and advisory and other board members, including Martha Sears. Many wise women and men contributed to our book in direct and indirect ways, and to them we will always be indebted.

First, we want to thank everyone at HCI Publishing and Tonya Woodworth our extraordinary editor, for believing in our work and the important legacy of attachment parenting in creating a better world. We are forever grateful to our agent, Nancy Rosenfeld and her unwavering support, compassion and enthusiasm.

We also wish to thank our advisory board members, who recognized early the importance of our mission and lent us their moral and professional support:

Elliott Barker, MD, founder of the Canadian Society for the Prevention of Cruelty to Children (CSPCC), without whose initial encouragement we probably would never have started API.

Elizabeth Baldwin, JD (deceased), who provided us with legal advice in our formative years and the courage to keep going.

Stephen Bavolek, PhD, researcher, parent educator, and principal author of the Nurturing Parenting Programs, whose experience and wise counsel has been instrumental in moving us forward from a "mom-and-pop" organization to one of professionalism based on research.

Sir Richard Bowlby, Bt, the son of Dr. John Bowlby, attachment advocate, friend, and ally, whose support and encouragement is a powerful validation of the work of API.

Barbara Clinton, MSW, director of the Center for Health Services at Vanderbilt University, who has always been there for us with her professional and motherly wisdom; she is our staunchest cheerleader and dear friend.

Isabelle Fox, PhD, psychotherapist, our tireless "ambassador" for API, friend, motivator, and role model of determination and fearlessness.

Jan Hunt, MS, author, founder of the Natural Child Project, friend, and strong advocate for children and families.

Alice Miller, PhD (deceased), author, therapist, and child advocate, for her pioneering work in awakening our collective conscience to the damage that has been done to children "for their own good." She has given us the missionary zeal we needed to fully engage in our roles as parents and as professionals to get this urgent message out to the world.

James McKenna, PhD, friend, outstanding researcher, and fearless advocate for the rights of parents and their babies.

Peggy O'Mara, editor of *Mothering* magazine, our friend and sister in this cause.

Bruce Perry, PhD, MD, strong voice for abused and traumatized children, whose eloquent words have given new awareness to the plight of children.

Raffi, singer, songwriter, recording artist, author, and children's troubadour, whose passion for children and his mission to promote the importance of honoring children has been a shining example to us and to all parents.

William Sears, MD, and Martha Sears, RN, whose work has given us and millions of parents the ability to see children in a new way and to be better parents. They have stuck with us through thick and thin, providing encouragement and advice when we most needed it. Thank you for being there for us.

Michael Trout, MA, director and founder of the Infant-Parent Institute, an early supporter and mentor who has always been there for us. Your work has been an inspiration.

Karen Walant, PhD, author, psychotherapist, and support-group leader who practices what she preaches in her family and in her work. We thank you for your years of support, encouragement, and friendship.

We want to thank our tireless operating board members, past and present, our staff, and our early supporters, for without their constant hand-holding, encouragement, and dedication, API would have folded up its tent long ago: Julie Artz, Miranda Barone, Rita Brhel, Zan Buckner, Kate Byrne, Adrienne Carmack, Beth Nielsen Chapman, Dave and Perry Clennon, Bill Corbett, Melissa Corbett, Carlotta Crawford, Mary Elizabeth Curtner-Smith, Avril Dannenbaum, Kathy and Joe Diaz, Linda Dicus, Lisa Dietlin, Don Duke, Laura Duke, Susan Esserman-Schack, Christy Farr, Lisa Feiertag, Karen Fletcher, Jill and Danny Flowers, Bob and Isabelle Fox, Ann Fundis, Wendy Goldstein, Michael Gomez, Macall Gordon, Samantha Gray, Kate Green, Lu Hanessian, Sarah Harding, Jane Hardy, Meredith Hays, Barbara Heaney, Molly and Don Henry, P. J. and Reedy Hickey, Amanda Hughes, Joyce Jackson, Jan Jacobson, Tricia Jalbert, Janet Jendron, Kathleen Kendall-Tackett, Kay and Stephen Knight, Rod Kochtitzky, Alison Krauss, Anna Krimshtein, Brandy Lance, Nancy Lansdell, Minda Lazarov, Nancy LeQuire, Liz Lockard, Dorothy Marcic, Dr. Susan Markel, Erika Maxwell, Delbert McClinton, Camille McNutt, Wendy Middlemiss, Jennifer Moquin, Ann Murray, Nancy Nance, Christine Orrall, Stephanie Petters, Lauren Porter, Dave and Stephanie Richardson, Anne Ross, Susan Savage, Amy Scott, Amy Silver, Jeanne Stolzer, Pam Stone, Susan Switzer, Sara Tavernise, Jennie Thompson, Anneloes Tijssen, Marian Tompson, Atsuko Uchida, Ray Westerhoff, Chris Wink, and Artemisia Yuen.

We are deeply grateful to the hundreds of API support-group leaders, past and present, who donated countless hours to facilitate local support groups to provide support and education to parents in their communities.

Most important, we want to thank our family members who supported us, whether directly or indirectly, in this long, amazing journey: Pauline Ellendorff, Tyler and Lori Ellendorff, John and Toni Lowery, John Lowery Jr., Kathleen Barnes Lowery, Tim Lowery, Les Baxendale, Charles and Jo Pearce, Morgan Kendrick, and Austin and Cameron Moore.

Introduction: Parents' Call to Arms

· ·

Our survival as a human community may depend as
much upon our nurture of love in infancy and childhood as upon
the protection of our society from external threats.

—Selma Fraiberg
In Defense of Mothering: Every Child's Birthright

Every Child's Birthright: In Defense of Mothering

A mother and father hold their newborn for the first time. As they gaze at his or her little face and body, they are in awe of the miracle of life they have created together. The birth of a baby symbolizes a new beginning, a renewed sense of hope, a sense of life's purpose, and a chance to leave a legacy for family and society. They wonder about the future that will unfold as both they and their baby grow. What kind of parents will they be? What kind of relationship will they have with their child? What kind of adult will their child turn out to be? How do they get there from here?

Parenting is the most important job we will ever have. Yet in our society, it is one for which we are the least prepared and for which we receive the least support. Babies are born without instruction manuals; every baby is unique, and no one book could possibly teach all that you need to know about your particular child. Only your child can teach you about his or her needs and personality.

Unfortunately, today's parents are challenged from all sides by the variety

1

of child-rearing advice now available. Since many new parents rely on the advice they get from others or from reading parenting books, they come to rely less on their own intuitive feelings or understanding of their child. This advice is often conflicting, so it's no wonder that many parents become confused or misdirected. Too often, the most popular parenting advice is based on someone's opinion rather than common sense and sound science. This undermines new parents' confidence in their own innate knowledge of their children. In some cases, popular advice is harmful to the child as well as to the parent-child relationship.

The Big Picture: How Parenting Affects Society

Parents can't raise children in a vacuum or expect that what they do within the home has no lasting impact. Most of us have experienced the effects of the way we were parented. Ideally, each generation does a little bit better than the generation before. Unfortunately, we still have a long way to go. As a culture, we seem content to spend billions of dollars trying to fix problems rather than to prevent them. As you read Chapter 1, it is our hope that you will recognize the endemic disconnect within our society, the root of many of our social ills, and the ways in which you, as a parent, play a role in prevention. We begin by examining the physical and emotional state of children in the United States—our most precious and vulnerable population.

"Parents of delinquent boys use frequent and violent punishment, issue numerous commands, provide little attention, are vague and inconsistent in giving direction, and practice little supervision of peer-group activities outside the home. That is, the parents of delinquents tend to be harsh, authoritarian, and lax in monitoring them, and they do not maintain consistent and high standards."[1]

Violence against and by children is committed in many parts of the world, yet the United States has the largest percentage of violence, mental illness, and incarceration of any modern culture. According to the National Council on Crime and Delinquency, "The U.S. has less than 5% of the world's population, but over 23% of the world's incarcerated people." These statistics include the highest rate of incarcerated women in the world.[2] Childhelp USA receives more than three million reports of child abuse each year. It is estimated that the actual rate of child abuse is three times this. *America's Cradle to Prison Pipeline*, a 2007 report from the Children's Defense Fund, states, "Our 'child and youth problem' is not a child and youth problem; it is a profound adult problem as our children do what they see us adults doing in our personal, professional, and public lives."[3]

Child and adolescent mental health experts are witnessing ever-rising rates of depression, anxiety, attention deficit disorders, conduct disorders, suicide, and other serious mental, emotional, behavioral, and even physical health problems in the United States. Since 1995, more than seventeen thousand patients at Kaiser-Permanente Hospitals have participated in a long-term study of the social, emotional, and, more specific, physical effects of childhood trauma: "Data resulting from their participation continues to be analyzed; it reveals staggering proof of the health, social, and economic risks that result from childhood trauma." This groundbreaking study, called ACE or Adverse Childhood Experiences, consists of detailed questions related to childhood experiences and trauma. The researchers found that the more adverse experiences a child had, the higher the risk of developing physical and emotional illnesses later in life and the higher the risk for early death.[4] According to the National Mental Health Association, six million children currently suffer serious emotional and mental health problems. The diagnosis of bipolar depression has increased 4,000 percent over the last five to seven years, translating into one million children being treated for bipolar disease alone. Something troubling is happening to our children.[5]

The big question is why? Many experts agree that this crisis is due to children feeling a deep lack of connectedness to their parents and their community. In the *Hardwired to Connect* report released by the Commission on Children at Risk in 2003, more than thirty researchers, community leaders, and scholars found that this lack of connectedness was of two kinds: "close connections to people and deep connections to moral and spiritual meaning."[6] These problems cross all racial, cultural, and economic status barriers. They are not limited to the uneducated or to those living in poverty. They reflect a more intrinsic kind of poverty—a poverty of the mind and of the spirit.

This information gives you a small snapshot of the lives of millions of children. While it may seem overwhelming, there is something that each of us can do, and it begins with growing a strong and indissoluble bond with our children.

MY MOTHER, A PSYCHOTHERAPIST, TURNED ME ON TO ATTACHMENT
PARENTING AND SENT US A SEARS BOOK—*THE BABY BOOK*—
AND A NOTE THAT SAID, "I'D HAVE HALF THE PATIENTS I HAVE NOW
IF EVERYONE WAS RAISED WITH ATTACHMENT PARENTING." AND SHE
REALLY BELIEVED IN IT. PEOPLE IN HER FIELD TALK ABOUT IT A LOT,
AND THE IMPORTANCE OF THE BOND BETWEEN PARENT AND
CHILD, EXPANDING OUTWARD TO PARENT AND FAMILY.

—Chris Wink, cocreator of Blue Man Group

Hope for the Future

Attached at the Heart is not a typical parenting book. Rather than dictate advice, it calls each of us to look deeper into ourselves and evaluate how we raise our children. It asks that we rethink our perception of children and see the world through their eyes. It sounds the alarm that our children are in trouble and that we, as parents and caregivers, are the only ones in a position to change this spiraling trend. Most of all, it is a book about hope. We can make lasting changes in the world by starting at home and strengthening our loving connections with our children, being more empathetic with them and with ourselves.

Of eighty-six juveniles who were incarcerated for at least one felony, 100 percent had been exposed to significant childhood trauma.[7]

Attached at the Heart offers hope that we can actively participate in reversing this dangerous trend, first by awakening our understanding of the emotional and psychological needs of babies and young children. Second, this book offers strategies that define attachment parenting as a way of helping us nurture these needs, to follow our parenting instincts rather than what culture dictates.

When you respond to your children's needs in a sensitive, respectful, and developmentally appropriate way, the parent-child relationship—and the family as a whole—is strengthened. A baby's first lessons of empathy and trust are embedded early on from daily experiences of feeling safe, secure, and protected by his or her parents. Babies need to know that someone will be there for them when they are in need.

Our purpose in writing *Attached at the Heart* is to inform, support, and empower parents. This book will teach you:

- the importance of being aware of how our own childhood experiences influence the way we parent;
- how to become more attuned to your child;
- to feel confident that you know your child better than any expert;
- how research supports attachment-parenting practices and the importance of sharing this information with pediatricians and other healthcare providers;
- the importance of making informed decisions about your children without fear of intimidation by others; and
- how to actively improve your family relationships and communities.

Why Attachment Parenting?

As you read this book, you will learn about those who came before us and pioneered the way for children and families. Numerous scientists and leaders have long believed that the parent-child relationship holds the key to the very survival of humanity; some believe it is the key to world peace. We call the type of parenting these scientists have observed in peaceful cultures around the world *attachment parenting*.

This style of parenting is designed to stimulate the optimal development of children. It calls for a new consciousness in child rearing and encourages parents to learn to trust their intuitive knowledge of their child in order to build a strong foundation of trust, allowing the child to develop his or her capacities for empathy and compassion for others. Attachment parenting will help you create a strong emotional connection or attachment with your baby, empower you as a parent, and strengthen your family.

Many parents have found that attachment parenting has helped them heal from their own childhood wounds by allowing them to give nurturance to their child that they didn't receive, at the same time educating them about new positive ways of child rearing and communicating. Attachment parenting gives parents permission to fall in love with their baby instead of worrying that they might spoil him or her. When we invest our time in our children's early years, we can take comfort in knowing that strong attachment relationships will positively influence the children's future relationships.

The concept of attachment parenting holds tremendous power—in the process of raising our children, we raise ourselves. Gandhi once said, "Be the change you want to see in the world." This sentence can easily be paraphrased to say, "Become the kind of adult you want your child to be." Gandhi understood the power of example that we as parents must provide—the onus is laid squarely on the shoulders of each and every one of us. Children will model our behavior before they heed our words.

We want to make it clear, however, that we all are a work in progress, and we do the best we can with what we know and where we are in our parenting journey. Attachment parenting is not a panacea for all problems, but it provides a good start in giving our children the most loving environment possible to achieve their fullest potential. As our children grow, they will make mistakes as part of their process of discovering who they are—our job is to maintain the heart connection and be there for them when they need us. It may take a few generations to really see the long-term benefit of our efforts, especially if there is a family history of dysfunction, depression, or addictions. Genetic influences, such as a child's temperament, also play a major role in how he or she experiences the home environment and the powerful forces of the culture.

Each of us has the potential to change the course of our familial inheritance and reveal the hidden potential within ourselves and our children, but we can't and shouldn't do it alone. We are social beings who need to be connected to others; we need an extended family. There is power in parents helping other parents that builds their confidence and skills. Our goal at Attachment Parenting International (API) is to create a tipping point of change in our society, to transform a world of war and violence into a world of compassion and peace. It can be done, and we hope you will join us.

CHAPTER ONE

CHARTING A NEW COURSE:
Breaking the Ties That Bind

Nothing is more important in the world today than
the nurturing that children receive in the first three years of life,
for it is in these earliest years that the capacities for
trust, empathy, and affection originate.

—Elliot Barker, MD,
The Critical Importance of Mothering

This quote by Dr. Barker, a long-time mentor of ours, a foren-sic psychiatrist, and the founder of the Canadian Society for the Prevention of Cruelty to Children (CSPCC), eloquently expresses the profound impor-tance of nurturing our young, yet it receives little importance or emphasis in our society. In fact, a nurturing parent—one who devotes time and attention to a baby or young child—is more likely to draw criticism from the public and media than praise.

We felt it important that parents see the "big picture," to understand why we wrote the book and how parenting attitudes and child treatment directly affect families, communities, and generations to come. It has been clear for some time that there is much we can do as a society to prevent mental illness and intergenerational violence, beginning with parent education and creat-ing community support for families, yet violence against children continues to rise.

The statistics of violence against children in the United States are staggering: Every day 5 children die from child abuse (a rise from 3.13 deaths every day in 1998), and it's estimated that 50 to 60 percent of child deaths from abuse are not documented correctly. Every year there are 3.3 million reports of child abuse involving more than 6 million children. Thirty percent of abused children become abusers as adults; 80 percent will develop at least one psychological disorder.[1]

As you read our book you will realize that much of what we write about or recommend is counter to popular societal beliefs. If you understand why you are consciously making certain choices and that they are supported by science, it will help build your confidence. Being confident in your decisions and choices will go a long way in deflecting criticism from well-meaning family, friends, and even doctors. Appendix A can help you deal with some of the myths people have about attachment parenting.

Because many of us have little or no experience with babies or children, it is difficult to know what to expect when we become parents. Maybe you have read a few books here and there, but without prior experience there's no way of really understanding the day-to-day reality. Most people don't think to discuss the kind of parents they want to be with their partners before having children, nor do they discuss the kind of adults they want their children to become. For many parents, the first baby they ever hold is their own. As important a role as parenting is for the future of families and society, there are no minimum requirements for education or standards of care. Many experts believe some form of child development and parent education should become a requirement in schools. Too often we spend more time and energy researching the details for buying a house or a car than we do for raising children, probably because we feel we will just learn on the job. Imagine you are about to climb the world's highest mountain. You would have two choices: you could begin your journey on your own and figure it out as you go (more difficult and reducing your chances for a successful climb) or you could prepare yourself physically, mentally, and spiritually, and your chances of achieving your goal would be much higher. Without a little knowledge and experience, we default to parenting the way we were parented, and for some families that may be fine, but for many families there is a lot that can be improved upon. The last twenty years have given us a wealth of research about what makes babies and young children tick. We know what children need from the adults in their lives to reach their best potential, and it doesn't require that we become perfect parents. Strangely, we begin this incredible, lifelong journey that radically changes us as adults, and most definitely has a lasting effect on our children (not to mention society as a whole), without any experience and very little knowledge.

> YOU KNOW YOU ARE FACE-TO-FACE WITH THE UNFINISHED
> BUSINESS OF YOUR OWN CHILDHOOD WHEN YOU RESPOND WITH
> STRONG NEGATIVE FEELINGS TO YOUR CHILD'S BEHAVIOR. . . .
> DISPROPORTIONATE LEVELS OF FEAR, SADNESS, ANGER,
> OR, CONVERSELY, ELATION OR RELIEF ARE SIGNALS TO THE
> PARENT THAT HE HAS JUST ACTIVATED AN OLD WOUND AND
> MIGHT DO WELL TO INVESTIGATE FURTHER.
>
> —Harville Hendrix, PhD, and Helen Hunt, PhD,
> *Giving the Love That Heals: A Guide for Parents*

The most natural thing parents can do is to raise their children the way they were raised. You are less likely to be troubled by conflicting advice if you had nurturing childhood experiences. Adults who had difficult childhoods for any reason—trauma, abuse, neglect, or separation because of divorce, for example—may have some challenges to overcome.

You Can't Give What You Don't Have

For some families, implementing attachment-parenting practices just seems natural, like it's the right thing to do. However, many parents find it difficult to give emotionally of themselves, especially if they didn't receive love and nurturing as a child. All those memories that were thought to be buried may resurface when you become a parent. Children's behavior at certain ages can trigger old wounds or "buttons." When children "push your buttons," it's usually because those buttons were installed a long time ago. You may have *thought* you had them under control—until you find yourself becoming angry, overreacting, or becoming irrational. These buttons, or unresolved issues, are what some call our "ghosts" from childhood. Our early childhood experiences create powerful forces that are extremely difficult to overcome on our own and will often require professional help. The first step toward healing is becoming aware—a person has to be conscious and aware of the past in order to not repeat it. For those parents who desire to break the cycle of abuse, becoming a parent can be the impetus for change.

Ghosts from the Past

It isn't necessarily just overt abuse or neglect that is damaging. Culturally accepted parenting practices can also be abusive or neglectful. These practices have deep roots that go back hundreds of years and have become traditional and are now being recognized by some as "normative abuse."[2]

"The prospect of having a baby brings forth memories of their own childhood and causes them to reflect on the parenting that they received."[3]

In most cases, parents cared for their children the way they were told to by the parenting experts of their day. They were simply doing the best they could with what they knew. Similarly, now that we know better, we must try to do better for our children.

Beginning the process of raising awareness starts with understanding how so many of us got to the point of trying to overcome our past. Until the evolution of our modern Western culture, children had to grow up fast and get to work, usually on the family farm. By the time they were eight, nine, or ten years old, their childhoods were over.

The period we call adolescence is a stage of development rather newly identified by child development researchers. With the identification of this new stage of development, coupled with new laws earlier in the twentieth century to protect children from abusive work practices, children were allowed to enjoy a longer childhood. All along the way, attitudes about children and parenting practices were largely influenced by strict religious dogma or experts in the fields of psychology and human development—such as Sigmund Freud, L. Emmett Holt, and the "father" of behaviorism, John Watson. Their parenting advice had negative and devastating effects on children and their families—sometimes for generations—ranging from sexualizing children to treating them as objects.

Over the years, thousands of parenting books have been written, each claiming to have the answer to raising good, obedient children, leaving many children feeling disconnected from their confused, anxious, or guilt-ridden parents. For hundreds of years, the treatment of children in many cultures has been harsh and disturbing. We know that the residuals of some of those abusive practices are still present today. While great strides have been made, we still have a long way to go. One classic example comes from the work of psychologist John B. Watson, who admonished parents not to hug, coddle, or kiss their infants and young children in order to train them to develop good habits early on. In 1928, Watson published his widely popular child-care book called *Psychological Care of Infant and Child*. In it, he said parents should:

> Treat them [children] as though they were young adults. Dress them; bathe them with care and circumspection. Let your behavior always be objective and kindly firm. Never hug and kiss them, never let them sit on your lap. If you must, kiss them once on the forehead when they say goodnight. Shake hands with them in the morning. Give them a pat on the head if they have made an extraordinary good job of a difficult task.[4]

In her book *Breaking the Silence*, actress and comedian Mariette Hartley writes about the heartbreaking legacy for her family and millions of other families created by the advice of her maternal grandfather, John Watson, or "Big John," as she called him:

> In Big John's ideal world, children were to be taken from their mothers during their third or fourth week: if not, attachments were bound to develop. He claimed that the reason mothers indulged in baby-loving was sexual. Otherwise, why would they kiss their children on the lips? He railed against mothers whose excessive affection made the child forever

dependent and emotionally unstable. Children should never be kissed, hugged, or allowed to sit on their laps.

"My mother's upbringing was purely intellectual. The only time my mother was 'kissed on the forehead' was when she was about twelve and Big John went to war. Although she was reading the newspaper by the time she was two, there was never any touching, not any at all. Grandfather's theories infected my mother's life, my life, and the lives of millions. How do you break a legacy? How do you keep from passing a debilitating inheritance down, generation to generation, like a genetic flaw?"[5]

Suicide and depression, the legacy left her by her family, resulted in her losing her father, an uncle, a cousin, and almost her mother. Not without her own emotional "demons," Mariette Hartley was able to break the chain through therapy and raising her awareness about life, love, and spirit. She became a loving mother of two children and continues to work as a successful actress while donating her time to suicide prevention.

New parents' own early childhood experiences have a major impact on their parenting attitudes and beliefs with the possibility of affecting the attachment process with their newborn child.[6]

When "Normal" Child Rearing Crosses the Line

Watson's legacy, like others', continues to permeate our cultural psyche in many ways—how we view children, how we speak to them, and how we treat them. To discipline children, our culture has accepted numerous ways of keeping kids in line. They are often talked down to or spoken to harshly, hit, humiliated, shamed, ignored, and, in some extreme cases, tortured—such as by placing hot sauce on a child's tongue or forcing a child to stand for long periods with his or her arms straight out. A nurse and lactation consultant at a local hospital recently shared this example:

I went into a mother's hospital room to help her with breast-feeding, and I saw her three-year-old daughter with her back to the wall with her arms straight out in front of her. I asked the mother if her child was playing a game, but she said, "No, she's being punished for misbehaving. She has to stand there for five minutes." It struck me that the mother thought there was absolutely nothing wrong with how she was disciplining her child.

These abusive forms of discipline have been so much a part of our culture that we sometimes don't think twice about them. We have learned to desensitize ourselves to the actual physical and emotional pain that is inflicted on children. After all, that's how we were raised, and we turned out okay—right? Maybe we were lucky and turned out well in spite of how we were treated; maybe we still suffer in ways we don't realize are connected to our early childhood years. Some of us were lucky enough to have strong, loving families with parents who did the best they could with what they knew then. We can understand that, embrace it, and even forgive because we know that there are no perfect parents, and their love far outweighs anything else.

Child abuse is a huge epidemic in the United States. Every day, five children die from abuse (up from three in 1998), and, of these, 80 percent are under the age of four.[7] We tend to think it only happens in families in poverty, but child abuse crosses all social, educational, and economic barriers and ranges from benign neglect to physical abuse.[8] If we are serious about breaking the cycle of abuse, we have to begin in the family. The Child Welfare Information Gateway website lists "nurturing and attachment" as one of the primary factors in preventing child abuse.[9]

Research has found six important protective factors for families and their children to reduce the risk of child abuse and neglect:

1. Nurturing and attachment
2. Knowledge of parenting and of child and youth development
3. Parental resilience
4. Social connections
5. Concrete supports for parents[10]
6. Social and emotional competence of children

A growing number of therapists are determined to bring attention to the dangers of "normal" or traditional parenting. In her book *Creating the Capacity for Attachment*, Dr. Karen Walant first described this type of treatment as "normative abuse":

> Our culture allows for a certain threshold of parenting practices that I term *normative abuse*. Normative, because these are included in some of the basic tenets of child-raising that are endorsed by the culture in which we live. Normative, because, like the generations before that believed "a child should be seen and not heard," these are parts of current parenting philosophy. Normative, because these are often tiny moments in a child's life, moments that may be followed by a loving interaction or a sweet caress. Normative abuse occurs when the attachment needs of the child are sacrificed for the cultural norms of separation and individuation. Normative abuse occurs when parental instinct and empathy are replaced by cultural norms.[11]

The word *abuse* is defined as "treating a living creature, whether animal or human, in a harmful, injurious, or offensive way."[12] Dr. Walant acknowledges that even though normative abuse in and of itself may not be *as* traumatizing as verbal, physical, or sexual abuse, it still has its damaging effects on the overall healthy development of the child.[13] Often we don't realize that damage is being done because we cannot see it.

Yelling, spanking, jerking, slapping, shaming, and humiliating are all ways that we can harm a child's dignity and our emotional connection. (Read more about the effects of physical punishment in Chapter 8.) You may know parents who are firm in their belief about the use of corporal punishment and crying-it-out methods as forms of discipline. Our goal is not to be judgmental or make this an indictment against parents who hold these beliefs. We've done some of the same things with our own children out of lack of knowledge and understanding. Our intent in writing this book is to raise awareness. Only when a person's awareness is raised can he or she begin to make conscious changes in behavior. So how do we get there from here?

WHEN WE SPOIL SOMETHING, WE DENY IT THE CONDITIONS
IT REQUIRES. . . . THE REAL SPOILING OF CHILDREN IS NOT IN THE
INDULGING OF DEMANDS OR THE GIVING OF GIFTS, BUT IN
THE IGNORING OF THEIR GENUINE NEEDS.

—Gordon Neufeld, PhD, and Gabor Maté, MD,
Hold On to Your Kids

Understanding Bonding and Attachment

Scientists haven't always been aware of attachment in humans but have long recognized the bonding that occurs in other mammals right after birth. You may have watched a family dog or cat have babies and noticed how the mother instinctively knew what to do—licking, cuddling, nursing, and protecting. You may have also observed that the babies had their own way of telling the mother what they needed—squeaking, crawling to get closer to the mother, searching for the nearest nipple to suck. Once satisfied, they become perfectly calm and content. Over time, as the babies grew, you may have noticed a special bond deepen throughout their development; the mother most likely became very protective and caring while the offspring began to explore and test their new skills, working toward their independence.

That special bond is called *attachment*, and it is a process that continues for a much longer time in human babies, usually for the first three to five years of life. It takes so long because only 25 percent of the brains of human infants are developed at birth, which means they will, in a very real sense, continue their gestation outside the womb, much like a baby kangaroo. Kangaroos are extremely dependent upon the mother for a much longer time than other mammals. Even chimpanzees, our closest genetic relatives, who are born with 75 percent of their brains developed at birth, remain very close to their mothers for several years.

Only in the last sixty years or so have professionals in the fields of psychology, anthropology, child development, and social work begun to recognize and accept how vital this process is in determining who we become. We are learning that attachment is at the core of our humanity.

Nature and Nurture

In the ideal home environment, babies flourish; their cognitive, emotional, and physical needs are being met by loving parents as they experience trust, empathy, and affection. They are stimulated and eager to learn new skills. During the first three years, under these conditions, their brains grow at the fastest rate of their lives—millions of cells waiting for "marching orders" before the brain starts pruning back unused cells. Brain cells designed for language and vision, if not stimulated by the environment by the age of six or seven, disappear forever. Children who are not spoken to, for whom language is not modeled, will lose the ability to speak, as scientists have learned from observing feral (wild) children and children neglected in orphanages. The brain is a "use it or lose it" organ, but it's also highly adaptable to even the most adverse environmental conditions.

The "use it or lose it" principle also applies to learning empathy, affection, and other positive aspects of social interactions and relationships. Brain researchers have found that a baby receives all kinds of sensory information from its mother's face and tone of voice, which is simultaneously associated with the physical sensations the baby is experiencing. If children do not receive love, affection, and responsiveness from their parents (or primary caregivers), or if they experience significant trauma and abuse, they may never learn what it means to love, to be affectionate, or to have empathy for another human being. All the while, their brains are adapting to their experiences (hardwiring), internalizing what their parents have modeled for them, making it more difficult to change as they grow older.

What is most striking is that neuroscientists have found that the critical period for the development of certain parts of the brain coincides precisely with the critical period for attachment development—during the first three years of life.[14] One such part is the orbitofrontal cortex, located above the eyes in the forehead area between the left and right hemispheres. Dr. Allan Schore from the Department of Psychiatry and Biobehavioral Sciences at the UCLA School of Medicine has described the orbitofrontal cortex as the key component to infant attachment and emotional regulation and believes that it plays a central role in the development of empathy and emotional memory.[15] The neurons located in this area are particularly sensitive to the emotional expressions of the human face. Schore believes that the effects of the attachment relationship and the process of mother-infant attunement have a direct impact on the development of the orbitofrontal cortex.[16]

Not only is the brain affected by the child's environment, but so is his or her genetic code. There is an exciting new area of study called *epigenetics*, which literally means "over or above" genetics. In other words, scientists are looking at other outside factors that influence gene expression or modifications without actually changing the DNA sequence, such as environment. In *The Relationship Code*, psychologist David Reiss and his colleagues at George Washington University describe the results of their twelve-year genetic study of parenting influences on genetic traits: "Many genetic factors, powerful as they may be in psychological development, exert their influence only through the good offices of the family; we'll be changing a genetic trait by changing the family environment."[17] In other words, "How parents treat a child can shape which of his genes turn on."[18]

For more than eighty years, scientists have been trying to figure out the mechanisms of what turns genes on and off, trying to answer the puzzling question of how humans are able to share essentially the same genetic code as all living things yet be so radically different: "How can the same DNA sequence lead to different outcomes?" And more important, "Why should we care?" Epigenetics has shown that something as simple as what a mother eats while pregnant can change the epigenetic state of her unborn child, and what a mother does with her infant during the first few months of life can affect her child later in life and even the attributes of her grandchildren. In a lab experiment, researchers fed two genetically identical mother rats a different diet. Their offspring were also genetically identical but looked completely different simply because of their mothers' diets; one was obese and had red fur, and the other was normal size with brown fur. The implications of this research mean that we all have the ability to make changes in our lives, our immediate families, and future generations. It also means, thankfully, that our genetic predispositions are not our destiny. Most stunning of all is that genetic scientists have found that only 1.5 percent of our genes contain genetic code. They have no clue what the other 98.5 percent of our genes actually do, but some hypothesize that humans complete their genetic coding after birth. Our genes become coded by our experiences through our environment. Lynne McTaggart, a science writer, wrote in her book *The Bond*, "Genes get turned on, turned off, or modified by our life circumstances and environment: what we eat, who we surround ourselves with and how we lead our lives."[19] Now that's an overwhelming but exciting thought, and this places a huge responsibility on each of us.

New research in the fields of neuroscience, genetics, child development, and psychology continues to provide evidence that there is a lot at stake for children and society. This is where the theory of attachment provides the glue that holds all the elements of child development together.

> JUST AS CHILDREN ARE ABSOLUTELY DEPENDENT ON
> THEIR PARENTS FOR SUSTENANCE, SO IN ALL BUT THE MOST
> PRIMITIVE OF COMMUNITIES ARE PARENTS, ESPECIALLY THEIR
> MOTHERS, DEPENDENT ON A GREATER SOCIETY FOR ECONOMIC
> PROVISION. IF A COMMUNITY VALUES ITS CHILDREN,
> IT MUST CHERISH THEIR PARENTS.
>
> —John Bowlby, MD,
> *Maternal Care and Mental Health*

The Legacy of John Bowlby and Mary Ainsworth

Two historical figures are largely responsible for our current understanding of children and what drives human relationships. In the late 1930s and 1940s, it was common for children to be admitted into hospitals without visitations by their mothers or fathers for long periods. It was the highest priority that hospitals remain germ-free, so parents were only allowed to visit once a week. Nurses were in charge of the physical care of infants and young children, but they didn't have time to hold or coddle the children because they had to keep up with their rigid schedules. As a result, the children's emotional states began to deteriorate quickly. They became sad, depressed, fearful, and unresponsive. James Robertson, a concerned individual in London, filmed this process and then shared the film with a British psychiatrist named John Bowlby. These films so disturbed and intrigued Dr. Bowlby that they led to his life's work of advocating for children and parents. Bowlby is considered the founder or father of attachment theory. It was his study of young delinquent boys that led him to understand the links between prolonged early separation from the mother (or primary caregiver) and later "affectionless character." His work was so radical that he was ostracized by fellow psychiatrists, who refused to believe that the environment had anything to do with how children turned out. Rather, they believed it was their genetic makeup.

Throughout it all, Bowlby never wavered in his convictions and maintained his position with confidence and dignity. Still, he had no way of actually proving his theory until Mary Ainsworth came into his life.

Dr. Mary Ainsworth, who was originally from Ohio and educated at the University of Toronto, accompanied her husband to England, where she began working for Bowlby as a research assistant. She later went to Uganda to study the weaning practices of mothers and realized that she was witnessing the natural process of attachment (bonding) of babies and mothers. Ainsworth used this knowledge to develop a procedure, called the "Strange Situation," to assess the quality of the child's attachment to the mother. Thousands of research studies later, this instrument is still being used today and continues to validate Bowlby's early conclusions.

The "Strange Situation"

Researchers have learned that the attachment process is a reciprocal one. In other words, both parent and child take turns initiating cues (signals) and responses—baby smiles, mother smiles back; baby cries, father picks baby up to comfort; baby signals he or she is hungry, parent responds by feeding; baby gazes at father, father gazes back, responding with loving interactions. All of these seemingly mundane daily activities are the basic elements of creating a secure attachment. It is not only the bond that the child feels toward the parent, but the bond that the parent feels toward the child. Bowlby and Ainsworth learned from studies done in Uganda and in the United States that attachment relationships fit fairly clearly into three categories: secure attachments, insecure-ambivalent attachments, and insecure-avoidant attachments.[20]

The Strange Situation procedure performed by Bowlby and Ainsworth was implemented by placing a baby with a stranger in a strange location (the research lab), then having the mother leave for a brief period. This allowed them to demonstrate that babies behaved in different ways depending on their relationships with their parents. The intent was to stress the baby for only a minute or two and then observe how it reacted to the mother leaving and when she returned.

The keys to the procedure are (1) to record how confidently and effectively the baby is able to separate from the mother and resume play and exploration of the toys, and (2) to record the mother's ability to soothe the baby on reunion. It is the detail of the reunion with the mother that is the key to assessing the quality of the baby's attachment to her—secure or insecure. Securely attached babies are likely to cry and protest strongly and quickly (other researchers believe that temperament and sex also play a role in their reactions). The babies become extremely upset, but when the mother returns (within a minute or so), they are quickly quieted and resume playing. Ainsworth noted that these children were the most nurtured at home as well.[21] It is an amazing process to watch, knowing that every action and reaction tells a part of the story.

The findings during the test by no means reflect that the parent-child relationship will always remain secure or insecure, since home environments are always subject to change, but it gives a good indication of the parent-child relationship at the time of the assessment and what could be a continuing pattern of interactions.

The three categories of attachment that Bowlby and Ainsworth created based on their observations are described here. Within each category, there can be varying degrees of attachment.

1. **Secure Attachment.** The infant actively explores, gets upset when mother leaves, is happy upon reunion, and seeks physical contact with

mother. Mothers of secure babies are typically loving and responsive to their infants, are quick to pick them up when they cry, and hold them longer and "with more apparent pleasure."[22]

2. **Insecure-Ambivalent (Anxious or Resistant) Attachment.** The infant stays close to mother, explores to a limited extent, becomes very distressed upon separation, and is ambivalent toward mother upon reunion but remains near her. Mothers of anxious babies were observed to be "more mean-spirited to merely cool, from chaotic to pleasantly incompetent. Though well-meaning, these mothers have difficulty responding to their babies in a loving, attuned, consistent way."[23]

3. **Insecure-Avoidant Attachment.** These infants show little distress when separated, ignore the mother's attempts to interact, and are often sociable with strangers or may ignore them as they ignore their mother. These mothers often have an aversion to physical contact themselves and speak sarcastically to their babies.[24]

A fourth category was added years later by Dr. Mary Main and her colleagues:

4. **Insecure-Disorganized or Disoriented.** These infants are the most distressed upon separation and are considered the most insecure. They seem confused upon reunion or would "act dazed or freeze"; they might "move closer but then abruptly move away as the mother draws near," exhibiting behaviors that appear to be a combination of resistant and avoidant.[25]

> "The self-organization of the developing brain occurs in the context of a relationship with another self, another brain. This relational context can be growth-facilitating or growth-inhibiting, and so it imprints into the developing right brain either a resilience against or a vulnerability to later forming psychiatric disorders."[26]

Attachment: An Idea Whose Time Had Come

Ironically, during the time Bowlby and Ainsworth were researching attachment theory, similar observations were being made in other parts of the world by professionals ranging from psychiatrists to anthropologists. Studying the dominant parenting practices of cultures around the world has given researchers deeper insights into why some societies are aggressive and others nonaggressive. In his book *Learning Non-Aggression*, anthropologist and human developmentalist Ashley Montagu answers the question of why aggression and violence are totally nonexistent in some nonliterate cultures:

> Years ago Margaret Mead was the first anthropologist to inquire into the origins of aggressiveness in non-literate societies. . . . [S]he pointed to the existence of a strong association between child-rearing practices and later personality development. The child who received a great deal of attention, whose every need was promptly met, as among the New Guinea Mountain Arapesh, became a gentle, cooperative, unaggressive adult. On the other hand, the child who received perfunctory, intermittent attention, as among the New Guinea Mundugomor, became a selfish, uncooperative, aggressive adult.[27]

Fully recognizing that there are no perfect cultures, through the years we have collected stories from around the world that have indirectly illustrated and validated attachment parenting principles. One of these stories takes place at the end of World War II, when a navy psychiatrist named James Clark Moloney was stationed in Okinawa. He and another doctor were told to be prepared for the devastation they would see—horrible bombings had forced thousands of people to flee to caves and the wilderness areas, exposing them to starvation, life-threatening injuries, and illness. They were told to expect that the psychological impact would be just as horrific, but, to their amazement, they found that the people were, for the most part, psychologically healthy. As Dr. Moloney started investigating why the Okinawan people had survived so amazingly well, he found that before the war they had no psychological wards in their hospitals, and there had only been one murder in their largest city in the last seventy-five years.

Dr. Moloney felt that a key component to the mental health of the Okinawans was how they parented their children. In contrast to the West, where bottle-feeding was quickly becoming the norm, Okinawan mothers breastfed, not only to nourish their babies, but also to give comfort. He noticed how the mothers would carry their babies on their backs in beautiful fabric carriers and let them nurse whenever they needed—not on a strict schedule. Most babies were nursed until at least two years of age or older, and, if the babies were not with the mother, they were carried by another family member—always in contact with someone they knew and trusted. Moloney was also impressed by the respect the adults showed for the children—for example, once when he was photographing a young child, he asked the father for permission to film. The father requested that he ask the child's permission—a revelation for this American doctor! Moloney reported that he never saw the use of physical discipline like spanking and referred to the Okinawans as "permissive" compared to standards in the United States. They talked to their children rather than using physical force, threats, or coercion. In spite of the fact that the parents were so "permissive," the children were very well-behaved and rarely cried. He became convinced that their style of parenting was the key to world peace.

Dr. Moloney traveled the countryside for many months, interviewing and documenting his findings in a film called *The Okinawan*. With great enthusiasm and hope, he took this documentary back to the United States and showed it to standing-room-only audiences in medical schools all over the country. Although these new concepts were fascinating, they were initially rejected with vehement opposition by most in the medical community, even though many of their ideas were put into practice years later. A small group of supportive doctors at Wayne State University formed a group called the Cornelian Corner, and became one of the first groups of mental health professionals to support his conclusions.[28] These new and foreign ideas, such as rooming-in, natural childbirth, and breastfeeding on demand, had begun to take hold in the late 1940s and early 1950s in a few experimental hospitals, with good success.[29] The Cornelian Corner began its own parenting classes, teaching a select number of American mothers the Okinawan style of parenting, including the idea of wearing their babies. An account of Dr. Moloney's experiences was written in an article published in the November 1949 issue of *Better Homes and Gardens* magazine, entitled "Is Your Wife

Traditional Okinawan Mother
Better Homes and Gardens, 1949.

American Mother
Better Homes and Gardens, 1949.

Too Civilized?" To illustrate Dr. Moloney's concept of the Okinawan style of parenting, *Better Homes and Gardens* used a photo of a young American mother with her baby happily secured to her back with a cloth fabric carrier— a very unusual sight in 1949! What Dr. Moloney was promoting then is very similar to what we call attachment parenting today. These pictures show an Okinawan mother wearing her baby on her back, an American mother wearing her baby in the 1940s, and a mother today wearing her baby in a sling.

Unfortunately, Dr. Moloney didn't witness an overwhelming acceptance of the Okinawan style of parenting, but in the early 1960s, he learned about the founding of a mother's breastfeeding group in Chicago called La Leche League International (LLLI) and spoke at one of its first conferences. LLLI became the primary organization promoting this new style of parenting until API was founded in 1994. The seeds of a new paradigm in parenting were planted.

World War II created so much devastation to the world population that scientists and researchers from around the world found unprecedented opportunities to explore and examine human behavior in a variety of contexts. The work of Dr. Alice Miller has shown how greatly culture shapes our attitudes about children. In her book *For Your Own Good: Hidden Cruelty in Child-Rearing and the Roots of Violence*, she gives us unsettling insight into prewar Germany and the parenting practices that were common at the turn of the twentieth century. She was fascinated that an entire society could fall under the spell of such an extremely authoritarian dictator, and she warns that unless we become more conscious in our parenting, we are destined to repeat the mistakes of past generations.

Dr. Miller researched some of the most popular parenting books in Germany during the years before and at the time that Hitler and his counterparts were children. She included passages from parenting experts of the day in her book, a compelling yet sad prediction of what laid the foundation for the Holocaust. In the later 1800s, Dr. Daniel Schreber wrote one of the most popular parenting books of the time, which went through forty printings and was translated into several languages. His advice sounds eerily similar to some parenting books that are on the shelves today. Here is an example of his advice (emphasis added):

> The little ones' display of temper as indicated by screaming or crying without cause should be regarded as the first test of your spiritual and pedagogical principle. . . . [N]ow you should no longer simply wait for it to pass . . . but should proceed in a somewhat more positive way by stern words, threatening gestures, rapping on the bed . . . or, if none of this helps, by appropriately mild corporal punishments repeated persistently at brief intervals until the child quiets down or falls asleep. . . . This procedure will be necessary only once or at most twice, and then you will be master of the child forever. *From now on, a glance, a word, a single threatening gesture will be sufficient to control the child.*[30]

Of course, parents must create safe, developmentally appropriate boundaries for their children. More about this is discussed in Chapter 8. However, the key goal here is to control the child's will before he or she remembers having a will. Domination, veneration for authority, and blind obedience are a recipe for creating a nation ripe for an authoritarian dictator, and, unfortunately, that's exactly what happened under Hitler's rule. Tragically, just like the children of American psychologist John Watson, Dr. Schreber's own children suffered from severe mental illness as adults—one committed suicide and one became a famous patient of Sigmund Freud whose case was well documented in his book *The Schreber Case*.[31]

Changing Course

The good news is that a growing number of parents and professionals have become increasingly interested in a style of parenting that actively promotes compassionate, respectful treatment of children and provides the much-needed support for the attachment relationship. The characteristics of this style of parenting are a hallmark of peaceful societies around the world and are more conducive to cooperation, compassion, and peace within the family and society. These practices have been used in some form for thousands of years—some call this kind of parenting "conscious parenting," "natural parenting," "compassionate parenting," or "empathetic parenting"—some American Indians refer to it as "original parenting." In many languages around the world, the word *parenting* doesn't exist. They don't try to define it—it's just something that comes naturally.

The most popularized term today for this style of parenting is *attachment parenting* (AP), which incorporates what we believe to be the best of most parenting practices from around the world and which has increasingly been validated by research in many fields of study, such as child development, psychology, and neuroscience.

Attachment parenting is a term that was coined by pediatrician William Sears and his wife, Martha, a registered nurse, more than twenty-five years ago, early in their book-writing careers. Martha told us the story of how they came up with the term:

When Bill wrote *Creative Parenting* [1982], he referred to it as "immersion mothering" and "involved fathering." At a talk one time in Pasadena, a grandmother came up to Bill and said she thought the term *immersion mothering* was a good one, because some moms find themselves "in over their heads." When he told me of this, I realized we needed to change the term to something more positive [!], so we came up with AP, since the attachment theory literature was so well researched and documented, by [John] Bowlby and others.

William and Martha Sears structured the practice of attachment parenting on what they call "The Baby B's" and offered them to parents as tools to help them build lasting bonds with their children. The Baby B's are listed in their book *The Attachment Parenting Book.* The basis for these tools came from observing and talking to the many parents in their practice who had great relationships with their children.

In creating API, we were inspired by the Baby B's, so with the Sears's blessing and input of parents, support-group leaders, and professionals, we modified and expanded them to create the Eight Principles of Parenting. We developed the Eight Principles of Parenting not as a checklist for attachment parenting but as guideposts for optimal child development supported by sound science. They are intended to provide guidance for parents as they face serious decisions and cultural pressures on a daily basis. These principles were created through the lens of attachment research and are designed to help parents become more attuned and connected to their children.

API's Eight Principles of Parenting

1. Prepare yourself for pregnancy, birth, and parenting.
2. Feed with love and respect.
3. Respond with sensitivity.
4. Use nurturing touch.
5. Ensure safe sleep, physically and emotionally.
6. Provide consistent, loving care.
7. Practice positive discipline.
8. Strive for balance in your personal and family life.

Although the Eight Principles of Parenting were initially developed for infants and young children up to the age of five years, there are common threads inherent in each of them that are applicable to all ages. Children are born with certain innate emotional needs or drives that we believe are the catalyst for developing secure attachment. With the help of Dr. Isabelle Fox, we have created the four P's of Innate Needs.

The Four P's of Innate Needs

Studies have shown that providing proximity, protection, predictability of care, and play in the earliest years is the best investment parents can make to create secure, successful, and loving adults.

Infants best survive and have the capacity to develop into secure and loving individuals when they experience four important behaviors from their parents or primary caregivers. In most cases, nature has ingeniously programmed mothers and fathers to provide these four critical responses to rear healthy children.

1. **Proximity** to mother or primary caregiver to meet an infant's innate need for security and familiarity of smells and voice of the mother or father. Proximity facilitates protection when needed, as well as timely responses to hunger, stimulation, and bodily care. Cosleeping, baby-wearing, and physically "being there" are behaviors that keep the infants close, and, as a result, their needs are more likely to be met promptly.

2. **Protection** from danger, predators, abuse, and neglect, or a baby may simply want to be protected from unfamiliar people, animals, or uncomfortable situations. Almost all species protect their newborns and attempt to keep them from harm's way.

3. **Predictability** of responsive nurturing, which builds trust. It provides the infant with a familiar set of arms, smell, voice, and patterns of response. Unfortunately, in contemporary society, when parents are absent a good part of the baby's waking hours, the frequent changing of substitute caregivers places the infant under unusual stress. The predictability of his or her world is shaken. Infants or toddlers without language or intellectual ability can't understand why, suddenly, a stranger

is feeding, holding, bathing, talking, and comforting them. Trust that their world is predictable and safe is undermined. For millions of infants and toddlers in day care, "caregiver roulette" has become the norm. (The infant never knows into whose arms he or she will land.) Such caregiver roulette occurs when caregivers change frequently, often every few months, and continuity of care is broken and trust is undermined. This can produce long-range negative consequences.

4. **Play.** New research supports the idea that play helps children form secure attachments and stimulates learning. Nurturing playful behavior is as important as nurturing any of the other senses. Rough-and-tumble play that is not hurtful or competitive stimulates a host of good hormones like oxytocin and endorphins. Researchers suggest that more play in childhood could prevent and reduce symptoms of ADD, ADHD, and impulsivity. The cocktail of good hormones that come from joyful play they call "joy juice" and can prevent or help alleviate depressive symptoms. It's a healthy activity for children and adults. The act of playing also promotes secure attachment and stimulates growth hormones.

By respecting and fulfilling your baby's innate emotional needs, you are nurturing the development of intrinsic core values—trust, empathy, affection, and joy that can last a lifetime. We think of AP as practicing the *golden rule* of parenting—treat our children as we would want to be treated. Our dream is that one day AP will become the mainstream way to parent, and, that as these children grow up, they will be the adults who will permanently change our culture to one of peace and respect for all living beings and the world they live in.

The following chapters are dedicated to defining the principles and providing practical strategies for everyday situations or decisions you will experience in your journey as a parent. We want to arm you with the best information available and provide you with the best resources so that you can investigate the principles more fully on your own. *You* are the expert when it comes to your child. Our hope is that after reading our book, you will feel more empowered to make changes and be the kind of parent and person you were meant to be.

The Four P's of Innate Needs are the foundation, or the roots as depicted here, that feed and nourish the secure attachment relationship, nurtured in an environment of empathetic and respectful care. The Eight Principles of Parenting are our guideposts to nurturing strong connections and robust growth. All contribute to producing a hearty plant: a child (and ultimately an adult) who will have better developed capacities for trust, empathy, affection, and joy.

CHAPTER TWO

PRINCIPLE 1: Prepare Yourself for Pregnancy, Birth, and Parenting

What Every Parent Needs to Know

Let's face it: You can do everything "right"—eating all the right foods, reading all the right books, and talking to all the right practitioners— yet you still can't control your pregnancy or birth. This can lead you to feel personally responsible when things do not proceed as expected. There is no "right way" to give birth. Birth is not a contest. It is a creative process, and as such, every birth is unique. If we give paints, brushes, easels, and canvases to a group of women and ask them to paint the same scene, each painting will be distinctly different—just as each pregnancy and birth will be a unique experience. . . . Birth is a normal event and no two are alike.

—Peggy O'Mara,
Having a Baby Naturally

The remarkable miracle of new life is a transformative experience for any human being. For most parents, the day their baby joined their family was the most profound experience of their lives. Pregnancy offers expectant parents an opportunity to prepare physically, mentally, emotionally, and spiritually for parenthood. Making informed decisions about childbirth, newborn care, and parenting practices is a critical investment in the attachment relationship between parent and child. Education is the key component of preparation for the sometimes complex decisions required of parents, and it is an ongoing process as each stage of growth and development brings new joys and challenges.

When preparing for the birth of a child, it is easy to get caught up in the material things associated with pregnancy, childbirth, and newborn care. Cute infant clothing, the latest maternity fashions, and all the baby gear can be an all-consuming (and expensive) part of preparing for a baby, but the lasting investment of preparation involves creating a peaceful, loving environment in which to grow, birth, and care for a new life.

Planning for Baby:
Preparing Your Body, Mind, and Spirit

Ideally, a couple planning to have a baby will begin to prepare themselves *before* becoming pregnant. Lifestyle choices, including eating a nutritious diet, avoiding the use of alcohol and drugs, exercising, and seeking emotional and spiritual health, will be a conscious choice for parents anticipating a healthy pregnancy.

Before getting pregnant, a woman will want to prepare her body by eating healthy foods. The amount of processed foods we eat is so much a part of our culture; many young people have never had a home-cooked meal from natural food sources. A practical guideline is to eat a wide variety of foods in as natural a state as possible. For instance, a breakfast of steel-cut oatmeal, yogurt, whole-grain cereal, or eggs, and whole grain toast, or some (preferably organic) fruits and juices, is an excellent way to start the day. Think about decreasing caffeinated drinks, or at least limiting them to only breakfast. Sodas and other highly sugared drinks (or carbonated drinks that are artificially sweetened) can be replaced with herbal teas sweetened, if desired, with a little honey, agave, or maple syrup and filtered water. These habits are wonderful to start before pregnancy so that healthy food choices will already be established when pregnancy occurs.

Because most of us have sedentary lifestyles, exercise is another important addition to a daily regimen. You may only have time for walking thirty minutes a day; this has tremendous advantages, but even better is mixing up your routine to include other forms of exercise like yoga, Pilates, and other stretching and balancing exercises. Good nutrition and exercise will help you be at an optimum weight before conception, so gaining the weight of pregnancy will not be a problem. Mothers who are more physically fit also have a much easier time giving birth.

Emotional preparation is a key factor in beginning a healthy pregnancy. Many women have mixed feelings about having their first baby and are not sure why they feel conflicted. Some women have a great fear of childbirth because of frightful scenes they have seen in movies or on television. A recent study found that far more mothers were exposed

"A pregnant mother's diet not only sensitizes the fetus to . . . smells and flavors, but physically changes the brain, directly impacting what the infant eats and drinks in the future. This highlights the importance of eating a healthy diet and refraining from drinking alcohol during pregnancy and nursing. . . . If the mother drinks alcohol, her child may be more attracted to alcohol because the developing fetus 'expects' that whatever comes from the mother must be safe. If she eats healthy food, the child will prefer healthy food. Exposure to odor or flavor in the womb elicits the preference but also shapes the brain development."[1]

to childbirth through television shows than through childbirth education classes.[2] This is a good time to read, ask questions, and do your own research about the normal process of childbirth. Learn about hospital routines in your area; for instance, how common are induced labors, ultrasound, epidurals, and cesarean sections? What are the pros and cons of these procedures, and what are the options in your community? Fear of the unknown is easily dispelled with good information. In her book *Immaculate Deception*, Suzanne Arms discusses the harmful effect of fear on a mother's birth experience:

A positive attitude is important, too. Nature is not prepared to handle inordinate fear and self-doubt. We hear so much about the harmful effects of cocaine and other drugs on a baby in utero, but we hear nothing about the harmful effects of our bodies being constantly flooded with stress hormones that weaken our immune system and inhibit normal birth. If, in addition to making our bodies fit, we do as much as we can to learn about birth as a natural process, we will do much to alleviate unnecessary fears and be able to face birth with calm and courage.[3]

Our culture has a powerful influence on our perceptions of the optimum birth experience. Declercq et al. found that:

> During pregnancy, mothers sought information . . . through a variety of sources, with first-time mothers naming books (33%) as their primary information source, followed by friends and relatives (19%), their provider (18%), and the Internet (16%). . . . Fully two-thirds (68%) had watched one or more of eight television shows specially created to depict childbirth, with more than half of the viewers regularly watching at least one of these shows. Far more mothers were exposed to childbirth through TV shows than through childbirth education classes. . . . [Only] 56 percent of new mothers took childbirth education classes. . . . As women neared the end of pregnancy, most felt confident, but a majority also felt fearful about their upcoming birth.

A few other troubling statistics were reported in this survey. "Despite the importance of early contact for attachment and breastfeeding, most babies were not in their mother's arms during the first hour after birth, with a troubling proportion with staff for routine, non-urgent care (39%)." And another surprising finding was that "just a small proportion of mothers visited multiple providers before selecting their own or sought a provider or hospital matching their own philosophy."[4]

Other issues from your own childhood may arise when thinking about becoming a parent for the first time. A couple can share their stories with each other, and if there are deep concerns, fears, or a history of abuse, this might be a good time to seek professional counseling to help see your birth and parenting experience in a positive light.

Preparing for baby is a perfect time for your spiritual growth; you might read books on spirituality together, talk to a counselor or minister about any questions or concerns you might have, and share your dreams and hopes for your child. If your partner comes from a particular religious tradition that you do not share, this is good time to discuss each other's spiritual beliefs more deeply, how they will influence your child-rearing decisions, what religious traditions will be taught to the children, and what compromises both of you would be comfortable making to incorporate the religious values you share.

Physician and educator Dr. Deepak Chopra and his colleagues offered a profound insight regarding the spiritual nature of the unborn infant when they wrote, "Throughout pregnancy your body is your unborn baby's universe. You are the rivers, sunlight, earth, atmosphere, and sky for this being growing within you.

The prospect of having a baby brings forth memories of parents' own childhood and causes mothers to reflect on the parenting that they received. New parents' own early childhood experiences have a major impact on their parenting attitudes and beliefs, with the possibility of affecting the attachment process with their newborn child.[5]

Your baby's body, mind, and soul are intimately intertwined with your own. Together you express the creative flow of life."[6] Embracing this "creative flow" in your life can set the stage for deep personal growth and spiritual development, which can give you an overall sense of inner calm, love, and happiness that will have lifelong benefits for you and your unborn child.

What Kind of Birth Experience Do I Want?

The two most important decisions a mom-to-be will make to help create a positive birth experience is the choice of obstetrician and where she will give birth. Being an active participant in your birth requires first that you think about the kind of birth experience you want and start looking at the birthing options in your community. To get the best prenatal and childbirth options, some couples have made the decision to move to a new area. These options vary widely in different cities and states, so it's important to do the research. If you have an API support group in your community, it is a great way to network with new and pregnant parents to find out about the options that are available.

Attachment-parenting advocates know that the most beneficial birth choice is one that has the fewest interventions and allows for the mother and baby to be awake, aware, and able to connect during and after the birth. "Making a decision on where your baby's birth will take place is second in importance only to making the decision to become parents in the first place!" advises Peggy O'Mara in *Having a Baby Naturally*. In making this decision, first look at the birth process through the lens of the attachment relationship. What would be the optimum experience for a baby entering the world? Imagine entering a peaceful, warm, quiet, welcoming environment, a tranquil place that closely resembles the dark, warm, and nurturing environment that the baby has been experiencing for the past nine months. Infants come "hardwired to connect" in the sense that they are programmed to expect the warmth of the human body, the familiar sounds of their mother's heartbeat and voice, and the warmth of mother's milk.[7] Amazing research has shown that when placed on the mother's stomach after an unmedicated birth, a baby can creep unassisted to the mother's breast, find the nipple, and begin to feed unassisted![8]

Most women in the United States use an obstetrician for their prenatal care and the birth of their babies. Some obstetricians are open and encouraging of a nurturing birth environment and have worked within hospital regulations to create a homelike atmosphere for their patients. Another excellent and safe option today in many hospitals, in birthing centers, and at home is midwifery care. Whether using a midwife in a hospital setting, in a birth center, or at home, many women have found that having this option gives them flexibility in their birth experience. For instance, some parents are interested in researching water birth (or laboring in water) as a more gentle approach to childbirth because they have seen videos or heard about the help this provides the mother in having a more relaxed and comfortable birth. It is a good idea for parents to compare different methods and philosophies regarding prenatal care and birth environments, classes offered, and each practitioner's statistical outcome and costs. Just because a close friend

Hospital birth centers are associated with lower rates of medical interventions during labor and birth and higher levels of satisfaction, without increasing risk to mothers or babies.[9]

liked a certain provider does not mean it is the best choice for you. Talk to other parents who have had a positive birth experience for recommendations, and then, after coming up with some questions, interview several providers before making a decision.

Choosing an Obstetrician

- Interview obstetrician providers before making a decision. Your best friend's provider may not be right for you. If the OB is in a practice with several other OBs, the chances of you actually having your OB on the day of your birth are slim. The other doctors may not be as willing as your OB to follow your birth plan. Find out! Share the Lamaze "Six Healthy Birth Practices" and/or the "Ten Steps of the Mother-Friendly Childbirth Initiative" (see below for more info) and discuss what you want. Choose an OB who is respectful of your birth preferences and who will make every effort to be there for your baby's birth.
- Ask the OB what his or her cesarean rate is. The World Health Organization has long recommended no more than 10–15 percent. However, due to elective C-sections and the overreliance on C-sections by doctors, rates have soared to 30–40 percent or more.
- Too often C-sections are justified because it is believed that the baby is too large to be delivered based on ultrasound or some other form of measurement. This is not a sufficient reason; it is based on the doctor's estimate rather than exact science. Anecdotally, many mothers have reported their babies were smaller than predicted rather than larger. Even if the baby is large, many mothers' bodies stretch and relax to accommodate the baby.

A great resource for developing questions for a healthcare provider and making an informed decision about where to have a baby is the "Ten Steps of the Mother-Friendly Childbirth Initiative for Mother-Friendly Hospitals, Birth Centers, and Home Birth Services," published by the Coalition for Improving Maternity Services (CIMS). If there are no "mother-friendly" hospitals, birth centers, or home birth services close by, investigate whether there are "baby-friendly" hospitals or birth centers by visiting the Baby Friendly Hospital Initiative website, www.babyfriendlyusa.org/. This initiative, developed by the United Nations Children's Fund (UNICEF), is now being adopted by healthcare systems all over the world. Baby-friendly hospitals and birth centers have implemented the Ten Steps to Successful Breastfeeding (Baby-Friendly Hospital Initiative) set up by UNICEF (outlined in Appendix B) to ensure that all staff and administrators have made a commitment to educate, support, and encourage mothers to breastfeed their babies, if at all possible. Parents are assured, among other things, that information they receive from all medical staff will be consistent and that the mother will be allowed to room-in with her baby.

Ten Steps of the Mother-Friendly Childbirth Initiative for Mother-Friendly Hospitals, Birth Centers, and Home Birth Services

To receive CIMS designation as "mother-friendly," a hospital, birth center, or home birth service must carry out our philosophical principles by fulfilling the ten steps of mother-friendly care.

A mother-friendly hospital, birth center, or home birth service:

1. Offers all birthing mothers:
   - unrestricted access to the birth companions of her choice, including fathers, partners, children, family members, and friends
   - unrestricted access to continuous emotional and physical support from a skilled woman—for example, a doula or labor-support professional
   - access to professional midwifery care
2. Provides accurate descriptive and statistical information to the public about its practices and procedures for birth care, including measures of interventions and outcomes.
3. Provides culturally competent care—that is, care that is sensitive and

responsive to the specific beliefs, values, and customs of the mother's ethnicity and religion.

4. Provides the birthing woman with the freedom to walk, move about, and assume the positions of her choice during labor and birth (unless restriction is specifically required to correct a complication) and discourages the use of the lithotomy (flat on back with legs elevated) position.

5. Has clearly defined policies and procedures for:
   - collaborating and consulting throughout the perinatal period with other maternity services, including communicating with the original caregiver when transfer from one birth site to another is necessary
   - linking the mother and baby to appropriate community resources, including prenatal and postdischarge follow-up and breastfeeding support

6. Does not routinely employ practices and procedures that are unsupported by scientific evidence, including but not limited to the following:
   - shaving
   - enemas
   - intravenous drip (IV)
   - withholding of nourishment
   - early rupture of membranes
   - electronic fetal monitoring
   - induction (rate should be 10% or less)

Other interventions are limited as follows:

- episiotomy rate of 20% or less, with a goal of 5% or less
- cesarean rate of 10% or less in community hospitals, and 15% or less in tertiary care (high-risk) hospitals
- vaginal birth after caesarean (VBAC) rate of 60% or more, with a goal of 75% or more

7. Educates staff in nondrug methods of pain relief and does not promote the use of analgesic or anesthetic drugs not specifically required to correct a complication.
8. Encourages all mothers and families, including those with sick or premature newborns or infants with congenital problems, to touch, hold, breastfeed, and care for their babies to the extent compatible with their conditions.
9. Discourages nonreligious circumcision of the newborn.
10. Strives to achieve the WHO-UNICEF "Ten Steps of the Baby-Friendly Hospital Initiative" to promote successful breastfeeding (see Appendix B).[10]

Childbirth Education Classes

One of the first steps toward creating a positive birth experience is deciding what kind of childbirth classes you want to take and finding out what classes are offered in your area, such as the Bradley Method for natural childbirth, Lamaze classes, or others. When interviewing different childbirth educators, find out what their classes have to offer, what various birth options are available, and what healthcare providers are supportive of more natural methods. Ask the childbirth educator if she will help you develop a birth plan. "A birth plan states, in writing, your vision of the upcoming labor and delivery. It crystallizes your beliefs, states your preferences, and outlines any procedures you would like to avoid."[11]

Couples often enjoy the social aspects of these childbirth classes as much as the information offered and can network with each other about this new world of becoming a parent. Appendix C suggests books, websites, and other resources for finding childbirth instructors and researching their philosophy about childbirth and their methodologies. It's important to remember that a onetime class at a local hospital won't come close to giving you all the important information you need to be prepared. For the best birth outcomes, parents need to be informed and active participants in all decisions that have to be made, as well as in the birth.

In 1972 a study was published in the book *Why Natural Childbirth?* The author, Dr. Deborah Tanzer, was a student of Dr. Abraham Maslow, the theorist who developed the "hierarchy of needs" scale and the theory of the "peak experience." Dr. Maslow defined peak experiences as those that make life worthwhile and give it meaning. Dr. Tanzer was curious to study mothers who were delivering babies by this new method of "natural childbirth," which was being touted as a rapturous experience by some mothers.

Early childbirth education can empower parents to be involved in the planning of their birth, often resulting in the use of less pain medication during labor.[12] Education about childbirth can significantly increase positive attitudes toward birth.[13]

In these studies, Dr. Tanzer found that, as soon as the natural childbirth classes were completed, the women who had taken them (called the "takers" in the study) showed greatly improved attitudes toward their pregnancies. Five times as many women reporting positive emotions after the birth had taken the childbirth classes, a statistically significant difference. Another important finding was that the takers felt they were much closer to being the type of people they wanted to be; in other words, their self-images were enhanced. Ironically, the takers (most of whom had little to no analgesia) reported significantly less pain than the nontakers. Almost equal numbers of the two groups reported high pain, but takers outnumbered nontakers eight to one in registering low pain.[14]

The issue that greatly interested Dr. Tanzer was a peak or rapturous experience. No one in the group who did not take the childbirth classes reported this kind of ecstatic experience, but ten of the takers in this study did. Overwhelmingly, it was the women whose husbands or partners were with them at both labor and delivery who reported a peak experience.

In summary, here are some of the key points from her research. First, certain fears, feelings, fantasies, needs, and responses seemed to be common to all women. Second, by the introduction of natural childbirth, the character of the total birth experience was changed radically and in a highly positive direction. Third, these differences in childbirth experiences included how the mother viewed herself, the baby, and the meaning of the experience; the women in the natural childbirth group emerged happier and healthier. And fourth, the biggest and most positive differences became apparent in the later stages of labor and during the actual birth of the baby, when the woman could begin to push and thus help to expel the baby. The act of pushing, the sense of meaningful activity, the participation in the great drama of the delivery room, the ability to welcome her new child in full consciousness, the joy in accomplishment—these seem to be the truly important facets of natural childbirth and for these mothers were the ultimate in a "peak experience."

We've talked to many women over the years who attended natural childbirth classes yet for various reasons did not have the "perfect birth" experience that they had wanted. Those women seem to have an easier time dealing with their disappointment than those who wonder what might have happened if they had been more prepared. It seems to be harder on a mother to accept a disappointing or difficult birth when she was not informed enough about the process of labor and delivery and the doctor was allowed to make all the decisions. We feel strongly that birth is such a transformative and empowering experience that each pregnant mother deserves to have the best information, enabling her to make the best decisions for her and her baby. The critical time to gather this information is well before the birth.

Mothers who experienced a positive relationship with their partners expressed more attachment to their infants. Overall, a mother's positive relationship with her partner had a positive influence in her attitudes toward pregnancy.[15]

To encourage positive birth outcomes, the Lamaze Institute for Normal Birth has identified and updated the Six Healthy Birth Practices, adapted from the World Health Organization, that promote, support, and protect normal birth. When adopted, these practices can have a profound effect—instilling confidence in the mother and facilitating a process that results in an active, healthy baby.

- **Healthy Birth Practice No. 1: Let labor begin on its own.** Letting your body go into labor spontaneously is almost always the best way to know that your baby is ready to be born and that your body is ready for labor.
- **Healthy Birth Practice No. 2: Walk, move around, change positions**

throughout labor. Moving in labor serves two very important purposes. First, it helps you cope with increasingly strong and painful contractions, which signals your body to keep labor going. Second, it helps gently wiggle your baby into your pelvis and through your birth canal.

- **Healthy Birth Practice No. 3: Bring a loved one, friend, or doula for continuous support.** In childbirth, as in many aspects of life, we humans do better when we're surrounded by those we trust, people who tell us we're doing well and encourage us forward. Good labor support is not watching the clock and checking IV lines and fetal monitor printouts. It's making sure you're not disturbed, respecting the time that labor takes, and reminding you that you know how to birth your baby.
- **Healthy Birth Practice No. 4: Avoid interventions that are not medically necessary.** Although research shows that routine and unnecessary interference in the natural process of labor and birth is not likely to be beneficial—and may indeed be harmful—most U.S. births today are intervention-intensive.
- **Healthy Birth Practice No. 5: Avoid giving birth on your back, and follow your body's urges to push.** Allowing a woman to find the positions of comfort and encouraging her to push in response to what she is feeling is beneficial to the birth process.
- **Healthy Birth Practice No. 6: Keep mother and baby together.** It's best for mother, baby, and breastfeeding.

Lamaze International recommends that care providers, hospitals, and birth centers adopt these Six Healthy Birth Practices as standards of care and encourages women and their families to choose care providers and birth settings that employ care practices that promote, support, and protect normal birth. All of these healthy birth practices can be found in their entirety and may be downloaded from www.lamaze.org.

Important Considerations While Pregnant

The purpose of sharing the following information with you is to empower you and to encourage you to ask questions, not to scare you. Many young parents-to-be are fearful of birth, and our intention is to prepare you so that you go forward with knowledge and the understanding that most births are low-risk and uneventful.

OB doctors and nurses are trained for all the "what ifs" that can happen, so they tend to view birth as a risky and "in need of control" event in life. Your provider may be in agreement with your birth plan or preferences, but what often happens once you are in labor at the hospital is that he or she becomes overreliant on technology and the clock, making everyone tense and anxious, slowing down the progress in a laboring mother. If a doctor or nurse expresses concern about something, such as that the baby's heartbeat is too slow or too fast or that labor is progressing too slowly, and starts mentioning the "c" word or Pitocin or epidural, always ask what other alternatives are available—such as walking around, sitting on a ball, quieting the activity in the room, dimming the lights. Seeds of fear and doubt will grow unless you are informed and have knowledgeable advocates with you, like an experienced doula.

Renowned midwife Ina May Gaskin has written and spoken many times about a "sphincter law" when referring to childbirth.[16] As funny as it sounds, she seems to be on to something. If a mother feels tense, upset, anxious, or rushed, her cervix will tighten up and slow down labor, much as with a bowel movement. The same holds true when delivering a baby: when the mother is in the right position, in the right state of mind, the uterus will take over and deliver the baby without the mother necessarily actively pushing.

> Fears about pregnancy and childbirth can increase the risk of emergency cesarean section and increase the risks of emotional instability after childbirth.[17]

Are Routine Prenatal Ultrasounds Necessary?

Ultrasound machines are intended to be used only for medically indicated situations—specifically, high-risk births. Routine ultrasound may lead to the implementation of more procedures, which can increase the risk of complications. Unless medically indicated, you can say "no, thanks" to your provider if asked. The Food and Drug Administration (FDA), the American Institute of Ultrasound Medicine (AIUM), and the College of Radiology strongly discourage this practice! The AIUM statement says, "The use of either two-dimensional (2D) or three-dimensional (3D) ultrasound to only view the fetus, obtain a picture of the fetus, or determine the fetal gender without a medical indication is inappropriate and contrary to responsible medical practice."[18]

There are concerns with routine ultrasounds for several reasons:

1. **The ultrasound waves heat human tissue, especially if close to or surrounded by bone (like the brain).** When you make a decision it's important to ask when the machine was last calibrated, how well trained the technician is, and how many ultrasound procedures he or she has done. The bulk of ultrasound studies were done in the 1990s when the intensity of the machines was 94 mW/cm2 (intensity of light measured at milliwatt per square centimeter), and that intensity has increased to 720 mW/cm2. Since the intensities have dramatically increased, few studies have been conducted, necessitating the need for much more research to ensure safety to the infant.[19]

2. **Doppler ultrasound machines are more powerful than the pulse-wave ultrasound.** The pulse wave is a preferred choice when having an ultrasound because the risk is lower for damage to delicate tissue.

3. **Beware of keepsake ultrasounds!** Keepsake 3D & 4D ultrasound machines and technicians are not monitored by anyone and are not safe. It sometimes requires several minutes of ultrasound to create a video, when only a few seconds is recommended to reduce the possibility of heating up delicate tissue of the baby.[20]

4. **Autism spectrum disorders (ASD)** have skyrocketed in the last twenty to thirty years from between 1 and 5 per 10,000, and, according to the Centers for Disease Control (CDC), as of March 2013, there has been a 72 percent increase in the diagnosis of autism over the past four years. Now one of every fifty children ages six to seventeen has an autism spectrum diagnosis. There are most likely

multiple environmental factors at play, and as parents it's important to be careful of the chemicals you use during pregnancy and after you have your baby. Dr. Jay Gordon, a pediatrician and passionate advocate for children, has written a provocative new book called *Preventing Autism: What You Can Do to Protect Your Children Before and After Birth* that raises awareness of the chemical soup we live in and educates parents about preventable toxic exposures in our food and environment that can negatively affect a developing or new baby. Some concerns have also been raised that there may be a causal link with ultrasound exposure, which has also increased in diagnostic frequency and intensity of exposure during those twenty years.[21] Currently, there are no studies that have shown a causal link, but it doesn't mean there isn't any. Given that we don't know the causes, why take a chance unless medically indicated?

Steer Clear of Ultrasound Parties

The newest trend in the United States is ultrasound parties at home. While there aren't conclusive studies of long-term damage (this is worth repeating), this doesn't mean they don't exist. "Ultrasound is a form of energy with effects in the tissues it traverses, and its use should be restricted to medical indications, by trained professionals, for as short a period and as low an intensity as compatible with accurate diagnosis."[22] The American Institute of Ultrasound in Medicine concluded, "There exists abundant peer-reviewed published scientific research that clearly and convincingly documents that ultrasound at commercial diagnostic levels can produce lung damage and focal hemorrhage in a variety of mammalian species. . . . The degree to which this is a clinically significant problem in humans is not known."[23]

Induction

"Be a pitter, not a sitter" is the slogan of one maternity hospital, but it also reflects the pervasive attitudes among many hospitals in the United States. The synthetic version of oxytocin, called Pitocin, is used routinely to induce and speed up labor, very often for the convenience of the doctors and hospital staff than for any legitimate medical reason. A mother can be in labor for many hours, as a result, it can be very inconvenient for a system that wants to get things done in a timely fashion, and there are likely to be cost concerns on behalf of insurance companies because of the extended stay. Once childbirth was considered a normal human process with a small percentage of complications; now every birth is treated as if it were a high-risk birth. With disregard for the natural unfolding of birth, unnecessary medical interventions are put in place, the means justifying the end—the birth of a healthy baby.

Sue Carter, a researcher at the University of Illinois, Chicago, who has studied the effects of human hormonal experience in early life, shared her concerns about the routine use of Pitocin. Speaking at a conference at Notre Dame in 2010, she explained that Pitocin is not well understood and should not be treated casually. She writes:

> There is growing evidence that early experiences, including physiological and behavioral changes associated with pregnancy, birth, lactation and the management of infants during the postpartum period, have the capacity to produce long-lasting changes in behavior. Routine manipulations, including the use of exogenous OT (in the synthetic form known as Pitocin) during labor and more recently the use of OT antagonists (blocks the oxytocin receptors to slow down labor), also hold the potential to influence the parent and offspring in ways that have not been investigated in humans.[24]

Dr. Carter is concerned about the routine use of Pitocin, because it is still not well understood. "Synthetic oxytocin could possibly create mental illness later in babies. It should not be treated casually."

The presence of a supportive companion during labor was associated with a striking reduction in the length of labor, with a consequent reduction in the rate of augmentation of labor with oxytocin. Fetal passage of meconium during labor was reduced, and this, together with the effect of the supportive companions on uterine action, resulted in fewer instrumental deliveries and cesarean sections.[25]

For the last several years, early inductions have become a trend at great risk to the infant and increased healthcare costs. The use of induction before a baby is thirty-nine weeks was routine for far too long. These preemies would require time in a newborn intensive care unit (NICU) because their lungs weren't fully developed, leading to all kinds of complications and sometimes lifelong problems for the child. The current recommendation by the March of Dimes and the American Congress of Obstetricians and Gynecologists (ACOG) is no inductions before thirty-nine weeks. Just recently the Georgia Department of Community Health announced it will no longer allow Medicaid payments for early deliveries for convenience. "They warn that choosing to deliver even one week early could threaten the development of the baby's lungs, brain, or other vital organs. . . . There is a short-term cost with babies having to stay in neonatal intensive care, as well as the long-term costs of caring for developmentally delayed children," said Dr. Dean Greeson, chief medical officer for Peach State Health Plan. "The state saw this as a way to get at both of those issues." When the cost of NICU can be as much as $15,000 per day, the officials project they will save as much as $7 million dollars a year.[26] This is, we hope, a precedent that these policies, which are in keeping with the ACOG and March of Dimes recommendations, will be adopted by all hospitals within the United States.

Epidurals

As with any procedure, ask your doctor or an anesthesiologist about the risks and benefits of an epidural for you and your baby so that you are fully informed, or do your own research beforehand. Epidurals can have an effect on the success of breastfeeding (initiation and duration), depending on how much anesthesia is administered and when, as in early in labor versus late in labor.[27]

If you choose to have Pitocin and/or an epidural (or don't have a choice), just be aware that it may take longer for your baby to get the hang of nursing and for you to establish a good milk supply. Trust it will happen, and, if you have a sleepy baby, use a breast pump to stimulate the breasts to produce until he or she is ready.

What Is a Doula?

Parents today have an incredible resource to use for an optimum birth experience: a doula (doo-lah). In the book *Mothering the Mother*, Marshall Klaus, John Kennell, and Phyllis Klaus explain:

> In searching for a term to describe the role, we wanted a word with a nonmedical connotation that would stress the value of a woman companion as attentive and comforting. We turned to the Greek word *doula* meaning "woman caregiver." Our first exposure to the word came from Dana Raphael's use of the term to describe "one or more individuals, often female, who give psychological encouragement and physical assistance to the newly delivered mother." We use the word in the now widely accepted sense of an experienced labor companion who provides the woman and her partner both emotional and physical support throughout the entire labor and delivery, and to some extent, afterward.[28]

Doulas of North America is a licensing organization for professional doulas. Its website has much helpful information, including the following description:

> Giving birth to a baby is so much more than a physical phenomenon; it engages parents-to-be in a transformational experience, a key life event full of emotion and meaning. A doula who accompanies a woman in labor mothers the mother, taking care of her emotional needs throughout childbirth. A doula also provides support and suggestions for partners that can enhance their experiences of birth. A postpartum doula continues that valuable emotional support and guidance, helping a family make a smooth transition into new family dynamics.[29]

A postpartum doula is one who helps the mother at home after the birth of her child. Postpartum doulas help continue the "mothering the mother" experience in a variety of ways. Some may help with breastfeeding, nutrition, emotional support and encouragement, light housekeeping, or child care for older children.

Denise Punger, a physician in Florida, shared her birth stories—one birth without and one birth with doula support—with the readers of *Attachment Parenting: The Journal of API*. Even though Dr. Punger had delivered more than two hundred babies in her residency, she was not aware that having a doula was an option for her first birth. She and her physician-husband attended childbirth classes, and they assumed that they would be prepared to have a wonderful natural birth experience. She invited her mother to be at the birth, not realizing until later that her mother had never witnessed a natural birth and was herself anesthetized for

Analyses suggested that continuous support was most effective when provided by a woman who was part of neither the hospital staff nor the woman's social network, and in settings in which epidural analgesia was not routinely available. No conclusions could be drawn about the timing of onset of continuous support. Continuous support during labor has clinically meaningful benefits for women and infants and no known harm. All women should have support throughout labor and birth.[30]

Denise's birth. When the day came to deliver, her labor was very long and difficult. Not having an experienced support person who was able to help her deal with the long hours of labor or to suggest strategies like walking or changing positions during her last stages left her feeling traumatized by the birth. She was able to deliver her nine-pound baby vaginally, but later, as she recovered from the birth, she knew that there must be a better way—to feel more empowered, supported, and nurtured through the birth—even though her family advised her to just try to forget about the experience.

Her next baby's birth was supported by a professional doula. The doula came to her house during her early stages of labor and gave Denise the loving support and wise counsel that she needed. She described how, with her doula, she walked around the neighborhood, stopping and breathing through contractions, rather than being forced to labor in a bed. As labor progressed, her doula suggested techniques for relaxing and letting her body do what it needed to do. She was amazed and grateful for the soothing words and birthing wisdom from her doula that gave her the confidence to actually enjoy the labor more and helped it progress more quickly. By the time they reached the hospital, she could feel the baby's head crowning and delivered another nine-pounder with a midwife in attendance.

Denise wrote, "In a way, I wish the obstetrician from my first birth had been at Scott's [her second son's] birth. He would have seen the difference a doula could make. If I delivered babies, I would insist that all my patients consider having a doula. It really makes me sad when I hear a mother tell another, 'You'll forget it all anyway.' Giving birth can be a rewarding physical and emotional experience—one that you will never forget."[31]

This model of "mothering the mother" has been found to have tremendous benefits for a mother in labor. Wise women from all cultures and eras have been a key component to any normal birth, and modern society is now recognizing the critical importance of nurturing parents during this transformative event. Health benefits range from shorter length of labor, lower incidence of forceps or vacuum delivery, and lower rate of cesarean birth to less postpartum depression and heightened satisfaction with the overall birth experience.[32] As with choosing any care provider, parents are encouraged to get references from other parents for finding and choosing a doula.

A Mother's Story: For the "Naturally Birthing Challenged"

I want to offer encouragement to moms who feel they missed the ideal birthing experience and/or who were separated from their babies at birth. I also want to share a few tips that would have helped me the first time and did help me the second time:

- Seek support for feelings of loss and recognize that you deserve validation.
- Have a doula, even for a scheduled C-section.
- Draw upon your spirituality, faith in your and your child's creator, and the knowledge that your baby will experience your emotional responsiveness for the entirety of his or her life and was birthed the way that baby needed to be birthed.
- Have the knowledge that despite all of the positive affirmations and the knowledge that our bodies were created to birth naturally, not all birthing bodies evolve equally through life, you are not a failure because

you required medical interventions, and you haven't messed up your kid for life because you required separation at birth.

- Surround yourself with friends who display empathy and support and are like-minded.

- Realize that your feelings of grief over having a C-section are completely separate from, and do not lessen, the love you feel for your baby. You can feel grief and love and thankfulness all at the same time.

- My dear husband suggests that in a hospital setting, you should question the staff. Don't expect them to remember your birthing plan (most won't). Kindly stand strong and stand firm, because you do have rights, and if there are no complications with your baby, you have all the rights to choose your baby's course of treatment. In doing so, you can get much closer to the birthing experience you've dreamed about.

—Kaylene Karras,
Attachment Parenting: The Journal of API

Vaginal Birth After Cesarean (VBAC)

Fortunately, for a mother who has had a cesarean section, the horizontal incision is more stable than the old style of a vertical cut from the navel to the pubic bone. This makes the possibility of a future vaginal birth possible, and thousands of women have experienced a successful VBAC. However, once a mother has had two cesareans, it is unlikely that she will be allowed to attempt a VBAC. It will take some research on your part to determine if this is a safe option for you. You will need to talk to physicians or midwives who support mothers in this decision and have delivered VBAC babies. The International Cesarean Awareness Network has excellent information to help you research this option.

A Fit Pregnancy Means a Healthier Baby

Exercise during pregnancy can be a challenge, especially if the mother is working and has limited time; however, the benefits are substantial. Many prenatal classes are offered in the evenings to accommodate working mothers, including prenatal yoga, swimming, and other exercise programs designed for pregnancy. These classes are also a wonderful way for a new mom to meet other pregnant women in the community. Mothers who exercise during pregnancy tend to have healthier pregnancies, and their labors are much easier and often shorter than those of women who have not exercised. Preterm births are 50 percent less common in mothers who exercise. Of course, it is always important to discuss your exercise regimen with your medical professional.

More than at any other time, pregnancy allows a woman the opportunity to fully understand the importance of how nutrition affects her health and the health of her baby. There is no question that the choices made will also have a direct impact on the birth experience. Research in this area has shown that malnourished mothers tend to have more premature births, lower-birth-weight babies, and more difficult labors. In this day of convenience food, it is surprising to see how many of us are not getting the proper nutrients, especially pregnant women who are now "eating for two." Take this opportunity to change your eating habits for the better.

When a woman has the excuse to eat for two, it's important to remember that overdoing portions will not be in the best interest of mother or baby! Remember that healthy weight gain is very individual and will vary, depending on many factors. Some mothers may actually lose a little weight in the early months, particularly if they have a lot of nausea. Others may put on quite a bit of weight in the early months, or notice a thickening in their midsection due to hormonal changes. If a mother is already too thin or too heavy before conception and uses this opportunity to change her eating habits for the better, she will find that her body will adjust beautifully to the best weight gain for her and her baby. A knowledgeable healthcare provider will give the guidance needed, including discussing the importance of prenatal vitamins.

However, it is still the parents' responsibility to do their homework on what food choices are the best for their family. If there are special dietary needs, such as a vegan diet or other diets not normally within the expertise of many care providers, parents will need to educate themselves and consult with their provider about optimal choices during pregnancy.

Some childbirth classes suggest the mom keep a food diary every day, which is a very helpful idea. Being conscious about food choices now will set a pattern for the choices made throughout the life of the child. What a life-long gift for a child to have parents who model good nutrition in the home!

How Will I Feed My Baby?

In Chapter 3, another important nutritional and attachment-promoting decision is discussed at length—the decision to breastfeed or bottle-feed your baby. In a recent study, 78 percent of the young mothers stated that they made decisions about breastfeeding before pregnancy or the first trimester.[33]

Looking through the lens of attachment, we learn nature's model of what the baby's expectations are from a biological perspective. A baby's primary need is to suckle, and he or she will be rooting and suckling immediately after birth, which will provide the first important immunization from the colostrum. We discuss this more thoroughly in Chapter 3, but suffice it to say that feeding your baby is such an important attachment-promoting behavior, it warrants much thought and careful preparation, especially if the mother has little experience with feeding a newborn—whether from the breast or bottle.

A positive birth experience and strong support system can strongly influence breastfeeding success, as well as reduce postpartum anxiety by helping parents develop strategies and coping skills for this stressful time.[34] Education of mothers, families, fathers, and healthcare professionals regarding the benefits of breastfeeding, as well as how to overcome barriers, has a positive impact on the number of mothers choosing to breastfeed.[35]

A mother who intends to breastfeed is encouraged to attend meetings of La Leche League International, an organization founded in 1957 to educate and support breastfeeding mothers. Most cities in the United States have meetings that are open to all women who are interested in learning more about breastfeeding, whether they have a baby or not. Even adoptive mothers who would like to learn if they can breastfeed (which they can) are welcome. At the very least, talk to a lactation consultant or experienced nursing mother to get accurate information about positioning the baby at the breast and getting off to a good start. Often, a mother will prepare for the birth, not thinking about the most important thing that she will do when she meets her baby for the first time—the baby will want to be cuddled and to suck!

The Emotional Highs and Lows of Pregnancy

A pregnancy can evoke strong emotions in parents-to-be regardless of whether the pregnancy was long anticipated or a complete surprise. The knowledge that they are bringing a baby into the world can bring excitement and joy to expectant parents but may also yield less positive emotions. Memories may be dredged up from the expectant parents' own childhoods, from a prior complicated pregnancy or birth, or from a previous loss. Time taken to reflect on individual childhood experiences and current beliefs about parenting is invaluable preparation. Explore different parenting philosophies and discuss parenting approaches that best nurture healthy attachments within your growing family. Work through negative emotions surrounding the pregnancy so you can focus on the joy of welcoming the baby.

Those experiencing negative emotions regarding the pregnancy or who have a history of depression should seek help from a healthcare provider. Meditation, centering prayer, yoga, visualization, and other relaxation techniques can help minimize stress surrounding the pregnancy while helping pregnant mothers prepare for the physical rigor of birth.

Studies have shown that the quality of a woman's relationship with her husband or partner has a substantial effect on the emotional and physical well-being of her baby. A

The decision to breastfeed is significantly related to the father's level of education and to his approval of breastfeeding. The strong approval of breastfeeding by the father was associated with a high incidence of breastfeeding (98.1%) compared to only 26.9 percent breastfeeding rates when the father was indifferent to the mother's feeding choice.[37]

Swedish study found that mothers who experienced a positive relationship with their partners expressed more attachment to their infants, and, overall, a mother's positive relationship with her partner had a positive influence on her attitudes toward pregnancy.[36]

The relationship with the spouse or partner will never be tested more than in the parenting journey. This will probably be the first experience of putting one's own needs aside and, together, putting the needs of another human being first—particularly in the early months of parenting when both parents are on call twenty-four hours a day! Some couples make the mistake of thinking that if there are problems in the relationship now, a new baby will bring them closer together. Take this time of preparation to deeply reflect on partnership—not only do you need to share your own childhood stories and reflect on their impact on each other, but also discuss what you might call your "parenting mission statement" or philosophy. For instance, how do you feel about traditional methods of raising children, such as letting the baby cry it out? Are you open to reading books and getting information about childbirth, child development, and positive discipline, perhaps by attending parent support-group meetings? Becoming parents can be one of the most meaningful, fulfilling times in your relationship, a time of great personal growth and joy.

Expectant parents who completed a brief relationship-strengthening class around the time their child was born showed lasting positive effects on each family member's well-being and on the family's overall relationships.[38]

In their book, *Giving the Love That Heals: A Guide for Parents*, married couple and authors Drs. Helen Hunt and Harville Hendrix share a profound discovery they made when working with couples:

As we became more and more interested in the relationship between parents and children, we came to a conclusion that amazed us: the people who were most successful in marriage relationships were the same ones who were most successful in parenting relationships. Why? . . . The people who did well . . . made a commitment to become conscious about the process. They were willing to see what was hidden in themselves and, without prejudice, to understand the connection between past wounding and present functioning. They were able to override their self-protective impulses in favor of responses that were less me-centered and more relationship-centered.

When you allow yourself to recognize the contours of your own emotional history and the shape of your current family interactions, you become empowered. You see yourself for who you really are and see your children for who they really are. Just this increased awareness alone, without any other help, means that you are more likely to avoid mistakes and are better able to act effectively to get what you want for yourself and the children you love.[39]

Preparation for becoming a parent starts with preparing for pregnancy and childbirth. As the journey unfolds, it is essential to learn about the upcoming developmental stages. Reading books about child development allows parents to have realistic expectations for themselves and for their child, allowing parents to be better prepared for the joys and challenges of each stage. In Part 4 of *Giving the Love That Heals*, the emotional developmental stages are thoroughly discussed, giving parents strategies for empathetic care.

Advanced preparation and education prompts discussion about parental concerns before they become crises. For example, if parents understand that it is normal for a newborn and young baby to awaken frequently to feed, they soon realize that sleeping through the night is a very unrealistic expectation. So often we see that simply knowing what to expect avoids a lot of anxiety and later discipline issues. This topic is discussed more thoroughly in Chapter 8.

Musings from a Mother of Multiples

I remember being pregnant with twins, and other AP twin moms (the very few that I could find) telling me the first year to eighteen months were going to be "brutal." Brutal? That's a really harsh word. Could they really be "brutal"? Yes, they could. And the first piece of advice I now give to any mom pregnant with twins is that the first year to eighteen months are going to be brutal—and yes, I do mean "brutal." As in, take a deep breath, jump into the swirling rapids, and fight for your very survival. You will lose yourself. It will strain your marriage. It will take you to the very brink of your sanity. You won't think you can handle any more. The days will fold together in a dark haze. And you won't remember most of it. Try to keep perspective. Count down the months. It is going to get better. Much better. Lean on your friends. Ask for help. Know that you can't do things the same way you can with a singleton, but you *can* be an attached parent—even though most people will tell you that you can't, even though at times you are sure it's impossible.

I quickly learned to avoid "twin parenting support groups." Being in a room full of mothers of twins was difficult. We were completely outnumbered by babies. Everyone was stressed and overwhelmed! And the only thing I had in common with any of those moms was the presence of two babies each. Nearly any question asked was answered with "one baby will just have to cry" or with some tool or trick to try to get the babies to be happy alone. I knew there had to be a better answer. I was lucky enough to find one other local AP mom of older twins to talk with, and many compassionate moms of singletons. My best support came from moms whose youngest was at least five. These were the moms who could hold a baby, change a diaper, or cut my food into small bites and feed it to me. They were the lifesavers. Other moms of infants could empathize, but with twins, what I needed was *help*. (*To be continued*)

—PAM S., MOTHER OF FOUR

[**Authors' Note:** *The following is a personal, deeply honest story from a mother's perspective in her experience with her twins, and not intended to reflect the experience of every mother of multiples. It's important to emphasize for parents of multiples to involve other extended family members, close friends, or hired help as much as possible, whether it is comforting one baby while the other feeds, cooking for and feeding the mother, doing household chores, or doing things with the older child. There are numerous ways moms of multiples can be helped and supported while still adhering to attachment-parenting principles. This mom didn't have any of these options available to her other than her four-year-old daughter and her amazingly supportive husband, who* *traveled a lot. Her story will not only help others, it helped her to better understand and process the tremendous physical and emotional marathon that she has endured. She's out of the darkness and into the light now with her beautiful and securely attached children.]*

Postpartum Depression

There has been much in the media recently about mothers who suffer from extreme bouts of postpartum depression or postpartum psychosis. Fortunately, new research is confirming that there is hope for women who suffer from different postpartum challenges. In her book *Depression in New Mothers,* Dr. Kathleen Kendall-Tackett discusses the importance of getting solid information and remembering that prevention should be the number one goal to help new mothers avoid spiraling into depression. Sometimes all a mother needs is support during and after her birth, a healthy diet, and plenty of rest to manage her symptoms. Other times, it is unclear whether a mother is depressed or perhaps suffering from a number of other conditions—like bipolar disorder, an eating disorder, or substance abuse—and needs professional help immediately. This book can help parents and professionals sort through these issues. Dr. Kendall-Tackett also has several excellent websites to help mothers, including www.breastfeedingmadesimple.com, which has information for breastfeeding mothers who may have questions about depression, medications that are safe for breastfeeding, and alternative therapies.

Important Decisions in the First Days After Giving Birth

So often we focus primarily on the birth of the baby, and critical decisions that must be made almost immediately after the birth are not given much thought! Most of these issues will be addressed by a professional childbirth educator, but, if not, please be aware of these topics, and do some reading and research to make informed decisions. Remember to consider these decisions through the lens of attachment: How will this affect not only my baby's physical health but also his or her emotional and psychological well-being? Examples of key issues for you to research follow.

The Circumcision Decision

If you give birth to a boy, you will be asked if you consent to his circumcision. This is not a decision you want to make on the spur of the moment, without reading and researching the pros and cons. Unless this is a religious tradition in your family, most parents do not give this much thought and will make the decision based on what the culture dictates. However, you owe it to your baby boy to research the issue.

It should be noted that Attachment Parenting International does not have an official policy on circumcision, but we all agree this is an extremely painful procedure and an important decision to be made with accurate information. Until recently, the American Academy of Pediatrics (AAP) didn't recommend routine circumcision, stating that the benefits did not outweigh the risk to infants; as a result, many insurance companies would not pay for the procedure. However, in 2012, it revised its statement, stating that after reviewing the literature, it was found that health benefits of circumcision outweighed the risks and can now be paid for by third-party insurance companies. That isn't the end of the matter; it has just stirred up more controversy.

In the same statement, the AAP admits that the health benefits aren't significant enough to warrant circumcising all male babies, and ultimately the decision is up to the parents. They cite that there is a slight decrease of urinary tract infections, transmission of HIV, and prostate cancer in circumcised males. The obvious question is whether it is ethical to cut off healthy human tissue from an infant to slightly reduce the chance of the child acquiring a sexually transmitted disease or perhaps developing prostate cancer later in life. It's a bit like removing an infant's tonsils or appendix in the event they might cause problems later in life.

Here is an excerpt from the AAP statement:

Although health benefits are not great enough to recommend routine circumcision for all male newborns, the benefits of circumcision are sufficient to justify access to this procedure for families choosing it and to warrant third-party payment for circumcision of male newborns. It is important that clinicians routinely inform parents of the health benefits and risks of male newborn circumcision in an unbiased and accurate manner.[40]

If you have decided to circumcise your infant son, the AAP recommends the use of a local analgesic to help reduce the pain. It is hard to believe that some doctors still perform this procedure without any topical pain medication for the baby. You may have to call around to find an OB (yes, obstetricians do the surgery, not pediatricians) who will be willing to use local anesthesia if your OB refuses. Ask ahead of time about this and also, as recommended, have the doctor inform you of the full risks and benefits of the procedure. (You can read the AAP policy statement on its website, listed in Appendix C.) You will need to find out the cost and whether your insurance company will cover the procedure.

Informed Consent for Vaccinations

Another decision you will be faced with once your baby is born is whether you want your child to receive routine vaccinations. You will want to discuss the pros and cons with your baby's pediatrician. Currently, there is a list of twelve different actual vaccination shots, but many combine vaccines, for a total of thirty-seven vaccines by the time a child is twelve years old. The first shot, the hepatitis B vaccine, is given right at birth. It protects against hepatitis B, a sexually transmitted disease. Why do infants need protection from a sexually transmitted disease? This question and many others are answered in *The Vaccine Book* by Dr. Robert Sears.

Dr. Sears has spent more than thirteen years of his medical career researching the pros and cons of vaccines, not only for parents but for himself as well. As he explains in his book, doctor training doesn't include education on the vaccines themselves, only the diseases. *The Vaccine Book* is an excellent resource (and the only one written) that lists all the current vaccines and the diseases they were designed to protect, as well as the likelihood of occurrence of each disease. It is a helpful guide to bring with you when discussing this issue with your baby's doctor.

Additives are a common concern with vaccines. This has led to a number of controversies surrounding possible links to medical problems in children—such as the epidemic rates of autism or developmental delays in the United States. Dr. Sears is emphatic that his book is not an "antivaccine" book but a balanced view meant to be an educational tool for parents and professionals. He made a diligent effort to refrain from bias and to perform his own research. He examined all the information he could find on every vaccine given in the first twelve years of a child's life. He methodically discusses each disease and vaccine as follows:

- What is the disease?
- How common is it?
- How serious is it?
- When is the vaccine given?
- Why are there so many doses?
- How is the vaccine made?
- What are the ingredients?
- Are any ingredients controversial?
- What are the side effects?
- Should I give my baby this vaccine?

Dr. Sears is concerned about the lack of information that parents and physicians have about this topic, as well as the consequences of not making an educated decision about how and why vaccines are given. He reassures parents that they can still fully vaccinate but should consider a different schedule, in which the shots are spaced out. Besides this carefully researched book by Dr. Sears, you will find many articles on the Internet concerning vaccinations.

Your responsibilities as a parent can feel very scary and intimidating when you are immediately faced with such tough decisions. Thus, it is imperative to take the time to research these issues thoroughly before your baby is born. When you come from a place of education and rational discussion, mixed with good old common sense, you have more confidence in your parenting and will make the best decisions for your baby and your family.

Look for These Important Social and Emotional Milestones in Baby's First Year

- **Birth to twelve weeks:** Locked gaze between parent and child. This is the baby's "quiet, alert" time, when he or she is open to learning. This milestone triggers the "falling in love" experience for parent and child.
- **Three to six months:** Mirroring and vocalizations indicate that the baby's development is on target. The baby can mirror some of her parent's facial expressions and make gestures and different vocalizations, from cooing to cackling with laughter, the building blocks of language.
- **Four to ten months:** Mutual play that is reciprocal between the baby and parent or caregiver, such as playing games like peek-a-boo. The baby is using smiles, vocalizations, and gestures.

Red Flags

In a twenty-two-minute video entitled *Creating Secure Infant Attachment: Helping Your Baby Get the Best Possible Start in Life,* Jeanne Segal, PhD, says, "Developmental problems require prompt, professional intervention. . . . The best way to identify infant behavior that signals developmental problems is to follow social and emotional milestones. Social and emotional milestones indicate that the attachment bond is on a secure track. If a parent can't pick up on an infant's cues or a baby isn't alert enough to engage in the earliest milestone behaviors, it's a red flag that signals a need to get help as soon as possible" (you can view the video at www.helpguide.org/video/attachment_sd.htm).

Attachment Parenting International Support Groups

Many times in this chapter we have mentioned the importance of support; it is critical for the birth, for breastfeeding, and for parenting in general. According to Dr. Bruce Perry and others, infants and children are biologically "designed to have four adults who are involved and a constant presence in their lives," referred to by anthropologists as "alloparenting." Mothers need to be "mothered" in the early weeks and months so they can effectively mother their infants. Parents of young children benefit, too, because they don't have to do it all on their own—and you shouldn't, either. Unfortunately, too many young families have felt alone and isolated.

API support groups are now available in many communities in the United States and throughout the world. Support is also available on our website and includes a parents' discussion forum on just about any topic related to parenting. With so much information now available on the Internet, parents have infinite choices for advice. It's really difficult to know what is good scientifically supported advice and what isn't. API's online resources are thoroughly vetted by the organization and its members, so parents can relax and trust the resources and information. In their book *And Baby Makes Three*, John and Julie Gottman report that support groups make a huge difference to the emotional health of a couple when they become parents: The couples who experienced the support groups changed in many ways. They learned that the stresses they were encountering as new parents were very common and not necessarily caused by a bad relationship.[41]

In today's world, where extended families live too far away to give the day-to-day support, knowledge, and care that existed in past generations, it is critically important for parents to find another way to create this support system for their family. API support groups are one way for new mothers and fathers to do this. These groups are a way to build friendships and a sense of community. They are also safe havens for learning about parental and partner roles. As each person becomes more experienced, he or she becomes a mentor to new members of the group. These groups are valuable resources when researching anything from childbirth methods and local medical care providers to family-friendly restaurants and fun activities within the community. Our hope is that all parents will seek support, and, if you don't have a group in your community, go to our website (www. attachment parenting.org) and learn how easy it is to get started.

CHAPTER THREE

PRINCIPLE 2:
Feed with Love and Respect
Beginning the Attachment Process

What is established in the breastfeeding relationship . . .
and the communication the infant receives through the warmth of the
mother's skin constitutes the first of the socializing experiences of life.

—Ashley Montagu, *Touching*

In his seminal book Touching, Dr. Ashley Montagu beautifully describes the beginning of the attachment process. Most parents today know of the health benefits of breastfeeding, but few understand that the initial feeding is nature's way of laying the foundation for a secure attachment. Whether a parent is breastfeeding or bottle-feeding, the purpose of this chapter is to help you understand how feeding your child with loving sensitivity enhances your future parent-child attachment relationship. We discuss breastfeeding first because it is a natural model of attachment and then apply many of the attachment principles seen in breastfeeding families to parents and caregivers who are bottle-feeding their babies.

First, feeding a child involves more than providing nutrients; it is an act of love. From satisfying the very intense hunger needs of a newborn to serving meals at the family dinner table, parents can use feeding time as an opportunity to strengthen their bonds with their children. The newborn's rooting, sucking, and crying reflexes ensure the close proximity of a mother or other dependable caregiver to meet his or her intense needs. The more parents learn to identify and meet their baby's needs, the more secure the parent-child bond becomes. We also discuss how parents can continue to respect hunger cues as their babies start solid foods and are able to feed themselves. It is so important that this process include offering nutritious foods, modeling healthy eating habits, and making mealtime an opportunity for love and connection.

Why Breastfeeding Is the Attachment Model

Dr. Montagu describes what the baby and the mother need at the moment of birth: "What the newborn is looking forward to . . . is a continuation of the life he enjoyed in the womb—in other words, a womb with a view—the child will also, by suckling, confer vital benefits upon the mother . . . producing massive contractions of the uterus . . . and [the placenta] is ejected. . . . Psychologically, this intensification serves further to consolidate the symbiotic bond between [the mother] and her child."[1] In other words, the baby and the mother have a reciprocal relationship from the moment of birth, and the act of suckling the baby soon after birth has tremendous physiological and psychological advantages for both mother and baby.

When a baby is first put in the breastfeeding position, he or she is experiencing a sensory bath of warmth, touch, smell, taste, and soothing sounds. The head is in the crook of the mother's arm, placing baby's field of vision approximately eleven inches away from the mother's face. Science tells us that newborns can focus only at about this distance, so we see how this close proximity to the mother is biologically programmed in the infant's brain.[2] Science also tells us that babies are hardwired to seek the human face as their first "imprint."[3]

Another attachment-promoting behavior we learn from the breastfeeding model is the importance of sensitivity to a baby's feeding cues. Since a breastfeeding mother does not have a bottle with ounces to look at, she is trusting that her baby will signal when he or she is hungry and when he or she is full. The baby may want to nurse again in an hour, or perhaps three hours, depending on how much he took in at the last feeding, how well it was digested, whether he just wants to suck a bit more—so many factors! A bottle-feeding parent can also trust that if the baby doesn't finish the bottle, it's important to not force him to eat more, or, alternatively, if he is hungry again in a short time, to be patient with his needs and trust his signals.

Breastfeeding on cue creates a close nursing relationship, ensures that the mother produces enough milk, and provides the baby with the nutrition and loving touch that is naturally designed for optimal brain development and growth. The mother is now the baby's environment. When the mother is holding her baby, she develops a unique ability to read her child's nonverbal cues, which enables her to respond empathically to the baby's needs even before she gets to the crying stage. A baby's cues may include squirming, making fussing sounds, putting her hand in her mouth, rooting, and turning her head toward her mother's breast. This sensitivity fosters a sense of trust; the baby trusts that her signals are being understood, and the mother learns to trust her own ability to read her baby's cues, laying a foundation for all their future interactions.

The Health Benefits of Breastfeeding for Mother and Baby

- Mothers calmer and less likely to overreact to everyday stressors.[4]
- Significantly decreased rates of diarrhea and sudden infant death syndrome (SIDS).[5]
- Reduced risk for multiple sclerosis.[6]
- Reduced risk for respiratory infections, otitis media (ear infections), and childhood cancer.[7]
- Reduced risk for insulin-dependent (type 1) diabetes (formerly referred to as "juvenile diabetes").[8]

- Protection from Hodgkin's disease among children who are breastfed for at least eight months.[9]
- Significantly higher IQ scores.[10]
- Reduced risk of breast cancer by 11 percent in premenopausal women who breastfed twelve months, and may be reduced by as much as 25 percent if breastfeeding up to twenty-four months.[11]
- Twice the rate of depression in women who don't breastfeed at all during a baby's first year. Lower scores on perceived stress tests in mothers who exclusively breastfed their infants.[12]

A healthy, happy baby develops secure attachments with her caregivers because she more easily reciprocates the loving, smiling behaviors that she receives. During times of sickness, breast milk provides the necessary nutrition and antibodies to fight germs, helping to shorten the duration of an illness or to avoid the illness completely. An unhappy or sickly baby may spend so much time and energy crying or fussing that—until she is feeling better—there is little time left for relaxing or playful interactions. Another amazing factor is that the colostrum (the first milk a mother produces) from the mother of a premature baby is higher in protein and other nutrients than that of a mother of a full-term baby. This suggests that even if a baby is too fragile to breastfeed, the mother should be encouraged to pump her colostrum for her baby.[13]

As a mother becomes more adept, she will find that nursing becomes easier, and she will appreciate its convenience—it is available anytime, anywhere, and satisfies many more needs than infant hunger. Being responsive to a hungry baby is so important in the early weeks, and having the ready breast can be a great help (more on this in Chapter 4). Bottle-feeding parents have found strategies to meet this need by having a minifridge with prepared bottles nearby and bottle warmers that can heat a bottle quickly, if needed. Be aware that microwaves are not recommended for heating bottles, whether they contain formula or expressed breast milk. Microwaves can cause "hot spots" that can burn the baby's mouth, even if you've checked the temperature on your wrist.

As the child gets older, nursing is a valuable mothering tool because it is naturally comforting to the baby. Nursing when a child is hurt or upset can help calm him and meet his needs quickly. "Comfort nursing" meets the baby's sucking needs and is one of the many wonderful benefits of breast-feeding. This aspect of nursing continues throughout the breastfeeding relationship.

Oxytocin, the Bonding Hormone

Breastfeeding is also an advantage for the mother's health and well-being. Breastfeeding triggers the release of the attachment-promoting hormone oxytocin into the mother's body. Often called the "mothering hormone," oxytocin has a calming effect on both mother and baby. Research on this amazing hormone gives us insight into the biological foundation for our early emotional attachments. Oxytocin is released through pleasant warmth and rhythmic touch. When a baby suckles at his mother's breast, an amazing chain of events ensues:

> The breast . . . is stimulated by the suckling of the infant. Nerve impulses travel from the breast . . . causing oxytocin to be released into the blood-stream. This blood-borne oxytocin reaches the . . . organized muscle cells that lie next to the milk-producing cells in the breast. These cells then con-tract and squeeze out the milk. All this is a reflex action. . . . Then when the woman sees her baby, hears the infant cry, or even just thinks about him or her, she may experience a tightening in her breast from the pressure of the milk, which may even begin to flow. . . . During nursing, oxytocin also produces other effects . . . women experience a warming of the torso when nursing. . . . To survive, infants need not only nourishment but also warmth, care, and protection.[14]

Oxytocin that is stimulated through breastfeeding and touch provides benefits for mother and baby. It plays an important role in milk produc-tion. Breastfeeding mothers are less anxious and more socially interactive.

Breastfeeding is associated with potent antistress effects. Breastfeeding is linked to important changes in digestive and metabolic functions in the mother. "Skin-to-skin contact in the immediate postpartum period gives rise to acute behavioral and physiological changes, such as increased interaction between the mother and infant, including reduced stress levels in both. Skin-to-skin contact between mothers, fathers, and infants is associated with increased bilateral social interaction and bonding as the child grows."[15]

The good news for a mother or caregiver who is not breastfeeding is that she can still receive oxytocin benefits from holding the baby skin to skin, especially within the first hour or two after birth, and also by giving and receiving nurturing touch through massage and gentle caress. Another advantage for mothers is that breastfeeding can reduce the risk of many devastating diseases, such as breast and other cancers.[16]

Breastfeeding and Sleep

One of the biggest complaints of new moms is that they don't get enough sleep. Dr. Kathleen Kendall-Tackett—a renowned researcher, author, and expert in breastfeeding as it relates to maternal depression and, more recently, maternal sleep and fatigue—says, "The biggest finding in the last [five to eight] years is that moms who exclusively breastfeed their babies *get more sleep!* The evidence is solid and consistent; there is something unique about exclusive breastfeeding." However, the findings weren't consistent if the baby was formula-fed, even part of the time. Only exclusive breastfeeding made the difference, which includes minimal to no pacifier use.

The other surprise finding came from a large study that Kendall-Tackett conducted, called the Survey of Mothers' Sleep and Fatigue, in which 994 out of 6,410 mothers were identified as having been sexually abused when they were younger. Women who have a history of sexual assault are at increased risk for depression, sleeping difficulties, and quality of sleep. After analyzing the data, she said she was stunned to find that those moms who exclusively breastfed their infants were at a much lower risk from the expected problems of depression, sleep difficulties, and poor quality of sleep. Once again, the potent physiological benefits of breastfeeding, such as relaxation and antistress, are able to mitigate these mothers' risks. Kendall-Tackett said the implications are huge, and that "exclusive breastfeeding can reduce risks for child maltreatment" and should be encouraged, especially with mothers who are known sexual abuse survivors.[17]

Maternal Depression

We know that postpartum depression can have a harmful effect on mothers and their ability to form secure attachments with their babies. Research in depression is showing a correlation between lower levels of certain hormones in mothers who experience depression, so it appears that anything we can do to increase the levels of these natural hormones may be a powerful aid in prevention. According to Kendall-Tackett,

> Prolactin is the hormone associated with the onset and maintenance of lactation, and sharply rises postpartum. . . . In one study, data were collected from twenty-three pregnant women, seventy postpartum women (at seven days postpartum), and thirty-eight nongravid [not pregnant] controls. Postpartum women had significantly greater levels of cortisol, prolactin, thyroxine, and estrogen than the nongravid women. The women with postpartum depression had significantly lower plasma prolactin levels than those who were not depressed. Women who breastfed were significantly less depressed than those who did not. Also, women with previous episodes of depression had significantly lower prolactin and TSH levels than those who had not been previously depressed.[18]

Fathers and Oxytocin

Fathers are not left out of the oxytocin equation. It has been shown that a live-in father's oxytocin levels rise toward the end of his mate's pregnancy. When the father spends significant amounts of time in contact with his infant, oxytocin encourages him to become more involved in the ongoing care in a self-perpetuating cycle. Oxytocin in the father also increases his interest in physical (not necessarily sexual) contact with the mother. Nature now provides a way for the father to become more interested in being a devoted and satisfied part of the family picture through his involvement with the baby. With all its powers, oxytocin is but one of a list of many chemicals that nature uses to ensure that baby finds the love and care he needs.

—LINDA PALMER, DC, "THE CHEMISTRY OF ATTACHMENT," IN
ATTACHMENT PARENTING: THE JOURNAL OF API

Breastfeeding Food for Thought

Some adoptive mothers have successfully breastfed their babies even if they have never been pregnant. Even if an adoptive mother is unable to produce enough milk to supply all of her baby's needs, by using an at-breast supplementer she is able to put her baby to the breast and feed him, stimulating her breasts to produce milk. While it is possible for some women to exclusively breastfeed an adopted baby or a baby born through a surrogate mother, La Leche League International's book, *The Womanly Art of Breastfeeding*, states that "the goal is less about the milk and more about connecting deeply to their new baby." They offer guidance for mothers interested in nursing without pregnancy and encouragement for building a good milk supply through new scientific advances in lactation.[19]

An at-breast supplementer is a device that allows a baby to nurse at the breast when the mother is not able to produce enough milk to support the baby without supplementation. Silicone tubing attached to a bag or bottle of breast milk (or artificial milk) is then taped to the mother's breast so that when baby latches on to nurse, she receives milk from the tubing in addition to any milk produced by the mother. This sucking can stimulate a mother's milk supply, especially in situations when an adoptive mother is attempting to lactate for the adopted infant.[20]

It is critical that partners and other extended family members understand how important it is for a breastfeeding mother to feel supported. Studies show that mothers have greater breastfeeding success when partners are knowledgeable and supportive of breastfeeding.[21]

Breastfeeding also helps the environment! There are no bottles to sterilize or products to dispose of, and it preserves another valuable resource—money. A breastfeeding family can save about $150 a month, not to mention savings in health care. Obviously, saving money and the environment can have psychological and emotional advantages.

Musings from a Mother of Multiples
(continued)

Little things seemed nearly insurmountable with twins. I tandem-nursed because I could not stand the thought of letting one of my boys cry while I fed the other. And I refused to believe that it was "necessary" to give them formula so that someone else could help with feeding. Some people suggested I pump, which I found ludicrous. I was nursing nonstop; when exactly was I going to pump? Tandem nursing was emotionally agonizing before the boys had neck control. I was using nipple shields because their little mouths were so tiny they couldn't get a good latch. Imagine holding a baby in each arm and simultaneously trying to place nipple shields! Those things seriously should come with duct tape or something! Thank heavens for my elder daughter. She learned to help me hold the shields in place until each boy could latch. Then, soon enough, one or both would lose their grip and a shield would fall off, invariably soaking me in milk, and I would have to call her back to help me reposition again. It was incredibly frustrating. Not to mention cold. My chest was always exposed, and I was perpetually cold. And I was thirsty. So thirsty. With a singleton, the common advice is to keep a water bottle next to your nursing chair. That doesn't work with twins. There is no arm with which to pick up the glass. I can remember sitting on the couch nursing both boys, and I could see the water bottle sitting there, and I would want a drink so badly that I would start to cry. And there was nothing I could do about it until someone came into the room to help me. I cried a lot in those early months. My husband did his best to make me laugh from time to time. And those moments were the best. It was so important to try to laugh.

Nursing got a little easier when the boys had head control. One thing I discovered was to get a long scarf to wear around my neck. Then when I was tandem nursing, I could hang the tails of the scarf between the boys to give me a little bit of cover. There is absolutely no way to pull up both sides of your shirt to nurse without exposing the entire torso! You also don't have an extra hand, so if a baby pops off to look around, there is no way to cover up the exposed nipple. Fun times! I found that sitting on the floor was much better than being in a chair. Often people would get up to offer me their chairs, and I would say, "No, no! If I drop one from down here it's less likely to result in an ER visit." Everyone laughed, but I meant it. At home I would pile pillows all around me. All the advice about properly positioning a baby is nonsense with twins. If their mouths are in proximity to the nipples, it's a good position! (*To be continued*)

—PAM S., MOTHER OF FOUR

[Authors' Note: *We really admire Pam's courage and determination, but please don't do this alone. The need for another adult to be in the home each day to help is very apparent from Pam's experience with her twins. An extra pair of hands and a loving heart could have held one infant while Pam fed the other baby or helped her with water and food for herself. Every mother needs to be mothered as she gets to know her babies. In many cultures it is customary to have many relatives or neighbors help nurture and nourish a new mother. If you're a mother of multiples or pregnant with multiples, start recruiting volunteers as soon as possible! If you can afford it, hire a postpartum doula or housekeeper who can do light housekeeping and help you when needed (or ask for a gift certificate for these services).*]

Can I Continue Nursing If I Become Pregnant Again?

For most mothers, breastfeeding a baby without supplementation will suppress ovulation, protecting her from conceiving another child for some time. This can vary from a few months to a few years, and from nature's viewpoint, we see that spacing our children gives the older baby time to grow and mature before a new sibling arrives.

If a mother gets pregnant while she's still breastfeeding, she can usually continue to nurse during a healthy pregnancy. Nursing an older child and a baby is known as *tandem nursing*. Deciding to nurse through a pregnancy can provide definite advantages to the attachment relationship between the mother and child. If the baby is still very young and breast milk is still a major part of his diet and emotional well-being, a mother might have an easier decision to continue. If the child is eating a lot of solid food and drinking from a cup, a mother may want to consider if her toddler still needs to nurse, and, if so, how often. Many mothers have found that their milk may diminish to the point that the toddler loses interest in nursing and gradually weans on his own. Every nursing mother and child pair is different, and it is important for a mother to get the support and information she needs to help her make the best decision for her and her child. The key is that the weaning process ideally be handled gradually with empathy and love.

If the older baby or child has weaned by the time a new baby is born, it is not unusual for him to want to nurse again when he sees a new sibling at the breast. Parents may refer to La Leche League International publications *The Womanly Art of Breastfeeding* and *Adventures in Tandem Nursing: Breastfeeding during Pregnancy and Beyond* for thorough discussions of the issues surrounding the decision to nurse through a pregnancy and beyond.

Bottle Nursing: Using Breastfeeding Behaviors to Bottle-Feed

Our culture often supports practices that create disconnection from our children. For instance, some parents have shared with us that they were given baby gear to encourage a "hands-off" style of parenting, including devices to prop a baby bottle so the baby does not have to be held during feedings. An API support group meeting may be the first place where a parent hears how important it is that babies be fed in the arms of a loved one.

API developed guidelines for bottle-feeding with a unique viewpoint. Because we encourage all parents to look at their parenting choices through the lens of attachment, we have coined the term *bottle nursing* because it reflects breastfeeding behaviors and has tremendous advantages for the parent or other caregiver and baby. These recommendations are applicable to infants who are bottle-fed breast milk, formula, or a combination.

To simulate breastfeeding, parents hold the baby in the crook of the arm, positioning the bottle alongside the breast. This position places the baby's face and cheek in contact with the parent's arm, and this skin-to-skin contact helps parent and baby feel more connected. Holding the baby during feeding also helps to prevent her from developing "flat-head syndrome," or plagiocephaly, which can happen when a child is left on a flat surface too frequently. When a baby drinks from a propped bottle, mother and baby miss an important opportunity to strengthen their emotional connection. Propping the bottle can also be a choking hazard.

Try to make feeding time a special time of calm for both parent and child. Maintain eye contact while feeding when the baby is alert and interested, and switch positions from one side to another; these help strengthen the baby's eye muscles. Talk softly and lovingly to your baby at feeding times. Parents should respect their child's hunger cues by avoiding feeding schedules. Following the child's cues helps to strengthen the attachment relationship and shows the baby that her needs are understood.

A Foster Mother's Story

We take care of our foster babies as if they were our birth children in every way, except that they are bottle-fed. We hold them as much as we can; I wear them in a sling all of the time when I am out in public, and we never take the car seat out of the car. We sleep in close proximity to them; we have a porta-crib next to our bed. We feed them bottles but use a breastfeeding model, holding them close, never propping the bottle, changing sides for eye-hand coordination, . . . demand-feeding, yet being careful not to overfeed them formula (which is not a concern with breast milk). We answer their needs as quickly as is humanly possible, helping them to feel as if they are the most precious beings on this earth.

—REEDY HICKEY,
FOSTER MOTHER OF THIRTY-TWO INFANTS,
ATTACHMENT PARENTING: THE JOURNAL OF API

With attachment in mind, mothers (or primary caregivers) who bottle-nurse choose to follow the breastfeeding model closely so that the baby associates feeding as a special time of holding and interaction; therefore, during feedings the mother is often the primary person who feeds him while using the bottle, though not necessarily the only person. The key is to avoid a lot of different people feeding the baby in order to help promote the parent-child or caregiver-child connection. This approach to bottle-feeding produces many benefits for mother and child. The mother will have an opportunity to sit down, to have a special time to bond and rest, just as a breastfeeding mother would be "allowed" to do. A new mother sometimes needs this excuse to rest, instead of feeling that she must do all the housework or other tasks while letting someone else feed the baby. With this behavior, the baby benefits from the consistency of his mother's presence while feeding and is able to gaze at her face, smell her scent, and feel secure in her arms. This enables their precious attachment relationship to deepen. A mother might say to a well-intentioned relative or friend who wants to feed the baby that this is their special bonding time and a rest time for Mom.

Sucking can remain a strong need well past the first year or two. Pacifiers, when used appropriately, can satisfy that need until the child outgrows it. Breastfeeding babies suck at the breast for comfort, so parents of bottle-fed babies can enrich their child's experience by either holding the baby in the feeding position when giving a pacifier or simply holding and comforting an older child. These modifications increase close physical contact and bonding time and can make weaning from the pacifier a more natural and gradual process.

As the baby gets older and is able to hold her own bottle, the parent may be tempted to allow the baby to feed herself or to let her walk around with a bottle rather than providing the comfort the child is seeking. If a child doesn't associate the bottle with being held or having undivided attention by the parent, she might use the bottle or a pacifier as a comfort tool or "transitional object." Toddlers who use the bottle, pacifier, or thumb for comfort—rather than being comforted by the parent—may have a much harder time giving up the bottle, pacifier, or thumb down the road. If they learn to come to a parent for comfort or cuddle time and perhaps a short time of sucking on their bottle or pacifier, eventually they will prefer the cuddle and gradually wean from the transitional object, much like a breastfeeding toddler weans from the breast. In the case of a baby or child who must be separated from the parents during part of the day, it is important that the parent evaluate how important a pacifier or other transitional object is for the security of the child. In some cases, it would be cruel to forbid the use of these comforts, so parents must use their best judgment.

Nurturing Yourself While Feeding Your Baby

Feeding time is the ideal time to take a break, rest, and refuel. For example, mothers can nurture themselves when feeding the new baby by sitting in a comfortable chair, having something to drink (like water or herbal tea), and making this a special time to connect with the baby. As mentioned earlier, the distance from a baby's eyes to the mother's eyes while feeding is about eleven inches, the perfect focal length for newborn vision. Nature provides this perfect visual field for the baby to study his parents' faces, allowing him to fall in love with his parents through sight, taste, touch, smell, and sound.

Just as a baby flourishes when fed by his mother, the new mother flourishes when nurtured by her partner. Sometimes mothers become so involved in the care of their infants that they don't recognize their own needs until they are in emotional or physical trouble. Mothers need frequent rest, plentiful fluids, and adequate nutrition.

A father's relationship with the baby is unique and extremely important to the child's overall development. It is important that fathers (especially those whose babies are breastfed) know they can still develop a close relationship with the baby in many ways other than feeding—such as holding or burping the baby after she has eaten, bathing her baby, changing a diaper, practicing infant massage, taking walks and naps together, and playfully interacting with her. When the father nurtures the mother, he nurtures his baby as well.

Musings from a Mother of Multiples *(continued)*

My hunger while nursing was insatiable. Crazy, wicked insatiable. I suggest to other moms of twins to go ahead and buy a case of protein drinks to have in the house because it simply isn't possible to eat enough calories to keep up. Complicating the issue is the fact that it is impossible to eat while holding two babies. With a singleton, I find I am constantly munching. With twins, both arms were often full and I couldn't reach to pick up food. My daughter often came to the rescue, feeding me bites of snack mixes and nuts all throughout the day. I would put a protein drink on the counter with a long straw so that I could bend down and take a drink. And I found that I ate a *lot* of calories in the car, because it was the only time I had one hand free. Still, I was almost always painfully hungry. There were times I was so hungry I had to put them down, even though they would scream the entire time I ate. It killed me, but I didn't know what else to do. (*To be continued*)

—PAM S., MOTHER OF FOUR

[**Authors' Note:** *Imagine how different her experience could have been if she had received help from others. Think SWAT team! As early as possible in your pregnancy, we would recommend getting volunteers from your friend or family networks or place of worship. If you don't attend a church, maybe a friend would be willing to ask for volunteers from her church to help for the first few months with providing healthy meals, snacks, or rocking the babies so Mom can eat and relax for a few minutes.*]

Introducing Solid Food

What does starting babies on solid food have to do with attachment parenting? A parent's sensitivity and attunement to the baby will be important in determining whether he is ready for solid food. As with all decisions, a parent must examine available options and make the best choice for the child—in this case, parents needs to opt for foods conducive to optimal brain and physical development. Babies fed the healthiest diet are sick less often, have fewer discipline problems, and achieve more in school. Babies start to show interest in solid foods toward the second half of the first year. Signs of readiness include getting a few teeth, drooling, showing interest in what the parents are eating, nursing more frequently, sitting up unassisted, and being able to pick up small pieces of food. Until these external signs are in place, it is unlikely that the baby is fully ready. It is important to remember that the child will let his parents know when he is ready. For instance, some babies who are prone to allergies may naturally reject solid foods until they are older.

Many experts agree that a baby is ready for solid food when she no longer thrusts out her tongue and she is able to pick up small items like dry cereal with her thumb and forefinger. When a baby is just learning to eat solids, offer breast or bottle first, followed by one solid food. Start slowly with foods that are not likely to cause allergies (delay dairy, eggs, fish, soy, peanuts, and any foods that other family members are allergic to). Introduce gluten-containing foods (wheat, barley, and rye) with caution. Gradually introducing gluten reduces the risk of celiac disease (an allergy to wheat gluten). Watch for signs that new foods agree with the baby and that he shows a genuine interest in them. Introduce new foods one at a time for at least five days before introducing another food. This allows time for any allergic reaction to manifest. Be aware that some babies do not like to be spoon-fed solid food. They would prefer to feed themselves, so give them the opportunity to have small bits of food on their plate or high-chair tray to try themselves. This is one way they learn to manage the amount of food they want to eat.

While the American Academy of Pediatrics recommends introducing solids at six months of age, breast milk or artificial milk will likely be a baby's primary nutrition source until about one year of age. It is normal for your child to eat only small quantities of solid foods during this time. Regardless of the amount consumed, mealtimes are an important opportunity for the child to explore new tastes and textures, to develop feeding skills, and to learn the social behaviors of the family's mealtime routines. (More information about introducing solids is available through the resources listed in Appendix C.)

Watch Out for Allergies

An important part of being attuned to your child and her sensitivities is to be conscious of how food can affect her moods, energy levels, and physical problems. Wheat, eggs, and dairy have been identified as the three most common allergens; however, acidic fruits or raw vegetables may also cause your child discomfort. Don't be alarmed if your child shows no interest in food before one year of age.

Some children need more time for their immune systems to develop before they are able to digest solid foods. Some of the signs of a food allergy are runny nose, itchy nose or eyes, rash, irritability, sleeplessness, diarrhea, or refusal to eat a certain food. Let your child be your guide, and allow your child to develop her taste for food naturally.

Food Additives and Hyperactivity?

For years, parents have reported to their doctors their concerns about hyperactivity in their children. Could it possibly be related to the foods they were eating? Most doctors did not see a relationship, but recently the prestigious British medical journal, the *Lancet*, published a study on children's behavior and artificial food additives. The researchers concluded the following:

> For many of the assessments, there were small but statistically significant differences of measured behaviors in children who consumed the food additives compared with those who did not. In each case, increased hyperactive behaviors were associated with consuming the additives. For those comparisons in which no statistically significant differences were found, there was a trend for more hyperactive behaviors associated with the food additive drink in virtually every assessment. Thus, the overall findings of the study are clear and require that even we skeptics, who have long doubted parental claims of the effects of various foods on the behavior of their children, admit we might have been wrong.[22]

Nurturing a Taste for Nutritious Food

Breast milk prepares infants for the various tastes of solid foods because it is flavored by the foods eaten by the nursing mother. In fact, a child's taste for certain food begins in the womb. That's why it's important for a mother to eat a variety of healthy foods. Generally, children develop their eating patterns from their parents; therefore, it's never too early for parents to begin improving their own habits. When parents offer only nutritious foods in the early years, children will develop a natural taste for these foods and learn important lessons about good nutrition.

What is considered "nutritious" food? Generally, a good rule for identifying nutritious foods is those foods that are in the most natural (least processed) state possible. Ideally, these foods are grown or raised organically (avoiding pesticides and growth hormones). Children who tolerate dairy products usually love cheeses and yogurt. Consider cheeses that are natural, such as Swiss, rather than processed cheeses like American cheese. Plain yogurt sweetened with a little maple syrup and fresh fruit makes a healthy snack. Foods containing dyes, preservatives, excess salt, and sugar should be avoided. Parents don't have to rely on baby food that comes prepackaged. By six months of age or older, babies are often interested in eating what their parents eat. Cooking foods with minimal seasoning can provide meals for the family and for the baby without any extra work or expense. Adults can always add additional spices or embellishments after cooking. Mashing or blending some foods prepared for an adult meal may make them palatable for a baby. They then can be frozen in small portions in an ice tray for future meals.

Remember that it is the parent's job to provide healthy choices and model eating nutritious meals. The child should be allowed to choose what to eat from these healthy choices and how much to eat. A growing child requires nutritious snacks (such as prepared finger foods) and meals throughout the day. Snacks or drinks that contain sugar will curb the child's appetite and negatively affect his willingness to eat more nutritious foods. Encourage your child to follow his bodily cues of hunger and thirst; this teaches him to eat when he is hungry and stop when he is full. Forcing your child to eat when he is not hungry, or to eat foods he does not want to eat, can lead to unhealthy eating habits and potentially to eating disorders. Never use food as a reward or punishment or make food or dessert contingent on behavior. Rather than restricting access to foods, consider having only healthy foods available in the home. Toddlers are busy and burn a lot of calories; they need to eat multiple small meals during the day and should not be expected to sit at a dinner table for long periods. Studies have shown that when offered a variety of healthy food choices, children will, over time, select a balanced diet (even if they only eat peas for one week and chicken for the next). Parents who have concerns about their child's eating habits, diet, allergies, or general health should refer to books related to healthy eating. A list can be found at the end of this book. *The Womanly Art of Breastfeeding* offers well-tested recommendations for healthy first solid foods and toddler foods, including for children with food allergies.

Gentle Weaning

The American Academy of Pediatrics 2005 Breastfeeding Policy Statement advises, "It is recommended that breastfeeding continue for at least twelve months, and thereafter for as long as mutually desired." It also states, "There is no upper limit to the duration of breastfeeding and no evidence of psychological or developmental harm from breastfeeding into the third year of life or longer." The World Health Organization adds that even though in Western cultures it may be unusual to see a child nurse past one year, worldwide it is normal for children, and it continues to be important nutritionally, immunologically, and emotionally to nurse beyond one year.[23]

As surprising as it may seem to some, nursing beyond one or two years of age is normal human behavior and continues to offer many advantages, not the least of which is to satisfy a strong sucking need. Although weaning begins the moment solid foods are introduced into a baby's diet, breast milk remains a beneficial component of the child's nutrition and overall good health. It is also an effective comforting tool, providing both mother and child with a special, relaxing time together to reconnect.

Food increasingly takes the place of breast milk in terms of caloric need, but nursing continues to meet many other needs, such as security and connection. La Leche League International and API recommend that weaning occur only when a child outgrows the need. In other words, the child is showing signs of readiness and may be nursing more out of habit than need. For instance, if you find that your toddler has been nursing every time you get on the phone, you might choose to find a quiet activity that replaces nursing at this time. If a child finds that this is the only way she can get your attention, you begin to see the difference between a habit and a need.

If weaning is initiated by the mother, it should be done gradually and sensitively. If there comes a point where the mother needs to wean before the child has displayed a readiness to wean, gentle techniques such as distraction, substitution, extension of time between sessions, night weaning, response by the father to baby's nighttime needs, or shortened nursing sessions may help. Local API or La Leche League support groups may offer more ideas or suggestions for weaning, or refer to *The Womanly Art of Breastfeeding* book. Fathers and other caregivers can also help mothers at this time by becoming more involved in the care of, and activities with, an older child. If the child reacts strongly to this change, the parents should assess the situation and the child's unmet needs and reevaluate the child's true readiness.

An empathetic mother understands that abrupt weaning from breast or bottle can affect the attachment relationship with her child, so it is important for parents to develop strategies for replacing the nursing frequency with extra attention. This may include more time for cuddling and reading stories, drinking from a cup when thirsty, and playing together.

Children under one year of age will need to be weaned from breast to bottle, and bottle-fed children should be weaned as gently from their bottles as breastfed babies are from the breast. Parents should remember that the weaning process takes time and patience; every child is different, so there is no timetable. Parents can learn more about these techniques in La Leche League International's book *How Weaning Happens* by Diane Bengson.

Mealtime: A Time for Promoting Connection in the Family

Many cultures around the world have preserved the tradition of family mealtimes as one of the most important times of the day. So often in American families, the TV is on and the family may sit in the living room or even go off to their bedrooms to eat their meals. Gordon Neufeld and Gabor Maté, in their book *Hold On to Your Kids*, reminds us of why this time is so important in family life:

> Since our sojourn in Provence, France, I [Gordon] have come to consider the family sit-down meal as one of the most significant attachment rituals of all. Attachment and eating go together. One facilitates the other. It seems to me that the meal should be a time of unabashed dependency: where the attachment hierarchy is still preserved, where the dependable take care of the dependent, where experience still counts, where there is pleasure in nurturing and being nurtured and where food is the way to the heart. What other activity can provide something for our children to hold on to, and invite our children to depend on us? What other activity provides us the opportunity to collect the eyes, coax the smiles, and get them nodding?[24]

Make mealtimes with your child an important family gathering time. Try to make at least one meal a day (dinnertime for most families) a time for connection and community. A couple can begin this ritual of creating a special time even before their baby arrives by turning off the TV, making a conscious choice to not answer the phone, and being present for each other at mealtime. Once this habit is started, it will be a natural part of the child's experience as he grows up. If parents keep their conversation positive, loving, and interesting, everyone will have a pleasant association with mealtime, which will help not only good digestion but also enhancing the attachment relationships that began when giving baby her first feeding soon after birth.

Breastfeeding Policy Changes in the Affordable Care Act

Employers (who participate in the Fair Labor Standards Act-FLSA) are required to provide a reasonable amount of break time and a space to express milk as frequently as needed by the nursing mother, for up to one year following the birth of the employee's child. The frequency of breaks needed to express breast milk as well as the duration of each break will likely vary. The space provided by the employer cannot be a bathroom, and it must be shielded from view and free from intrusion by coworkers or the public.

For a list of state laws to protect breastfeeding mothers go to:

www.ncsl.org/issues-research/health/breastfeeding-state-laws.aspx. For information about breastfeeding policies and updates on the federal law in the workplace go to: www.usbreastfeeding.org.

CHAPTER FOUR

PRINCIPLE 3:
Responding with Sensitivity
Learning the Language of Love

Here's how the early mother-infant communication system works.
The opening sounds of the baby's cry activate a mother's emotions.
This is physical as well as psychological. Upon hearing her
baby cry, a mother experiences an increased blood flow to her breasts,
accompanied by the biological urge to pick up and nurse her baby.
This is one of the strongest examples of how the biological signals of the
baby trigger a biological response in the mother. There is no other
signal in the world that sets off such intense responses in a mother
as her baby's cry. At no other time in the child's life will
language so forcefully stimulate the mother to act.

—William Sears, MD, "Bonding with Your Newborn," in
Attachment Parenting: The Journal of API

Of the eight principles of parenting, we believe responding with sensitivity is one of the most important. It is the foundation that
strengthens all the other principles, and it is the basis for developing a secure
attachment relationship with your children. Sensitive responsiveness implies
the ability to set aside one's own needs for the needs of the baby; it presupposes

a change in consciousness of the parents and the capacity to feel empathy—to see the world through the eyes of their child. Babies communicate their needs in many ways, including body movements, facial expressions, and crying. They often try to tell us that they need our attention long before they begin to cry, if we only understood their attempts. As you learn to understand and respond to your infant's cues (signals), through consistency you will build a strong foundation of trust and empathy.

Researchers have found that human infants are born with the expectation to be responded to rather quickly. When responses are consistent, babies begin to learn the first lessons of empathy and trust. Often parents wait until their baby is crying before responding, and then they have a very distraught baby on their hands who is much harder to calm down. For instance, a hungry baby (or one who needs comforting) will typically turn his head toward the breast and open his mouth wide, he may put his fists in his mouth and suck on them, or he may simply start making sucking movements with his mouth. By paying attention to his subtle signals, you will begin to understand what he is trying to communicate long before the tears begin to flow. If a baby fusses and seems restless but quiets down when you pick him up, you are fulfilling his need for closeness, warmth, and comfort.

Neuroscience studies are showing that there is more to these interactions than meets the eye. A mother and baby's brains can actually become synchronized, and it is that synchrony that they call *neural resonance*. Neural resonance very simply means that mother and child are better able to read and interpret each other's emotions, and brain waves become very similar. In her book *The Bond*, Lynne McTaggart describes her experience as a first-time mother. She felt ill prepared, even though she studied pregnancy, birth, and parenting with the same passion as an investigative journalist. She describes how she, alone, was able to calm her crying baby, no matter how much her husband tried. She later realized that she was—in a very real sense—a "metronome" for the baby's brain waves: "Our brain waves had coordinated into a single undulation. . . . Opening yourself up to a pure connection with someone else, as occurs with someone else, as occurs with a mother and child, creates a neural resonance effect between you."

What Is Empathy?

The word *empathy* means experiencing as one's own the feelings of others, or the capacity for this. When you respond to your baby (or any other human being, for that matter) with empathy, you convey these implicit messages:

I want to understand how you feel.   *Let's work this out together.*

I hurt when you hurt.   *I'm here if you need me.*

We're in this together.   *You can trust me.*

Your feelings matter to me.   *You matter to me.*

I trust you.   *You can count on me.*

I respect you.   *I see the world through your eyes.*

I will help you feel better.   *I'll always be here for you.*

I honor you.   *I love you no matter what you do.*

I care about you.

The implicit messages of empathy to yourself as a parent:

I see myself in you.   *I am not afraid of your feelings.*

I was once in your booties.   *I am secure in myself.*

I understand myself.   *I trust myself.*

I accept myself.   *I know myself.*

I am strong even in my weakness.   *I accept you in all of your expressions.*

I am not afraid to feel.   *I do not reject you when you are not*

I honor myself.   *reflecting back what I wish or need.*

—Lysa Parker and Lu Hanessian

Building a Strong Connection with Your Baby

Harville Hendrix, a renowned psychotherapist, and his wife, Helen Hunt, wrote *Giving the Love That Heals* to help parents understand how imperative it is that they strengthen the attachment with their baby. This advice comes from many years of experience working with individuals and couples using

Imago therapy, which they developed (they are also the parents of six grown children):

> For the first eighteen months after birth, your baby is totally dependent. He is bonding with you and learning that his needs will be met. *During this period, the most important thing you can do is be reliably available and reliably warm.* This means responding to what he needs when he needs it, regardless of whether it is convenient. When you do this, you are ensuring that your baby will survive and that he will maintain that sense of connection with the universe that is the foundation of his future security in the world." [1]

Building a strong connection with your baby involves not only responding consistently to her physical needs but also spending enjoyable time interacting, talking, and playing with her, a natural and fun way to meet her emotional needs. When your baby gazes into your eyes, it is her invitation to you to connect with her; she may smile at you with the expectation that you will smile and talk back to her. Later, as she begins to understand the rhythm of the sounds of language, she will attempt to make her own sounds to communicate back to you in the form of babbling, expecting you to talk back. Hendrix and Hunt advise that parents meet the emotional needs of their baby by speaking in a soothing, soft tone of voice:

Mothers of securely attached infants tend to be more sensitive, reliable, and accepting of their infants. [2]

The synchrony, or dysynchrony, of interactions between parent and infant have been found to determine security of attachment. Mothers who were found to be inconsistent, intrusive, and overstimulating were more likely to have insecure attachments with their babies. [3]

Parental warmth and positive expressiveness with children was strongly correlated with children's development of empathy and social functioning, especially in older children. [4]

> As the baby begins to experiment with facial expressions and sounds that will eventually enable her to verbalize her communications, it is important for the parents to validate her nonverbal communication by mirroring them. This means reproducing the sounds and expressions in order to allow the baby to gain confidence in her experimentation. When in doubt how to mirror, smiling works wonders. [5]

Researchers have found that mothers who are depressed have difficulty picking up on a baby's facial or body signals and are out of synchrony with their babies.[6] When a baby's frustrated attempts to engage his mother are not responded to, he will eventually stop trying to communicate his needs to her. This can affect his brain development, lower his IQ, and put him at risk of becoming depressed as well.[7] Researchers have also found that when mothers respond quickly and appropriately to their babies' cues over time, these children develop better language, cognitive abilities, and self-esteem.[8]

Many societal challenges can interfere with a parent's ability to develop a responsive relationship with his or her baby. For example, parents may believe myths about spoiling a baby, or they may follow advice (often unsolicited) from well-meaning family, friends, and medical professionals, the media, and self-proclaimed "parenting experts." More often than not, this advice conflicts with the science of normal child development. The parents' own intuitive feelings become suppressed, which can undermine their confidence and create unnecessary stress.

> Mothers who accurately perceived the urgency of their infants' cries consequently responded appropriately. The benefit to infants . . . proved to be higher cognitive development and language-acquisition scores. The mothers who responded to their infants' cries inconsistently were found to have lower self-esteem and lack of social supports.[9]

In the course of a child's development, she begins to form attachments with the person who spends the majority of time nurturing and caring for her. Frequent holding throughout the day and playful interactions with your baby will increase bonding and promote a secure attachment. Many new parents are relieved to learn that most babies need a lot of close physical contact.

It is impossible to spoil a baby when satisfying his need to be held. When you listen to your baby, you will find he is most content and happy when being held close to you—this is because he is experiencing life as part of you, not as a separate being. Who doesn't want a happy, contented baby? Soon enough, your baby will be squirming in your arms to be put down.

In the first six months or so, your baby may seem perfectly happy being held by and interacting with other people. Then, around eight to nine months of age, she may suddenly begin to respond with fear and anxiety to strangers and less familiar family members. Attempts to separate her from Mom will be met with desperate clinging and crying. Rest assured, this is normal developmental behavior, which most babies experience as they develop more awareness of the world around them. It is actually a good sign that she wants to remain close to the person to whom she has become attached. Knowing this should make it easier to cope with, rather than allowing yourself to become overly concerned or frustrated. This is an important phase of development, and the baby's feelings require that you continue to be sensitive in your responses, to help her feel safe and secure. This is *not* the time to teach your baby to be independent or to self-soothe. The intense fears of separation will gradually subside as your child matures over the next few years, depending on her temperament. It may take considerably longer to pass for more sensitive children, especially if they have to learn to be comfortable in the care of nonparental adults. Follow your child's cues rather than forcing her to accept the well-meaning actions of strangers or expecting her to overcome stranger or separation anxiety before she is developmentally ready. This can also be an intense time for Mom; she will need a lot more support and understanding from her family and friends.

> THERE IS THE LANGUAGE OF THE EMBRACE, THE
> LANGUAGE OF THE EYES, THE LANGUAGE OF THE SMILE, VOCAL
> COMMUNICATIONS OF PLEASURE AND DISTRESS. IT IS THE ESSENTIAL
> VOCABULARY OF LOVE BEFORE WE CAN SPEAK LOVE.
>
> —Selma Fraiberg,
> *In Defense of Mothering: Every Child's Birthright*

Responsiveness and Development

Responding sensitively to your baby teaches him that he is loved and that he can trust you to be there for him. In the beginning, infants don't understand what love is. What they know is that when they feel hungry, uncomfortable, insecure, and frightened, they need someone to respond to them. From a biological perspective, they are born with three basic survival needs: proximity (close physical contact to Mom or the primary caregiver), protection (the need to feel safe and secure), and predictability (knowing that Mom or Dad is consistently available and that their needs will be met).[10]

From a neurological perspective, it's important to understand how responsiveness plays a significant role in brain development. As we discussed in Chapter 1, a baby's brain is greatly underdeveloped at birth (only 25 percent is developed), making him highly dependent upon his parents for everything, especially food, warmth, and comfort. Brain researchers have found that the mother's face, emotional expressions, and tone of voice have a direct impact on the development of the brain. The development of critical parts of the brain coincides with the period in which that attachment develops—during the first three years.[11]

Emotional Regulation

Because of their neurological immaturity, infants cannot be expected to figure things out on their own—to soothe themselves—especially during the early weeks, months, and sometimes years. *You* are the emotional regulator for your child until her brain growth has caught up and he is developmentally capable of regulating her own feelings. This is a gradual process that happens over the first few years.

When faced with stressful or fearful situations, your baby or young child needs calm, loving, and empathetic parents to speak affectionately and reassuringly to him. Using comforting touch such as holding, massage, or stroking also helps children learn to regulate their emotions and intense feelings. The sucking reflex remains strong for babies and toddlers and goes a long way in helping to comfort them.

Sue Gerhardt, author of *Why Love Matters: How Affection Shapes a Baby's Brain*, describes a parents' role: "Parents are really needed to be a sort of emotion coach. They need to be there and to be tuned in to the baby's constantly changing states, but they also need to help the baby to the next level." For instance, she writes that with the help of parents, children will begin to identify specific feelings with words like *frustration, irritation, anger, silly, funny, joyful*—a wide range of emotions. Parents can do this by "helping the baby to become aware of his own feelings, talking in baby talk, and emphasizing and exaggerating words and gestures so that the baby can realize that this is not mum and dad just expressing themselves, this is them 'showing me' my feelings."[12]

The Sensitive Baby

Most parents find that caring for their baby is more intense than they expected. A so-called fussy baby is a sensitive baby and can magnify the intensity of your parenting experience. You may find yourself quickly overwhelmed. "High-need" is a term used to describe a certain temperament of baby who is very sensitive and who may experience more periods of fussiness than other babies. Sensitive babies can become overstimulated in a variety of ways, such as by cold air, bright lights, sudden noises or movements, or too many different adults giving her attention.

If a child's need for comfort is not met by an emotionally responsive adult, the child's nervous system can, over time, remain in a hyperaroused state.[13] Uncomforted stress can lead to a host of physical ailments later in life, including eating and digestive disorders, poor sleep, panic attacks, headaches, and chronic fatigue.[14] If left to cry alone in childhood and without therapy in later life, the higher-level brain functions that regulate antianxiety chemicals in the brain are impaired. This may result in clinical depression.[15]

Sensitive babies tend to be more vocal about what they need, and adults may incorrectly perceive them as too demanding. Instead of perceiving the baby's "fussiness" as disapproval, try to see it as a signal that he is overwhelmed with his own feelings and needs, and he is seeking help to find his equilibrium. High-need babies may well require more soothing, but in the aftermath of such consistent responsiveness, these children often develop a peace about them that shows they have been deeply nurtured. Margot Sunderland, a child psychotherapist and author of *The Science of Parenting*, describes the mechanisms that work in a baby's brain to help him cope with stress later in life: "If you consistently soothe your child's distress over the years and take any anguished crying seriously, highly effective stress response systems can be established in his brain."[16] So don't worry that you might be "giving in" by responding to their cries; they often grow up to be delightful, spirited children with strong leadership qualities. In time, as your baby matures and you become more attuned (tuned in), you will know intuitively when he gradually becomes capable of waiting a few minutes for your response.

Responding at Night

Cultural expectations have led us to believe that babies should sleep through the night for at least a good six to seven hours. This ongoing myth keeps many parents frustrated and can cause them to become desensitized and less responsive if they feel they are reinforcing a negative behavior, such as waking, fussing, and crying. Researchers have found that infants have different sleep rhythms, with more periods of light sleep, and aren't naturally designed to sleep for long stretches of time in their early months—especially breastfed babies.

The reality is that your baby still needs to be cared for during the night. Allowing a baby to cry for prolonged periods with the intention of teaching her to sleep on her own causes the baby to experience abnormally high levels of stress hormones (cortisol), creating an unbalanced chemical state in his brain. Researchers have found that responsive mothers help a baby's stress hormones normalize more quickly.[17] Minimizing stress for your baby is important; children who experience high levels of cortisol are at risk for emotional problems later in life.[18] More information on responding to a child's nighttime needs is available in Chapter 6.

When Baby's Cries Overwhelm You

Remaining sensitive and empathetic when faced with a crying, inconsolable infant can be very hard for many parents. It calls for awareness and a lot of patience. This doesn't typically come easily or naturally—especially if you weren't raised that way. At times, you may find it difficult to be emotionally responsive, especially when you are feeling exhausted or are experiencing a lot of stress in other areas of your life. Hendrix and Hunt write in *Giving the Love That Heals*, "If you find yourself reacting strongly to your child's dependence on you, then you may have been wounded at this stage [of development]. You can use this insight to focus your attention on issues that you need to work on in your efforts to become a conscious parent."[19]

Whether you are balancing the needs of a new baby and an older sibling or the demands of being emotionally responsive to a high-needs baby, fatigue, frustration, and exhaustion can cause you to overreact, so don't take this lightly! Even the best of parents can become dangerously overwhelmed without support and rest. Call in the reserves (Dad, Mom, a friend), and allow yourself some time alone to rest, collect your sense of calm, and practice personal reflection so that you don't take your baby's crying personally or fall into the mind-set that the baby is being manipulative.

Symptoms of burnout or inability to cope with baby's needs are signals that you need extra support or professional help. We discuss this in more depth in Chapter 9.

Musings from a Mother of Multiples
(continued)

There was so much more crying with twins than with a singleton. It simply was not possible to meet their needs the way I could meet the needs of one. I would get horrible guilt if one cried more than the other. It's awful, but sometimes I would put them both down to do something I could have done holding one because I just couldn't bear to pick. Other times I would hold one for a few minutes while the other screamed, and then switch. It was gut-wrenching, and I spent a lot of time crying myself. Sometimes I would wear earplugs as I tried to comfort them because the agony of two crying babies rattled me to the core. The earplugs took a little bit of the edge off so I could stay calm and focused on them. Whenever possible, I held them both. That in itself was hard. My back and arms ached. I had to lean backward to adjust my center of gravity, and then I couldn't see the ground in front of me. I couldn't cradle both horizontally, so they had to be upright even when they would have preferred another hold. I was terrified I was going to trip and drop them both. I became very strong. I had the muscles of a weight lifter! I just kept telling myself that I could do anything for a year. I would think of the hardships our ancestors endured. It was just one year. I could do it.

The first year was totally about survival. I took things fifteen minutes at a time. I tried to smile and laugh some, but I cried a lot more. It was so hard to feel uniquely bonded to each. Those fun infant moments, where you gaze into a baby's eyes or stroke his hair while he sleeps, they just didn't happen. Not often, anyway. The mechanics of holding two meant that I was rarely gazing into their eyes. I remember another mom saying I could surely tell them apart because "I was the mom." I just cried. I couldn't tell them apart as well as my husband and daughter could, who often saw them side by side in my arms. Later I would learn about them as unique kids, but in the beginning, they almost felt like one being. I was so overwhelmed by meeting their needs and making sure they could be attached to me as their mom that I didn't have time to stop and get to know them as my individual sons. It's hard to describe. I have a singleton now, my fourth child, and only now do I really see how much I missed of that first year. Even little things were overwhelming, like I couldn't enjoy bathing one because I only had a few brief minutes before the other, waiting in a bouncy chair nearby, would start crying. I couldn't help one toddler walk unless there was someone else home to help the other. So many things were about timing—just rushing through the motions and moving on to the next baby. Diaper changes were horrid. Every baby wants to be picked up and comforted after a change, but the first boy would have to wait for the second change, and then they had to share my arms. They usually didn't seem to mind sharing. They would snuggle in to each other, grip on to each other. It was all they had ever known. But I knew. I had a singleton, and I knew how much more each "should" have. It made me sad that I couldn't give them what I felt they needed. At the time I was sure they would not be properly attached, that I wasn't doing "good enough." It was a dark time. But they are older now, happy, and securely attached. My husband likes to remind me that even on my "worst attached" day, our kids get more connection than on some kids' best days. Kids are resilient, and while I would never advocate testing that resilience unnecessarily, it does seem at some level twins just "know" they are rough on a mom. They forgive a lot. And they have each other. (*To be continued*)

[**Authors' Note:** *Children are forgiving and resilient, especially when they know they are loved. We can't quiet our child's every cry or heal every hurt, but we can be there for them, to comfort the best we can.*]

Why Do Babies Cry?

Remember that infants cry to communicate their needs and feelings. Here is a list of some of the most common reasons babies cry or appear "colicky." In time, you will develop a mental checklist and go through it quickly as you try to determine how best to help your fussy baby. It is helpful to try different approaches—your baby will let you know when her need is being met. Sometimes the only thing you can do is hold her.

- Hunger
- Fatigue
- Loneliness
- A need to be held
- A need for skin-to-skin contact
- Discomfort, irritability, or gas (also known as "colic")
- Feeling too hot or too cold
- Perception of the mother's stress
- Sress from too much stimulation
- Understimulation (needs more loving interactions with parents)
- Surprise from loud, sudden noises
- Food sensitivity to something directly ingested or passed through the mother's milk
- Unidentified pain or medical problem such as ear infection, gastro-esophageal reflux, urinary tract infection, or anemia

Toddlers and Beyond

Toddlers still need a sensitive and responsive parent as their bond to you continues to grow. You can maintain your responsiveness by using the following tips:

- As your child grows, responding with empathy, respecting your child's feelings, and trying to understand the need underlying his outward behaviors will help you continue the close connection you nurtured when your child was a baby. Young children continue to need a lot of loving attention. As toddlers begin to demonstrate more independence, parents can support their explorations by providing a safe environment for discovery and staying nearby to respond when the child needs it. By showing interest in their toddlers' activities, participating in child-directed play, and sharing in their excitement, parents build their children's confidence and help them develop skills. Throughout the early years, children require frequent feedback from their parents as they try new things.

- Parents are instrumental in helping their children develop social skills. Parents can set up appropriate playdates for their child, monitor the children's play, and intervene using positive discipline techniques to keep the children safe and teach effective communication techniques and concepts of fair play. While some toddlers are ready for, and do enjoy, more formal preschool environments, it is not necessary for the socialization of young children. When evaluating any program in which parents are not included, consider your child's readiness to separate from you and the amount and type of support provided by the adults supervising the program.

- Parents are the child's first teachers and begin teaching from birth. Enrich your child's experiences on a daily basis as much as possible. Seek out activities that you can do simply that don't require spending money. Children really love learning and soak up everything like a sponge. Parents who are attuned intuitively help stimulate that learning environment by following their child's current interests, answering questions, and responding to daily "teachable moments." You can read, sing, play learning games, create projects, and follow your child's lead in play. Toddlers are also capable of playing alone or alongside Mom or Dad as they do other chores around the house. Toddlers love to mimic what they see you do, so give them opportunities to perform tasks like folding towels or washing the car. They learn that working can be fun, and it makes them feel like they are a helping member of the family.

Responding to Toddler Tantrums and Strong Emotions

You've seen it happen: you're in the grocery store or restaurant and a young child has a meltdown—whining, crying, or maybe screaming on the floor. You may have thought, "That child just needs a good spanking," but in reality, that child needs a parent who remains calm. It is critical to respond to children's strong emotions, even when they act out with negative behavior or tantrums. How do you do it? You can start by not taking his behavior personally and by trying to see the world through his eyes, with the understanding that it's up to you to help your child regulate his emotions. The best prevention is to avoid putting yourself and your child in a situation you know will likely lead to a meltdown, such as shopping when your child is tired or hungry. Plan ahead as much as possible and keep in mind the low tolerance level of children; they can get bored rather quickly.

> Mothers whose behavior toward their preschool children is responsive, nonpunitive, and nonauthoritarian are more likely to have children who exhibit prosocial behavior.[20]

If you do have to go shopping, talk to your child ahead of time and explain what you're going to do and what your expectations are for her. Make sure she is fed or you have snacks with you. Try creating a game of shopping by giving your child some item to look for in the store. Keeping their little minds busy (distraction is easy at young ages) will keep them from getting quickly bored and becoming cranky.

Temper tantrums are an outlet for emotions that are too powerful for a young child's undeveloped brain to manage in a more acceptable way. Tantrums represent real emotions and should be handled empathetically. A parent's role during a tantrum is to acknowledge and validate the child's feelings and provide comfort, not to get angry or punish her (even if you feel the urge). Remember that as children grow they develop empathy and improved social skills when you respond with love and affirmation.[22]

Parents bring the baby into this more sophisticated emotional world by identifying feelings and labeling them clearly. Usually this teaching happens quite unself-consciously.[21]

In the heat of the moment, it is likely that your child will not be able to talk about his feelings or will need your help to give his feelings the right words. He might respond best to soothing words and physical comfort. To calm an upset child, remain composed and try techniques such as distraction, cuddling, or, if it is more comfortable for the child, holding or sitting next to him while talking gently to him (assuming you're not in the middle of the grocery store). You will likely have to experiment to find out how your child responds best—every child is different, as is the situation. You *can* learn to model appropriate ways to deal with young, fragile emotions by using empathy and compassion for the child who is tired, frustrated, hurt, or angry. You can read more information about handling tantrums and strong emotions in Chapter 8.

Helping Children Learn to Express Feelings

Children learn empathy from parents who have been responsive to them. Once the child is three, four, or five years old, parents are better able to use language and reason to express empathy; this helps children understand their feelings and the feelings of others. The seeds of empathy are growing during the early years, and you will begin to see the results of your efforts when your child begins to show kindness toward another child or concern for a child who is hurt.

Many parents tend to forget that children, like adults, need to learn how to express their feelings. It's hard to do without the appropriate words, and many adults are not even literate when it comes to adequately expressing their own needs and feelings. A program called Nonviolent Communication (NVC), also called Compassionate Communication, offers resources to teach adults successful ways of expressing feelings that meet deep emotional needs. (Read more about NVC in Chapter 8, and visit the Center for

Nonviolent Communication's website, www.cnvc.org.) Being sensitively responsive to your baby is the beginning of teaching compassionate communication skills for life.

Just for Dads

In the early weeks and months, a father can feel like second fiddle to the mother and baby. They seem to have a nice thing going, but when and where do fathers fit in? According to Dr. William Sears, fathers are often portrayed as well-meaning but bumbling when it comes to caring for newborns. He has found that "fathers have their own unique way of relating to babies, and babies thrive on this difference. . . . Studies on father bonding show that fathers who are given the opportunity and are encouraged to take an active part in caring for their newborns can become just as nurturing as mothers. A father's nurturing responses may be less automatic and slower to unfold than a mother's, but fathers are capable of a strong bonding attachment to their infants during the newborn period."[23] Attachment researchers have found that babies are born with a drive to initially form a close emotional bond (attachment) to one person, usually the mother or the primary caregiver. As the baby matures, she is more able to expand her universe to be more inclusive of the father and others in her life.

Mothers can and should actively promote bonding with fathers. Dads can be great at comforting, burping, bathing, dressing, and diaper changing. In fact, fathers' unique styles of interacting and playing with the baby should be honored and encouraged. You may find the child begins to prefer Dad for diaper changes or giving a bath. Nestling on Daddy's chest for comfort or sleep creates a very special bond that is sacred. But when hunger pangs begin or discomfort occurs, your baby will likely cry for the parent to whom she is most attached—usually Mom. Fathers are more likely, but not always, to remain the secondary attachment figure in the child's life until two to three years of age, or sometimes longer, depending on the temperament of the child. But take heart, this is normal child development. Before long, your child will be begging to go with Dad or do things with him that will create precious lifelong memories for everyone.

Research on Fathers

The Fatherhood Initiative reports that the degree of father closeness determines the likelihood of adolescents engaging in risky behaviors such as drinking, smoking, and using hard drugs and inhalants. The report states, "Given that father closeness reduces adolescent drug use, and that father closeness is highest in intact families, adolescents in intact families are at the lowest level of risk for engaging in drug use. The level of risk of adolescent drug use increases in blended families, is still higher in single-parent families, and is highest in no-parent families [families in which neither parent is involved, such as a state-run institution]. On measures of smoking, drinking, and the use of inhalants, father closeness has independent, positive, and powerful effects on adolescents. On the other hand, there is no direct correlation between mother closeness and any of the measures of adolescent drug use. In other words, efforts to reduce adolescent drug use must emphasize the strengthening of father-adolescent relationships, regardless of the type of family structure in which the adolescent lives. The strengthening of father-adolescent relationships is especially important for the millions of adolescents living in father-absent homes, where limited contact with nonresident fathers is inadequate.[24]

What About Boys?

As a culture, we have always had different perceptions and expectations of boys. People often fear that if boys are nurtured too much, it somehow warps their personalities and makes them too dependent and too sensitive. Conventional attitudes about boys permeate all aspects of society (e.g., parents, grandparents, teachers, and coaches) and has created what William Pollack calls a "boy code"—myths that boys' behavior is driven solely by their hormones and not the environment, boys need to learn to be tough at an early age, and so on. This code has only served to force boys to become disconnected from their feelings—less sensitive and more aggressive.

New research has begun to reverse this trend by emphasizing the importance of mothers and fathers in nurturing strong emotional connections with their sons. For instance, Dr. Pollack found from his research that "the absence of a close relationship with a loving mother puts a boy at a disadvantage in becoming a free, confident, and independent man who likes himself and can take risks, and who can form close and loving attachments with people in his adult life."[25] Research conducted by the Fatherhood Initiative showed that "adolescents who are close to their moms and dads have less of a need to seek out affirming relationships outside of the home, which can lead to risky behavior (gangs, smoking, drinking, and drugs)."[26] Eli Newberger, MD, in *The Men They Will Become*, says, "It is easy to slip into the habit of touching an infant boy mainly when he needs to be fed, cleaned up and changed, or comforted in irritability. . . . Every boy needs a lot of touching given just for the pleasure it will provide; and a parent needs the heartwarming feedback of a happy boy."[27]

This research points to the protective benefits of nurturing a strong connection with young boys by both mother and father. If you have a family in which the father is not involved, it's important for your child to develop a loving relationship with a father figure, such as a brother, an uncle, or a grandfather. Your sons may be fathers themselves someday, modeling what they learned from both sexes—the skills to nurture their own children.

How to Be Responsive in Spite of Life's Challenges

When life throws you some curves, you do the best you can with what you're given. Some situations may not be ideal for raising your child. If your life situation puts an emotional strain on your relationship with your child, your efforts to maintain sensitivity and responsiveness with your baby will help minimize the negative effects.

Single Parenting

There are no two ways about it, single parenting is really tough! If at all possible, consider moving in with grandparents or other family members to have a built-in support system for parent and child. Another option is for single parents to seek out other single parents to share an apartment or home with, as well as support each other in parenting. It's critical to be on the same page as far as parenting values and child care for these types of arrangements to work successfully. Single parents may find that cosleeping with their baby after work or school provides a wonderful opportunity to reconnect and be responsive at night. If grandparents or others care for the baby during the day, be sure they know that you want them to be consistently and sensitively responsive to your child, because crying it out is not acceptable.

If you feel alone and isolated, create your own extended family with your network of friends or seek out other single parents in person or online. Find a local API support group or consider starting one with other like-minded families.

Adoption

Adopted infants will bond sooner if the care and responsiveness of the parents is consistent and loving. If an adopted child has a history of trauma, developing trust may take longer, and her needs may be more intense. Regardless, it is critical that the adopted baby learn that her new parents are consistently available and responsive. If adoptive parents find this challenging in any way, then professional help from therapists knowledgeable about adoption and trauma can be a valuable and critical resource. Children who are adopted from foreign countries adjust much more easily if the adoptive parents bring an item from the orphanage that will help make the child feel more secure, like a special blanket or toy. If the child is eating solid foods, continue to provide similar foods until the child becomes adjusted to her new life and new experiences. The following website offers a lot of good information about attachment parenting for the adopted child: www.adoptivefamilies. com. For the Eight Principles of Parenting for the adopted child, go to www .attachedattheheart.com.

Divorce

Here again, consistency is key. Divorce situations can be very difficult and will vary depending on the parents involved. To prevent breaks in the attachment process, it's important that both parents commit to open communication, keeping prolonged separations to a minimum, with day and nighttime routines as consistent and as developmentally appropriate as possible. For the children to make a reasonably healthy adjustment to losing the intact family, both parents will have to make their child's emotional welfare the top priority. In many cases, this means setting aside differences and working together to be active in their child's life and activities. Most important, both parents need to remain sensitive to their child's feelings and be responsive to his emotional needs. API's website contains information regarding visitation and overnights. A strongly recommended book that focuses on maintaining the attachment relationship is *Creating Effective Parenting Plans: A Developmental Approach for Lawyers and Divorce Professionals* by John Hartson, PhD, and Brenda Payne, PhD. It can be purchased through the American Bar Association website (www.abanet.org). Also recommended is *The Unexpected Legacy of Divorce: A 25-Year Landmark Study* by Judith Wallerstein, Julia M. Lewis, and Sandra Blakeslee and *What About the Kids? Raising Your Children Before, During and After Divorce* by Judith Wallerstein.

Children with Special Needs

Children born prematurely, with physical handicaps or challenges, or with other forms of disability are no different from nonchallenged children in their psychological and emotional needs. It's important to understand that *you* are the expert about your child and that when you feel connected and tuned-in to what your child needs, you will respond intuitively. Challenged children often spend much of their childhood experiencing a maze of different doctors, hospitals (sometimes multiple surgeries), therapists, and teachers. As a result, it's critical that parents establish a strong bond with their child because it will strengthen their ability to be fierce advocates for him, and that bond will give their child the love, support, and courage he will need. You can find additional resources about this topic and others in Appendix C. Also, visit our parent forums on this and other topics at www.attachmentparenting.org/forums/.

Having More Than One Child, Twins, and Other Multiple Births

If you've had your first baby, you may now wonder, "How will I be able to parent the next one with the same devotion, care, and empathy? Won't the older child suffer when a new baby takes her place? How should I space my children for optimum attachment? What about birthing twins, triplets, or other multiples? Is it possible to practice the attachment parenting principles when there are so many needs to fulfill?" These are common questions for all parents, no matter what philosophical view they may have about parenting.

Most of us will have one baby at a time, and spacing our children is a definite consideration when thinking about the attachment needs of each child. Many child development experts feel that at least two and a half to three years between children is beneficial, because the older child has the language and cognitive skills to understand the needs of an infant and can more easily delay his needs than a younger child. The older child may have less jealousy and be able to help in some ways, like bringing diapers or sitting with books and toys while the baby is being fed. Having babies really close together is almost like parenting twins, because they will have similar needs and will probably be in fairly close developmental stages. We advise parents of closely spaced babies to get a lot of help and support, just as if they had given birth to multiples, because the older child will probably not want to be separated from Mom for very long. This is especially true if he is still nursing or is too young to understand where Mom has gone. He only knows that he needs his mother, and Mother needs to be supported in parenting both babies.

We are always amazed to hear the stories of parents who have successfully parented multiples—their stories inspire the rest of us with singletons, and we can learn a lot from their experiences. Organization, prioritizing, and support are the key components to keeping balance in the family. One mother of triplets (and an older child) we worked with said that if it weren't for the volunteers from her church, she never would have been able to successfully breastfeed her babies. She was able to pump enough milk so that while she was nursing two, the third baby could get a bottle if needed, and by the time they were a few months old, she was able to nurse them all without bottles. Volunteers did her laundry, took her older son for outings and preschool, and brought her family meals. When Mom and Dad can focus on the children and their needs, and the community helps support the parents, everyone can keep their sanity, their sense of humor, and their stamina! Best of all, the attachment needs of each child can be met, and parents find that somehow they do have the ability to give tremendous stores of love to each child they are blessed to parent.

Musings from a Mother of Multiples and an Older Sibling
(continued)

Things were so much easier at home. I think if I hadn't had an older daughter, I would not have left the house for the first year. I had to go out because she needed to have a "normal" life. It felt so much like I was depriving her. Between my bedrest during the pregnancy, the NICU weeks, and the first several months at home when I just couldn't manage to leave the couch, let alone the house, she lost nearly half a year of her normal activities. When the boys were a few months old, I felt I *had* to leave the house for her. It was overwhelming to get anywhere. The amount of things I needed to carry with me was crazy. I received a huge Skip Hop Duo Diaper Bag, and it was fabulous. Now with a singleton, I can't imagine how I ever filled it up! I learned to go places where there would be other moms who could help me. When I saw the same moms frequently, my boys got to know them and were happier in their arms. I worried a lot about my daughter in the first year. Books on new siblings talk about sitting with the baby on one side and the sibling on the other, sharing things together. That was impossible. She had been completely displaced; there was no place for her on my lap. I included her as much as I humanly could, but it never felt like enough. Some people told me I should send her off to school, but I knew that then there would be even fewer shared moments. It really was just a matter of surviving the first year. Things got a little better with every milestone . . . with neck control, with sitting, with walking . . . the older they got, the more she could be involved and the more we felt like a family again. (*To be continued*)

—Pam S., mother of four

A Mother's Story: Sacred Love

Within hours of my firstborn child's birth, I got the distinct sense that he wanted a fourth trimester. Here I was, full of breathless anticipation, unspeakable bliss, and mortal terror, and there he was looking at me square in the eye, as if to say, "Work with me, Ma."

I had prepared as so many mothers do for their first baby. But I could have never known the profound effect of meeting someone else's needs because I never took the time to know what they were in the first place.

My son was poised to show me the difference between unmet needs and fulfilled ones, from the time he was a newborn to today, nearly ten years later, as a boy embracing his emerging self-reliance.

They called him a "high-need" baby. What did that mean? *Aren't we all high-need humans?* I thought. They called him "fussy." *Isn't that a judgment of him?* I reasoned. And in calling our babies names—fussy, demanding, good, easy—wouldn't this usher in our fears, fueling our defenses? How could I love my baby unconditionally, I wondered, if part of me was *afraid* of him? And wouldn't he sense that subtle rejection somehow?

As with any burgeoning conviction, I was tested. In those early months, he was averse to the car, the bath, clothes, diaper changes, the telephone ringing, lights, appliances, distant lawn mowers outside his window, being rocked back and forth as opposed to side to side, and the sound of his Velcro diaper tab being pulled ten times a day. Friends, relatives, our pediatrician, and perfect strangers told me to "put him down or he'll think the world revolves around him." What they (and we) didn't know was that the world actually *was* revolving around him—he had vertigo.

We didn't discover this until he was five and could finally tell us. During those five years, we followed his lead. The road to uncovering and defining his complex sensory sensitivities was, at times, confusing and circuitous. Along the way, we had to find out what drives him, what motivates his reactions, what stirs him and soothes him in order to begin to know him in tiny increments every day. *This*, I thought intellectually, *was the easy part.* After all, as his mother, I loved the minutiae of his existence, reveled in his perfect beauty, even as I stared with drunken love at his crossed eyes and pimply face a mere four weeks after our first glimpse of each other. I was prepared to love him with all my heart. What blindsided me was my fear.

He cried inconsolably, and I felt my own helplessness. He wailed, and I felt his disapproval. He couldn't sleep, and I felt forsaken and fragile. As he grew, I spent more than a few nights blinking in the darkness, wondering if I had chosen the right school or teacher or therapy or doctor or response.

It was all about me. And yet, it was not about me at all. It hit me. How could I respond to him with sensitivity, taking his needs and feelings seriously, without taking them personally? How could I get out of the way enough to parent in the moment, allowing him—and me—to flourish as mother and child, so that both of us are organically changed in the process?

I realized, in those moments, that intuitive, conscious, attached parenting requires something that none of us learns on the playground, in the classroom, or on the job: *grace*. The only way I got a taste of its delicacy was through my own painful rites of passage. Those times, as a mother, when I've had the whistle blown on my own pretense and defense. I now know that a baby is wise and forthright enough to smoke a parent out of her hiding places. The same goes for that same baby standing tall enough to reach my collarbone when he hugs me.

I need my maternal radar more now than I ever did. He needs me to move away—closer. His space is sacred. And yet, he needs to share that space. He needs my sensitivity to his changing moods, perceived overreactions, and quirky preferences. But more than my understanding, he needs my authentic presence. Responding to him is no longer about meeting basic needs, but about recognizing individual, deeply personal ones—and respecting them, in spite of my fear. I have learned to respond to what's invisible. Because I want to see him with my heart, not my eyes.

—Lu Hanessian,
Let the Baby Drive

CHAPTER FIVE

PRINCIPLE 4:
Use Nurturing Touch
The Healing Power of Physical Closeness

It is through our hands that we speak to the child,
that we communicate. Touching is the primary language.
The newborn baby's skin has an intelligence, a sensitivity that we
can only begin to imagine. How, then, ought we to touch—to handle
—a newborn baby? Very simply: by remembering what this infant has
just left behind. By never forgetting that everything new and unknown
might terrify and that everything recognizable and familiar is
reassurance. To calm the infant in this strange, incomprehensible
world into which it just emerged, it is necessary—and enough—that the
hands holding him should speak in the language of the womb.

—Frederick Leboyer, MD,
Birth Without Violence

For infants, touch is as vital as the air they breathe and the
milk they drink. From Dr. Montagu, we learn that touch is the foundation
upon which all senses are based, the "mother of the senses," and the earliest

sensory system to become functional in all species. It is the one sense that we cannot live without, as has been tragically demonstrated in orphanages and hospitals where untouched babies used to die of a strange disease called "hospitalism" or "marasmus," known today as "failure to thrive." Dr. Montagu reported that as late as the 1950s, the death rate of infants under one year of age in various United States institutions for abandoned children was nearly 100 percent. These babies were only touched during routine examinations or when they needed a bottle or a diaper change.[1]

Touch: A Matter of Life and Death

Dr. Fritz Talbot of Boston was one doctor who decided to try something different. He remembered a trip he made to Düsseldorf, Germany, before World War I, where he toured a children's clinic. As he was shown about the wards, he noticed a large old woman who was carrying a very sick infant. When he inquired who the woman was, the attending physician said, "Oh, that is Old Anna. When we have done everything we can medically for a baby, and it is still not doing well, we turn it over to Old Anna, and she is always successful." So what was Old Anna's secret? It was what we would call tender, loving care as she rocked and held these fragile babies. Dr. Talbot introduced this kind of care when he returned to Boston, and his methods spread. In 1938, Bellevue Hospital in New York established the rule that every baby should be picked up and "mothered" on the pediatric wards; that year the death rate fell from 35 percent to less than 10 percent.[2]

Today we have new policies that dictate how child therapists can deal with traumatized and abused children. Naturally, we want to protect our children from abuse and unhealthy touch, but blanket policies such as the ones described below are not the answer. Dr. Bruce Perry, senior fellow of the Child Trauma Academy, writes:

I certainly don't have all the answers, but I do know that many of our current childcare practices are hurting our children. For example, in California, at a large center serving three- to five-year-olds, staff members are not allowed to touch the children. If they want to be hugged or held, the adults are supposed to push them away! This is a classic example of how a seemingly good idea—wanting to protect children from sexual predators—can have serious negative consequences.

Children need healthy touch. As we've seen, infants can literally die without it. It's part of our biology. Unfortunately, we've become so afraid of unhealthy touch that we may actually make it more likely by failing to meet the needs of children for healthy physical affection. This can make them more vulnerable to pedophiles, not less, as children will tend to seek out those who appear affectionate towards them.[3]

The *Oxford English Dictionary* defines *touching* as "the action or an act of touching (with the hand, finger, or other part of the body)" and "exercise of the faculty of *feeling* upon a material object" (emphasis added). The word *feeling* has an interesting double meaning here, because the tactile faculty we refer to as "feeling" is directly related to the complex language of our entire range of emotions. This double meaning is no accident—feeling and emotion are interrelated and stem from our earliest relationship to touch. Each neural or muscular stimulation and its related emotion make an indelible imprint on the developing brain.

Nurturing touch begins in the womb. Even before an embryo develops eyes or ears, his skin is highly developed. Research has shown that a fetus as young as nine weeks will bend his fingers as if to grip something if his palm is touched. The amniotic environment is a soothing, rocking, gentle environment, and the baby's skin is like an external nervous system, the medium by which the external world is perceived.

When we observe the behavior of our closest mammalian mothers, their inborn behavior after a relatively short labor is to stimulate their babies through licking. This is nature's way of ensuring that a baby's urinary, gastrointestinal, and respiratory systems are activated. The purpose of a human mother's much longer labor is to massage the human baby in utero, stimulating the baby's systems so that the mother can concentrate on giving her baby a different kind of postlabor experience. A reciprocal process begins immediately after birth—the mother's gentle touch as she holds and caresses her baby begins the all-important bonding and attachment process; the baby's sucking helps to expel the mother's placenta.

Dr. Montagu explains the need for physical contact with the newborn: "During the birth process, mother and infant have had a somewhat trying time. At birth, each clearly requires the reassurance of the other's presence. The reassurance for the mother lies in the sight of her baby, its first cry, and in its closeness to her body. For the baby, it consists of the contact with and warmth of the mother's body, the support in her cradled arms, the caressing, the cutaneous [skin] stimulation it receives, and the suckling at her breast, the welcome into 'the bosom of the family.' These are words, but they refer to very real psycho-physiological conditions."[4]

Studies in Uganda have shown that babies who are carried in upright positions are quicker to walk and develop faster in other areas, too: the upright position heightens a baby's visual alertness while developing muscles in the back and neck. Carried around all day, babies become familiar with their worlds as they watch from their secure vantage point. Because they're held close and upright, they stay calmer—studies show that they even cry less than babies who aren't carried regularly.[5]

Human Babies—Cache or Carry?

Anthropology also teaches us a great deal about what human babies are designed to expect from their caregivers, based on very real biological needs. Mammalian behavior is divided into four distinct categories in the ways in which the mothers carry their young; *cache* and *carry* are two examples. The *cache* mammals are those that leave their babies in hiding for long periods so the mother can hunt for food. These mothers have milk high in fat and protein, allowing their babies to sleep for long periods of time in order not to attract a predator with their cries. The *carry* species are those mammals whose babies are relatively immature and must be on their mothers' bodies or in very close proximity. These mothers produce milk that is low in fat and protein, which digests quickly, guaranteeing that the baby will be hungry more frequently. This forces the mother to stay close by, ideally having the baby on her body so they can move together quickly if needed to escape a dangerous situation. Human babies are by far the most immature babies born, needing constant care, including feeding, holding, rocking, and other soothing behaviors. Unfortunately, Western culture has traditionally treated human babies as if they were more like cache animals, trying to invent ways to keep them quiet and alone for as long as possible, especially at night. This can force babies to go against their biology and, in some cases, lead to failure to thrive.

Researchers in the United States and England have found that on average, babies in Western cultures are touched or held for only approximately 25 percent of their daytime hours. By nine months of age, the touch time goes down to 16 percent. Even young infants in a model day care center were touched only 14 percent of the day. In contrast, studies done with the !Kung San tribe in Africa found that infants are in touch with their mothers for approximately 70 percent of the day and in someone else's arms the rest of the time. These babies cry much less than Western babies.[6]

Attachment parenting encourages parents to find a happy balance in their ability to keep their babies physically close. Seventy percent may seem overwhelming for some parents, especially if they have a physical challenge to holding their babies that much, but being aware of the biological needs for babies to be held and soothed encourages us to find creative ways to meet these needs.

Why Is Touch So Important?

Nurturing touch has so many advantages; for instance, it stimulates growth-promoting hormones. Growth hormone emanates from the hypothalamus, and touch is what sends a message to the pituitary gland to release this hormone. A Duke University researcher discovered that when baby rats were not licked by their mothers, it took only forty-five minutes before the growth hormone was suppressed.[7] As Dr. Tiffany Field, the director of the Touch Research Institute at the University of Miami, explains, "Our fingertips contain an incredible pharmacy. Slide them across the trunks of preterm infants and the pressure stimulates a branch of a cranial nerve called the vegetative vagus, which, in turn, stimulates the gastrointestinal tract, releasing hormones like glucose and insulin [which aids in gastrointestinal food absorption, thus enhancing digestion]." Researchers also found that premature infants who were gently stroked produced more immunoglobulin, which protects against respiratory infections. More research tells us that nurturing touch improves intellectual and motor development immediately from birth.

Skin-to-skin holding of newborn infants had as many beneficial effects as an analgesic. Researchers compared differences in crying, grimacing, and heart rate of babies held skin to skin or not held during a heel lance procedure. They found that crying and grimacing were reduced by 82 percent and 65 percent, respectively. They noted it prevented the explosive rise in heart rate that normally accompanies heel lance.[9]

It also helps regulate babies' temperature, heart rate, and sleep-wake patterns, especially when the baby is held skin to skin. These babies not only gain weight faster, they also nurse better, are calmer, and are able to be more quickly soothed when they cry.[8]

Parents also benefit from practicing nurturing touch. As discussed in Chapter 3, the hormone oxytocin (the "mother love" hormone) is released through loving touch, so babies, mothers, and fathers all benefit from massage, hugs, and snuggle time. The calming effects of skin-to-skin contact help parents get to know their babies better, strengthening the emotional bonds between parent and child. Additionally, an inverse relationship exists between nurturing touch and adult physical violence. Cultures that rate high in physical affection, touch, holding, or carrying rate low in adult physical violence. The cultures rating low in physical touch have high rates of adult physical violence.[10]

Kangaroo Care

Doctors in Bogotá, Colombia, discovered an amazing solution to their lack of funding for incubators for premature babies: their mothers' bodies! They called this type of care Kangaroo Mother Care, or "K-care" for short, which creatively describes how a baby is held skin to skin on the mother's chest. Babies who were able to breathe on their own were placed between their mothers' breasts for warmth, and the mothers were encouraged to let their babies suckle as frequently as they could. The nurses soon realized that these babies grew faster, gained significantly more weight, and slept better, and their heart rates and temperatures stabilized more quickly. Fathers were also given the opportunity to hold their infants, and the results were remarkably beneficial for the babies. Many of the newborns were able to leave the hospital sooner, and the mothers and fathers felt much more confident about their abilities to care for their babies once they returned home.[11] More recent research has shown that if a K-care baby's body temperature cools down, the mother's body warms up, and if the baby's temperature gets too warm, the mother's body cools down.

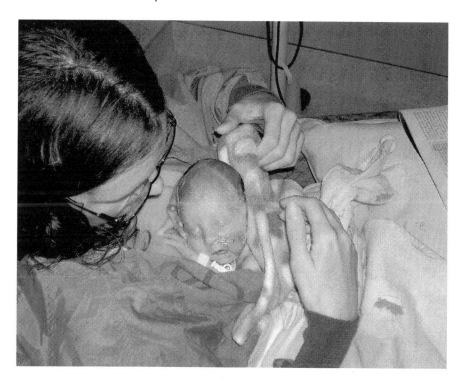

Dr. Nils Bergman first introduced K-care to hospitals in South Africa in 1995. His website, www.kangaroomothercare.com/, has excellent information and research, with significant contributions by his colleague Susan Ludington-Hoe. They provide much research that demonstrates the profound physiological and attachment benefits to premature and full-term

Kangaroo Mother Care (KMC), a technique first developed in 1978 to deal with overcrowding of neonatal units in Colombia, uses mothers or fathers as incubators. Babies weighing less than two thousand grams (four and a half pounds) at birth are attached to their caregivers' chests in skin-to-skin contact and kept upright twenty-four hours a day. The study showed that KMC is at least as good as traditional care with incubators, improves breastfeeding rates, and improves bonding between parent and infant. Parental confidence and sense of fulfillment are also improved. Two decades of implementation and research have made it clear that KMC is more than an alternative to incubator care and should be encouraged even in affluent settings, say the authors.[12]

babies and their parents, especially when done within the first hour after birth. Now many hospitals practice K-care around the world, so if you deliver a preemie, be sure and ask whether you can practice K-care with your baby.

How You Can Provide Nurturing Touch

Parents can meet their children's need for loving contact in many ways. Skin-to-skin holding in the form of kangaroo care is beneficial for all newborn babies and helps them transition peacefully to the outside world. Part of your birth plan could include instructions on how you would like your baby cared for directly after birth. Many hospital nursery nurses are directed to scrub the baby, sometimes with rough washcloths, but you may request that the baby stay with you, and, if possible, that Mother or Father give her her first gentle bath with warm water and a gentle approach.

One study showed that premature infants who received three fifteen-minute periods of massage a day for ten consecutive days experienced a 47 percent increase in weight gain. By eight months of age, these babies showed advanced weight gain and better intellectual and motor development.[13]

Premature babies who were held skin to skin with their caregivers had less severe infections, less time in the hospital, and were breastfed longer than the control group.[14]

Premature babies who were touched and held gained weight faster and were healthier than the control group.[15]

Breastfeeding provides an excellent opportunity for a mother to snuggle with her undressed infant. If a mother or other caregiver is bottle-feeding, the baby can still be held skin to skin to give the baby that important touch time. For instance, the baby's clothing can be removed and the mother can hold the baby in the same feeding position as a nursing mother, as discussed in Chapter 3. Bath time is another opportunity for skin contact. The calming effects of nurturing touch are increased with the warmth of the bathwater, and studies have shown that this simple technique can foster more secure attachments with babies.[16] Many parents find that it is safer and easier to bathe with their infants rather than bathe the baby in a sink or other hard surface; this, too, increases opportunities for nurturing touch.

Infant Massage

Massage is perhaps the best way to provide nurturing touch to infants, and the benefits continue as children get older. Massage can soothe a colicky baby, help a child unwind before bedtime, and provide playful interaction between parent and child. While all parents can use massage as a special way to connect with their babies, it is a particularly wonderful tool for fathers to nurture their attachment relationships. Vimala McClure, the founder of the International Association of Infant Massage, writes, "The bonds of trust and love, the lessons of compassion, warmth, openness, and respect that are inherent in the massage routine will be carried by your child into adulthood. Especially if your parenting practices reflect the same values of infant massage, your child will be more likely to respond to others with empathy and warmth, to respond to social problems with compassion and altruism, and to experience life as a joyful adventure in which he has the opportunity to love and be loved—to help others and extend himself in genuine service to humanity."[17]

One of the University of Miami Touch Institute's discoveries in the early 1990s was that the benefits of touch therapy are mutual. So vibrant is the power of touch that the massage giver enjoys as many significant health benefits as the massage recipient. For one study, the institute recruited retiree "grandparent" volunteers and trained them to massage premature, drug-exposed, "failure-to-thrive" newborns, orphans, and abused children. After a month of massage, the infants were more active, their alertness and tracking behaviors improved, they slept better, and they were more sociable and easier to soothe. But the children were not the only beneficiaries. The retirees showed a dramatic decrease in depression, increased feelings of self-worth, improved sleep patterns, and fewer doctor visits. They reported less anxiety and drank fewer cups of coffee, and their levels of urine cortisol, a stress-related hormone, decreased. In fact, the positive effects on the "grandparents" were greater after giving a massage than after receiving one.[18]

Parents who practice infant massage report many benefits, including some that they never would have associated with nurturing touch. Recently, writer Jennifer Mahal shared this story in the *San Diego Union-Tribune* when she interviewed parents who were taking a baby massage class in a San Diego elementary school:

Itzel Serrano used to hate being put into her car seat. The five-month-old would fuss and kick when her father, George Serrano, strapped her in. That was before George and his wife, Aracely, took a class in infant massage offered by the Kids on Track pilot project in the Chula Vista Elementary School District. "Before, I would pick her up and put her in the car seat, but now I tell her. I show her the car seat. I tell her we're going for a ride," George said, watching Itzel, his first child. . . . "She responds much better."

Communication and bonding between parent and child is what the five-week class is all about, instructor Elaine Lopez said. "It's not about the strokes, it's more the bonding and attachment," said Lopez, who teaches a group of five to seven parents to massage their babies by demonstrating on a doll named Lucy.

"How a baby is viewed influences how a baby is cared for," said Suzanne P. Reese, an international instructor with Infant Massage USA. "Infant massage works as a way to create greater understanding between children and adults because it is all about nurturing," she said. "It's simple and effective and you don't need the electronic tools and gizmos and gadgets. . . . It's the love from your heart to your hands."

Studies done by the Touch Research Institute at the University of Miami School of Medicine show that infant massage can help preterm babies grow and develop, can help preschoolers behave better, and has positive effects on the parent-child relationship. Enriquez, who brings her three-year-old son, Gael Ontiveros, with her to the weekly sessions, said learning how to massage Valeria has helped her discover her daughter's likes and dislikes. "She loves to have her toes rubbed," Enriquez said in Spanish. "She'll put her foot on me and wait very still."

Parents are taught to ask their babies' permission before starting massage. They warm drops of oil in their hands, making a swishing noise that acts as a cue to the baby. Martha Hernandez said her five-month-old, Edwin, is antsy before she starts. He calms "the minute I do the massage," she said.

The class cycles through a series of massage strokes with names such as water wheel, open book, sun and moon, and Indian milking. Although Lopez teaches the massage strokes as a series, going from hands and feet to the stomach and the back, she tells the parents to pay attention to what their child wants and follow the little one's lead. "This is really child-led, it really truly is, because it's all about the baby," said Lopez, a mother of three. That means if a child needs to eat during class, they eat. If they want their back rubbed instead of their front, so be it. "Sometimes [Itzel] doesn't want to be massaged," George said. "Sometimes she just wants to play."

No fancy lotions or salves are used. Parents learn that babies can be massaged with 100 percent cold-pressed olive oil. "They can use what they use in a salad," Butler said, noting that babies often like to suck their fingers and toes. "We want them to be able to do it and not have to buy costly products." Parents are encouraged to incorporate massage time into their family's lives. Many families add it to their child's bedtime or bathing routines. Lorena Lopez sets aside time for her nine-month-old, Raul Grajeda, and her four-year-old, Rene Grajeda. She said doing massage has allowed her to connect with both sons. "Rene has his time and Raul has his time," Lopez said through an interpreter. "It's important to be able to do this, with our lives being so hectic."

The commitment of the parents coming to the class has impressed the instructors. "These moms are so dedicated. They have a million things on their plate—cooking, cleaning, taking care of their husbands—but they're taking this hour and a half," instructor Elaine Lopez said. The instructors said during the last session, one mother walked several miles to the class because her car broke down and she didn't want to miss it. "I think those babies are experiencing a lot of love," Lopez said.[19]

The Benefits of Infant Massage

- promotes bonding
- encourages relaxation
- makes baby feel loved
- promotes better sleep
- facilitates body awareness
- boosts immune system
- promotes sensory stimulation
- improves skin condition
- improves blood circulation
- aids digestion and waste elimination
- balances respiration
- helps parents learn to read babies' cues and better respond to their needs
- helps build parents' and babies' self-esteem

—FROM "FREQUENTLY ASKED QUESTIONS," INFANT MASSAGE USA WEBSITE

Infant massage classes are now available in most communities. Although this practice has been used in many cultures around the world for centuries, it is relatively new to parents in Western cultures. As research catches up with the miraculous benefits to babies and parents, the practice is now being promoted by hospitals and infant development experts around the world. Resources for classes are available in Appendix C.

"Babywearing"

In 1990, a study was published by Dr. Elizabeth Anisfeld and her team of researchers at Columbia University, who wanted to determine if close physical contact would increase infants' security of attachment. The mothers who participated in the study were low-income inner-city mothers, married and single, who had just delivered in an inner-city hospital. One group of moms was given soft baby carriers (called "Snuglies"), and the other group was given plastic infant seats to use to carry their babies. The researchers wanted to determine if this factor alone would correlate to the security of attachment of these babies to their mothers at thirteen months of age. By three months of age they observed a marked difference in the degree of responsiveness and sensitivity from the mothers using the soft carriers. At thirteen months, using the Strange Situation experiment, they found an astounding 83 percent of the infants who were carried in the soft carriers were securely attached, whereas only 38 percent of the infants carried in plastic infant seats were securely attached. They concluded that the close physical contact alone was related to sensitive responsiveness, which led to secure attachment of baby and mother.[20]

Today's AP Mother

All over the world, mothers have found this simple tool to be the greatest mothering technique ever invented. In Western culture, it is a relatively new practice and is commonly referred to as "babywearing." This refers to carrying a baby in a sling or other soft carrier and provides the same benefits as carrying the baby in one's arms. Carried babies cry less and are more calm and content.[21]

Many pediatricians are concerned about a new phenomenon they are seeing in their practices, of babies with "flat-head syndrome," or plagiocephaly, caused by babies spending too much time lying on their backs.[22] Babies who are carried rather than spending all their time in plastic seats or car seats do not have this problem. Another advantage is that infants who are carried can see the world at their parents' level but can also snuggle in when feeling overwhelmed or overstimulated. Babywearing also meets a baby's need for physical contact, comfort, security, stimulation, and movement, all of which encourage neurological development. Many parents find babywearing extremely effective for meeting a child's need for nurturing touch while on the go or doing everyday tasks around the house.

My Baby Doesn't Seem to Like a Sling—Help!

Q I recently received a baby sling as a gift, but my baby doesn't seem to like it. When I put him in it, he starts to fuss. He is three months old, and I've carried him in my arms a lot up to this point. Is there anything I can do to get him to accept being in the sling? If not, can I still be an attachment parent without using a sling?

A Using a baby sling or other soft baby carrier is a great way to ensure that your baby gets lots of holding and carrying as you move through your busy life. The hands-free aspect makes it easy for you to get other things done at the same time you are meeting your baby's needs for touch, closeness, movement, and your presence. Up to now, you may have been meeting these needs by holding your baby in arms. It is certainly possible to be an attachment parent without using a sling by continuing to carry him in your arms and finding other high-touch ways to stay connected, like infant massage. But don't give up on the sling just yet! Slings are convenient and make it easier to hold your baby longer.

Here are some suggestions that may help: *The Attachment Parenting Book* by Dr. William Sears and Martha Sears has an excellent chapter on baby-wearing. The authors point out that using a sling can take a little practice and might feel awkward at first but will become second nature after a while. One of their suggestions is to put on the sling in the morning when you're getting dressed. Then you already have it on and can put your baby in it whenever you'd like during the day instead of first putting him down, which isn't always convenient to do. This is a good way to get used to wearing the sling and will make it easier for you to try it with your baby.

- Babies can often sense when you are stressed or upset and become upset, too, so try to stay calm and patient as you introduce the sling.
- Double-check to be sure that you are wearing the sling correctly and that you know how to position your baby in it comfortably. Your sling probably came with detailed instructions and maybe even an instructional video, which you may want to review.
- You may find it helpful to talk to another parent you know who is experienced in wearing a baby. She or he can help you make sure that there is nothing you've overlooked, and give you tips on adjusting the sling to fit you and your baby comfortably.
- Every baby is different, so you may need to experiment to see what works best for yours. You can try putting him or her in the sling at different times—when he or she is sleepy or wide awake, calm or fussy, and so on, to see when he or she is most agreeable to being in it.
- You may also want to try different positions. From three months or a little older, many babies like facing forward in the sling; if possible, get an experienced babywearing parent to assist you.
- If you are breastfeeding, you can nurse your baby while using the sling, and it may be a good way to get your baby to stay interested in staying in the sling longer.
- Some parents find that a little distraction helps as they get their baby settled into the sling. When you first put your baby in it, try walking around, patting, and talking to him reassuringly. Movement is usually calming, so this may help him get used to the sling without starting to

fuss. Another idea for distraction is to have your partner or someone else talk to him for a little while or show him a toy to engage him for a few moments when you first put him in the sling.

- Don't put a time limit on getting your baby to accept being carried in the sling. Keep in mind that you are making a change in his or her routine, and it may take a little while for him or her to get used to this new way of being held.[23]

Many creative and fashionable baby and child carriers are available and are used around the world. Various types of carriers can distribute the weight load of the child across the caregiver's body differently and allow the child to be positioned in several ways. Try multiple carriers and positions to determine what is most comfortable for parent and child, recognizing that carrier needs may change as the child grows. Some API support groups offer a "sling library" to give parents the opportunity to try on and experiment with different slings or carriers. It is now easy to buy carriers at most baby retail outlets and, of course, on many websites.

Most soft baby carriers can be used for discreet breastfeeding. This helps mothers who are uncomfortable breastfeeding in public—or those whose babies nurse frequently because of growth spurts or teething—to nurse their babies on cue while going about their daily business. Soft carriers may offer more comfort and protection for babies who are otherwise easily distracted from nursing.

Gentle movement may be helpful as a child acclimates to a new carrier. Walking or swaying with the baby in the carrier may approximate the baby's experience in the womb and make the carrier feel more familiar and comfortable. Parents can also support the baby with their hand(s) until both parent and child feel comfortable that the carrier is secure.

As children grow, they continue to need nurturing touch for comfort and connectedness. Babywearing can continue for as long as is comfortable for both parent and child. Many carriers can accommodate growing toddlers. Soft carriers provide special security to the older child in busy and crowded locations and keep busy hands from the temptation of touching breakable objects! An overwhelmed toddler may be comforted by the familiar security of being carried. Be assured that carrying a baby into toddlerhood and beyond will not "spoil" the baby. Parents can follow the child's lead and try not to make her feel bad about still wanting to feel the closeness that carrying provides. If you find your child is too heavy to hold comfortably, take a few minutes out, if possible, to provide attention or comfort in your lap.

Many devices can be used to hold a baby or young child independently that, if overused, do not promote attachment (swings, jumpers, plastic carriers, strollers, or car seats when not being used for safety reasons). Parents using these devices should be sensitive to the baby's behavior and body language, and they must be conscious to avoid the overuse of these products. If using a stroller or baby carriage, use a brand that allows the baby to face the parent rather than looking away. Some children like the security of seeing their parents, especially since very young babies don't yet understand where their parents have gone when they are out of sight.

In one study, mothers were asked to carry their three-week-olds in their arms or in a soft body carrier for at least three hours a day until the babies were three months old. The babies who received more carrying—four and a half hours compared to a little over two and a half for the control group—cried 43 percent less than the control group. And they cried 51 percent less in the early evening when babies are presumed most fussy. Furthermore . . . they found that infant crying did not peak at six weeks of age in the infants who were held more [as found by an earlier study conducted in 1962 by T. Berry Brazelton].[24]

Nurturing Touch and the Older Child

Frequent hugs, snuggling, back rubs, and massage all meet the older child's need for touch, as does more physical play such as wrestling and tickling. Use playfulness and games to encourage physical closeness in a child who is resistant, and remember that touch is an ongoing need throughout life.

Children need various types of play, from rough-and-tumble wrestling to imagination games. Many girls and boys, even sometimes as babies, enjoy some rough-and-tumble play, and it can strengthen attachment. Often parents find themselves specializing in only one type of play and may even be uncomfortable with other types, especially if they were not touched very much in their own childhood. This can be especially true for play that on the surface seems harsh or mean but may in reality only be wrestling on the floor or a child enjoying a ride on Daddy's back. These types of play serve an important purpose for children who are working through emotions, processing the images they see in the media, and exploring their own ability to control aggression. Children benefit immensely when each parent can actively engage in all types of play, including those that require parents to challenge their own comfort levels. It is important, however, for parents to respect the child's boundaries. Sometimes eye contact, a wink, or a smile is enough to connect with an older child, and wrestling or tickling should never be forced or overdone.

Parents should also remember to use nurturing touch with partners and other loved ones! We all know how much we appreciate a hug, a neck massage, or even a warm handshake when we interact with family, coworkers, and friends. All humans thrive on touch and the reconnection it provides. We share Sharon Heller's vision as she concludes her book, *The Vital Touch*: "I can't deny that this book is a call to arms and that the victory parade I envisage will be a march through the malls with more babies strapped on our hips, our backs, our fronts, or our shoulders. I believe this will be good for all babies—and especially those content only when held. Each tender touch buys love stock kept in a permanent reserve, always there to be drawn from. What better security could parents offer?"[25]

Bowling Alone

"In 1995, Robert Putman, a professor of international affairs at Harvard University, released an article that caught the attention of the U.S. government and became the subject of widespread response and social concern. The article, entitled "Bowling Alone," spoke of the decline of what Putman called "social capital," which refers to an individual's network of social connections. He noted with statistical evidence that while individually centered activities (such as bowling alone, computer games, and virtual reality) are on the rise, participation in community-based activities such as bowling leagues, PTA meetings, religious groups, Boy Scouts . . . and voting are seriously declining. He quoted a poll in which Americans were asked if they could trust most people. In 1960, 58 percent of Americans said that they did, whereas in 1993, only 38 percent responded in favor of trust. . . . A touch-starved nation very quickly becomes a trust-starved nation."[26]

CHAPTER SIX

PRINCIPLE 5:
Ensure Safe Sleep,
Physically and Emotionally

The Critical Importance of Nighttime Needs

The reality is, no babies need to sleep through the night.
That is completely a cultural construct. It is usually not the babies that
have the sleep problems—they can sleep where and when they need—
but it is the parents who have the sleep problems. These are
usually induced by the notions of the baby being separate from the
parent. It is not that the baby can't sleep, they just can't sleep how
the parents want it, when they want it, and in a solitary environment.
Biologically speaking, this is unnatural for them,
and their emotions rightly tell them so.

—Dr. Jim McKenna, "The Greatest Gifts We Can Give Our Children,"
in *Attachment Parenting: The Journal of API*

"Is your baby sleeping through the night?" is often the
first question a new parent hears. For many parents, this question undermines their confidence and creates unnecessary anxiety. The truth is that

most young babies do not sleep through the night. This is simply a myth that continues to be perpetuated in our modern society—a myth that Dr. Jim McKenna calls "a cultural construct," since many cultures around the world don't have that expectation. Babies have needs at night just as they do during the day—to be fed, to be comforted, and to be protected. They may feel fear and loneliness, sadness, or too cold or too hot—and therefore they need the reassurance of a loving parent to help them feel secure during the night. Attachment Parenting International (API) encourages parents to respond to their children's needs at night just as they do during the day. This requires exploring a variety of different safe sleeping arrangements and choosing the approach that best allows parents to be responsive at night. Some of these approaches are explored in this chapter.

Understanding Infant Sleep Patterns

Many physiological and developmental reasons account for the ways babies sleep. Human infants are designed to feed frequently because mother's milk is lower in fat and digested very easily. Their immature brains are so underdeveloped that they need frequent feeding and skin-to-skin nurturing to stimulate healthy growth. Dr. William and Martha Sears explain infant sleep patterns in their book *Nighttime Parenting*: "In the first few months, most babies sleep fourteen to eighteen hours per day without any respect for the differences between day and night. A baby's sleep pattern resembles his feeding pattern: small frequent feedings and short frequent naps."[1] Adults and infants also sleep differently: adults have fewer periods of rapid eye movement (REM) sleep (also known as active sleep) and more periods of deep sleep or "quiet sleep," whereas infants have frequent periods of REM sleep and fewer periods of quiet sleep.

During REM sleep, our brains are actively dreaming, which seems to stimulate the development of higher brain functions. Sleep researchers believe that the more complex the brain, the more REM sleep is required to help in its development. From a biological perspective, infant sleep patterns appear to increase the baby's ability to survive, allowing her to feed more often and maintain close contact with the mother. The younger the human being, the more REM sleep she requires, which increases the probability of wakefulness, especially during the transitions from active sleep to quiet sleep, which tend to occur on average every ninety minutes.

As we get older, periods of REM sleep lessen greatly. Infants' sleep patterns gradually adjust to adultlike sleep patterns beginning around the age of two or three years.

Sleeping Like a Baby

When it comes to sleeping like a baby, we know the following:

- Most babies don't sleep through the night but may wake up every one and a half to two hours to be fed.
- Babies weren't designed by nature to sleep seven to eight hours straight. In fact, some experts feel it could be dangerous for an infant to sleep that long.
- When you bring your newborn home from the hospital, it's a good idea to begin a routine of sleeping when the baby sleeps to catch up on the hours you missed during the night.
- You will feel more rested if you keep your baby close by or in bed with you, as long as you follow safe cosleeping guidelines.

What Exactly Is Cosleeping?

Cosleeping and *bedsharing* (also referred to as "sharing sleep" or the "family bed") are terms often incorrectly used interchangeably to describe a sleep arrangement in which family members sleep in the same bed. References to these words often lead to confusion about publicized information on safe versus unsafe infant sleep practices. *Cosleeping*, however, is an umbrella term that is used to refer to infants and their adult caregivers sleeping in "close proximity," though not necessarily in the same bed. Bedsharing, one form of cosleeping, is sharing the same bed with an infant. Cosleeping is encouraged by API and the American Academy of Pediatrics (AAP) and governed by safe practice guidelines. Unsafe infant sleep practices, including sleeping with an infant on a couch, recliner, or other nonbed surface, are not accepted forms of cosleeping or bedsharing.

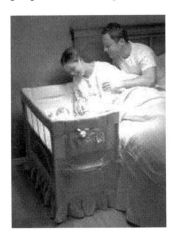

The Benefits of Cosleeping

From a purely practical standpoint, parents report that they get more sleep with fewer interruptions when they cosleep. They don't need to get up to attend to baby's needs, which keeps parents from having to wake up fully during feedings. Cosleeping improves a mother's milk supply, increases the number of feedings, and increases the duration of the breastfeeding relationship. This can also suppress ovulation, helping to prevent another pregnancy.[2] While the American Academy of Pediatrics does not support bedsharing, it does recommend that infants sleep in the same room as the parents separately and in close proximity.

Babies feel warm, secure, and protected; therefore, they fret and cry less. Research has found that mothers tend to be more responsive when cosleeping, which may be a protective behavior.[3] Mothers worry less about their infants at night when they can reach out and touch them, and both parents develop a closer bond with their baby. In addition to these benefits, cosleeping also enhances the breastfeeding and attachment relationships. A study of military families found that cosleeping was associated with parental reports of higher social and life skills and less psychiatric treatment.[4] Another study found that cosleeping is associated with family nurturance, less use of transitional objects, flexibility in family structure, and parental reports of higher adaptive functioning on the part of the children.[5]

From a physiological basis, when cosleeping, the baby experiences more periods of light sleep, which stabilize the heart rate and breathing pattern, and the risk of sudden infant death syndrome (SIDS) decreases. We have had mothers over the years report to us that they believe they were able to save their children's lives—some from sleep apnea, some from other unforeseen occurrences—because they were bedsharing. The following story powerfully illustrates the importance of mother-baby togetherness at night:

> I had decided to cosleep with my son for many reasons. I enjoyed looking at him cradled in my arms, nursing him at night was easier, and, as a first-time mother, having him right there relieved any fears that something may be wrong. On the night of his six-week appointment, by my side was the best place for him. I was wary of having my son vaccinated because of the controversies, including their possible link to autism. Having an autistic younger brother myself made my fears seem reasonable. But after his physician assured me that any chance of a reaction was remote, my son Angus received his DTaP [a combination vaccine that protects against diphtheria, tetanus, and pertussis (whooping cough)], along with his other shots.
>
> We had an early appointment that morning, and we returned home to what seemed to be a normal day. Angus became grumpy later in the afternoon and had a slight fever, as well as some redness around the injection site, but the nurse on call said that this was normal and to give him ibuprofen. By 8:00 PM, we were both tired, and he fell asleep at my breast as he had done since his birth.
>
> At about 11:00 PM, I felt something slapping against my chest. It was not hard but was repeated rapidly. I had a night-light on, and when I looked next to me, I saw my son thrashing his arms about and an expres-

sion of a silent scream on his face. He was not breathing. My reflexes took over, and I sat up and yanked him into the air and to my chest. As I raised him up, I heard him inhale deeply, and he began to scream. I called the doctor and found that he had indeed had a reaction to the shots and to give him Benadryl. Within thirty minutes of that dose, he calmed down and was able to sleep again, though I could not.

I know that if Angus had not been sleeping there by my side, I would have woken up to a crib death. Because of cosleeping, my son is alive. Angus is now five years old.

—*Lilith M.*

Are There Dangers with Bedsharing?

A little historical background may help put the concern of danger into better perspective. It's important to know that infant solitary sleep is a relatively new practice that has evolved in the Western world only within the last one hundred years. Recently, various medical and professional organizations have discouraged parents from sleeping with their children for fear that it contributes to an increase in SIDS. However, new research demonstrates that sharing sleep, when practiced by informed parents, can be safe and beneficial. In fact, many cultures around the world, where millions of parents routinely sleep with their children, have reported some of the lowest SIDS rates. In some of these cultures, such as China and Japan, it is virtually nonexistent. Dr. James McKenna, one of the few cosleeping researchers in the world, offers important advice to all parents about solitary sleep:

> Now we at least know that if you're going to put a baby alone in a crib in a room by itself, you would put a baby on its back, and at least that's a big step up in the chances of the baby surviving. But what we also now know is three to four studies show quite conclusively that putting babies to sleep in a room by themselves at three to six months of age doubles their chances of dying from SIDS. Indeed, when cosleeping is defined by the baby sleeping within the proximity of a responsible adult caregiver, and not necessarily bedsharing, the hypothesis that cosleeping reduces the chance of SIDS has in fact been confirmed.[6]

British researcher Dr. Helen Ball found that breastfeeding mothers were more likely to sleep on one side in a protective position—tucking their knees up under their babies—and awaken more quickly than bottle-feeding mothers. Further research by Dr. McKenna and his colleagues found that when studying mother-infant breastfeeding pairs, babies were largely responsible for positioning themselves during the night and spent most of their sleep on their sides or backs, just inches away from their mothers' faces. Mothers reported that they got a better quality of sleep when their babies slept nearby.[7] For those reasons, McKenna recommends that bottle-fed babies sleep on a separate surface yet close to the mother.[8]

Parents often worry that they might roll over and suffocate their baby during the night, but remember that just as we are able to sleep in a bed without falling out of it, sober parents are acutely aware that a baby is in the bed. Research conducted by Dr. Miranda Barone put this worry to the test and videotaped mothers and babies sleeping together. "In more than 1,000 hours of observing forty mother-infant pairs, no mother was ever remotely close to overlying or suffocating her infant. Instead, maternal and infant behaviors were beautifully synchronized—when one moved, the other responded, without fully awakening."[9] In fact, she says that in the context of attachment relationships, her study found that the "attachment behavioral system [such as the need to be physically close to the caregiver and other sensory needs] operates twenty-four hours per day and does not deactivate during sleep, where infants spend 60 percent of their time."[10]

Musings from a Mother of Multiples (continued)

I was very lucky that my boys had the same natural sleep patterns. From completely anecdotal evidence, this seems to be much more common with identical twins than with fraternal twins. Still, it was a challenge to do it safely. I made a bit of a "nest" for myself in our king-size bed. I'd lie on my back without a shirt, with a pillow next to my body on each side and a pillow under my knees. I'd lay my arms on top of the pillows, and then each boy would lie on one arm, so that he was on his side, half on my torso and half on my arm. I made sure there was no way he could come into contact with a pillow. From this position, I could easily nurse whichever boy woke without disturbing the other. I'm quite sure it looked absolutely ludicrous, but it was the only way I could get a little sleep. In hindsight, I wish I'd gotten a photograph.

At night was the only time I was ever calm. I know it sounds strange, but there in the bed I was able to meet the boys' needs and do a little relaxation myself. I would do progressive relaxations and meditations. I would smell the boys' hair and look at their faces. It was the calm between the storms of my days. My husband mounted a TV on the wall for me, and I kept the remote beside me where I could reach it without disturbing a baby. I watched shows and movies on closed captioning so there was no noise.

We put night-lights all over the room so there was always a dim glow. And we set up a baby monitor in reverse, so that I could talk softly and ask my husband for things when he was in the other room.

My nights were a blur of sleeping and waking. I tried to stay as semi-asleep as possible as I nursed. Every once in a while the boys would get off sync, and I'd be awake every hour nursing one or the other. When this happened I'd try to wake the sleeping boy and nurse him at the same time to get them back together again. It usually worked, but sometimes it didn't, and those days were really rough. I think I survived because I went into it with the expectation that I just wasn't going to sleep for six months or so. Then when I did manage to sleep for an hour or two, it felt like a bonus. After a few months of very little sleep, I started having very short, bizarre dreams. I'm sure it was a symptom of extreme fatigue. But in a way those dreams became an anchor, something to laugh about in the morning. (*To be continued*)

—PAM S., MOTHER OF FOUR

[*Authors' Note: What would it look like if this mom had received help at night with her babies? Grandmother, auntie, friend, or postpartum doula could care for one baby if he got "off sync" so mother could nurse and doze with one at a time. Some dads are able to take off work and provide the extra arms, too, of course. If a mother is getting seriously sleep-deprived, it's important to seek help. If support can be arranged only during the day, finding ways for Mom to take a nap will ease the lack of sleep at night.*]

America's Anti-Cosleeping Campaign

In September 1999 and again in May 2002, the U.S. Consumer Product Safety Commission (CPSC) issued warnings about the practice of cosleeping as dangerous and life-threatening. This can be confusing for parents when in fact the American Academy of Pediatrics is in favor of cosleeping, or sleeping in close proximity. What the CPSC is really warning against is bedsharing. As a result, a nationwide campaign began in conjunction with the Juvenile Products Manufacturing Association (JPMA) that discouraged and frightened parents from bringing their infants to bed. Because of this confusion, parents reported sleeping on couches or recliners with their babies, which is many times more dangerous than bedsharing. Ironically, if a baby's death occurs in this unsafe environment, it is reported as a "cosleeping" death. A groundswell of opposition came from researchers, psychologists, parents, and others who protested the lack of solid science behind the campaign. They found that the data was collected anecdotally and inefficiently

> Every day dozens of babies are injured in falls from cribs, according to what may be the first study focusing on nonfatal crib-related injuries in children younger than two. In nine out of ten cases, the child was alone when the fall occurred; most of the injuries were to the head and neck. The study, published in the journal *Pediatrics*, analyzed nationally representative data for 181,654 injuries related to cribs, playpens, and bassinets from 1990 through 2008. Of those injured, 2,140 children, or 1.2 percent, died—most from becoming caught or wedged in the crib.[11]

from newspaper clippings, coroners' reports, and death certificates, with very little information from the parents. Even today, no standard interview questions or protocols are used to collect information after a baby dies at home. Additionally important is the need for what researchers call a "control group" of infants in order to make legitimate comparisons for all the factors involved in the children's sleeping environments.

In the 1990s, researchers in the United Kingdom conducted the largest case-control study ever done on infant deaths, called the Sudden Unexpected Deaths in Infancy (SUDI) study, carried out by the Confidential Enquiry into Stillbirths and Deaths in Infancy (CESDI). They included information from 450 sudden or unexpected infant deaths and 1,800 matched "control" infants. According to one of the researchers, Dr. Peter Fleming, a professor of infant health and developmental physiology at the University of Bristol and pediatrician at the Royal Hospital for Children in Bristol, "The CESDI study showed that for infants who shared a room with a parent, the risk of SIDS was approximately half that for infants who slept alone. In other words, putting a baby to sleep in a separate room (rather than the room in which the parents slept) doubled the risk of SIDS."[12]

In the United States in 2002, scientist Dr. Tina Kimmel reviewed the CPSC data and analyzed data from the CDC's Pregnancy Risk Assessment Monitoring System (PRAMS), which surveyed mothers with infants from two to six months of age, and included the question "How often does your new baby sleep in the same bed with you?" At the time of the report, only five states kept the data. However, from that information, Dr. Kimmel was able to determine that not only was it safe to sleep with your baby but "it was actually less than half (42 percent) as risky, or more than twice as safe, for an infant to be in an adult bed as in a crib."[13] With all the safety mechanisms in place to make cribs safer, still more infants die alone in cribs than in the family bed, yet there has never been an outcry to ban cribs.

Dr. Fleming questions the logic behind this sweeping campaign:

> No one would suggest that because sleeping in a crib can be hazardous under certain conditions, no baby should sleep in a crib. By analogy, therefore, it is equally illogical to suggest that because under certain circumstances bedsharing can be hazardous, parents should not bedshare with their baby. Given the near universality of the practice of bedsharing at some stage, it is far more logical to identify the conditions under which bedsharing is hazardous and to give parents information on how to avoid them.[14]

The blanket condemnation of bedsharing without any attempts to educate the public about how to do it safely is a big concern of many parents and professionals. The bottom line is that many parents are going to do it at some point, anyway, so they need to be well versed in safe cosleeping guidelines. Dr. McKenna expressed his disappointment and concern with the short-sighted focus of the anti-cosleeping campaign:

By refusing to point out that cosleeping, and cosleeping in the form of bedsharing, can be practiced either safely or unsafely, and that sleeping next to a baby is not inherently dangerous, especially for a breastfeeding, sober mother, the CPSC misses opportunities to educate millions of parents about how to cosleep safely. Its actions suggest instead that parents are neither educable nor intelligent enough to make their own decisions about how, or whether, to cosleep."[15]

Dr. Fleming agrees: "Rather than issuing broad statements, not based upon good evidence, to suggest that parents should not bedshare with their babies, I suggest that giving them accurate information, based upon careful studies of healthy babies as well as babies who have died, will allow parents to make safe and appropriate choices."[16]

Regardless of the research, some parents just don't feel comfortable sleeping, or are unable to sleep, with their baby in the bed. If you're one of those parents, then it's important to know that it's okay. You can still practice attachment parenting without sleeping with your baby—it's about being responsive to your baby and being in close proximity during the night. We uphold a parent's right to choose, to make informed decisions that feel right for everyone. The American Academy of Pediatrics provides safety guidelines for the use of cribs and other separate sleeping surfaces on its website (www.healthychildren.org/English/news/Pages/AAP-Expands-Guidelines-for-Infant-Sleep-Safety-and-SIDS-Risk-Reduction. aspx).

In 2009, the Alaska Division of Public Health examined thirteen years of infant deaths that occurred while bedsharing to assess the contribution of known risk factors. Their conclusion was that 99 percent of all bedsharing deaths occurred in association with other risk factors, such as smoking (75%), substance abuse, or placing the infant prone for sleeping. This suggests that bedsharing alone does not increase the risk of infant death.[17]

Study Recommendation

In 2010 the following findings were published from a survey of nearly 5,000 families with infants up to 12 months of age in the United States.

- Despite ongoing anti-bedsharing campaigns, U.S. parents continue to bedshare in high numbers.
- Bedsharing families cite both ideological and pragmatic reasons for sleeping with their babies.
- They appear well aware of prohibitions on bedsharing, but, consistent with the results of previous studies, the majority continue to bedshare.
- In a possible attempt to avoid bedsharing, 55 percent of mothers feed their babies at night on chairs, recliners, or sofas. Forty-four percent (25 percent of the sample) admit that they fall asleep with their babies in these locations. Of all sleep locations, chairs, sofas, and recliners are by far the most dangerous and dramatically increase the risk of suffocation.

Safe-sleep campaigns should include information on safe bedsharing. In the absence of this information, parents are likely to continue bedsharing but may do so in unsafe ways. Alternatively, safe-sleep campaigns could provide other strategies, such as encouraging babies to sleep on adjacent, yet separate, surfaces.[18]

What About Cosleeping with Nonbiological Parents?

Many adoption agencies are beginning to support cosleeping with adopted babies for a couple of very good reasons. First, many internationally adopted babies come from countries where it is the custom to sleep with the baby. Second, adopted babies seem to adjust much better and are more likely to form a secure attachment with their adoptive parents sooner when the parents sleep with them.

In the case of stepparents, the biological parent will need to discuss this openly to gauge the stepparent's feelings about bedsharing. If the stepparent has a close, loving relationship with the baby, has mentally and physically taken on the role of a parent, and agrees to follow the safe-sleeping guidelines, then the biological parent may decide that it would be safe to cosleep. Any parent, biological or step, who is a deep sleeper should not sleep with an infant in the bed, because he or she is less likely to be as aware of the baby.

Some may have an unspoken fear that sleeping with a young child may stimulate sexual feelings—especially in a nonbiological parent. It's important to remember that sexual abusers are not born but created by their own horrible experiences in childhood and that a normal, healthy adult will not be tempted to abuse a child, whether or not they share bed. It is, however, imperative that biological parents take time to get to know a person very well before inviting him or her into the family and the family bed. A stepparent may feel uncomfortable with the situation based on his or her personal beliefs or childhood experiences—these feelings, if that is the case, should be respected and alternative arrangements discussed.

Sharing Sleep with Multiples

It can be a little more complex to cosleep with more than one infant. Dr. McKenna recommends bedsharing with one baby at a time while the mother is breastfeeding. If the mother is single or otherwise doesn't have a partner to help care for one of the babies in the family bed while she cares for the other, then she can make sure, such as in the case of twins, that both are in front of her and she is sleeping in a protective position with her knees bent upward. Two or more babies in the family bed make it a little more difficult for everyone to be comfortable or safe. If you share the bed with twins, be aware that as they grow they will begin to move around in the bed and can fall onto the floor if the bed isn't securely protected or if the mattress isn't on the floor (please read the Safe Cosleeping Guidelines that follow).

Parents of multiples can consider placing young infants in the same bassinet, crib, or cosleeping device (called *cobedding*) while in the same room with the parents. This practice may be frowned upon by your pediatrician or others, but in his book *Sleeping with Your Baby*, Dr. McKenna writes, "Nowadays when you hear a recommendation against cobedding, it often illustrates cultural biases against cosleeping in general where medical authorities assume, without any data, that if some instances of bedsharing between an adult and a baby are dangerous, then certainly two infants of equal body size must likewise pose a mutual threat."

For more information about safe cosleeping with multiples, we recommend you read Dr. McKenna's book, as well as *Mothering Multiples* by Karen Gromada.

Safe Cosleeping Guidelines

API recommends the following research-based guidelines that, when followed, allow parents and infants to share sleep in the safest way possible. These guidelines should be followed regardless of where the baby sleeps:

1. Place your baby to sleep on her back. This helps protect her from sudden infant death syndrome (SIDS).
2. Choose a firm mattress, free from fluffy bedding, bumpers, and stuffed animals. Never place your baby—or fall asleep with your baby—on a couch, recliner, beanbag chair, foldout couch, inflatable bed, or water bed to sleep.
3. Keep baby cool. Adjust clothing and room temperature to keep baby from overheating. UNICEF recommends a temperature of 60 to 64 degrees Fahrenheit for nighttime sleep.
4. Use a fan in the room where baby sleeps to help circulate air and maintain a cooler environment.

If your baby sleeps with you:

1. Breastfeed your baby. Breastfeeding mothers spend more time in lighter stages of sleep, making them more aware of the baby. They also tend to sleep in a protective position (with knees bent upward), which prevents baby from moving down under the covers.

2. Place the baby next to the mother rather than between the mother and father.

3. Use approved side rails or bed extenders when placing your baby in the family bed. Fill in any crevice between the bed and the walls or furniture with a rolled-up baby blanket or towel. Do not bedshare on a water bed or soft memory foam mattress topper. Placing the adult mattress on the floor (like a futon) creates the safest possible sleep environment.

4. A baby should not be left to sleep alone on an adult bed, even during naps. If parents do not have access to a crib or cosleeping device for naps, place a smaller, firm mattress or futon on the floor.

5. Be mindful about sharing sleep and settle the baby safely next to Mom in a planned environment rather than falling asleep from exhaustion on the couch, a recliner, a beanbag chair, or another unsafe place to share sleep.

6. Only primary caregivers should sleep with an infant. Do not allow babysitters or older siblings to sleep with the baby.

If your baby sleeps in a crib, the
crib must meet CPSC safety guidelines:

1. Slat spacing should be less than 2⅜ inches.
2. Slats must not be loose or broken.
3. The headboard and footboard must not have cutout designs.
4. Corner posts should be no more than $1/16$ inch higher than other rails.
5. Use firm, tightly fitting mattress with tightly fitting bottom sheet.
6. Remove loose bedding, bumper pads, and soft toys.

When You Should Not Bedshare

Parenting and infant care should focus on both health and safety. Bedsharing with an infant is healthy and safe in most cases, but there are situations that require parents to use a bassinet or crib instead.

You should *not* share a bed with an infant if any of the following apply:

1. You use alcohol or drugs. Using any substances that interfere with your judgment or level of consciousness at night will interfere with your ability to be aware of your baby. These substances include over-the-counter medication such as sleep aids or cold medication.
2. You smoke. A higher risk of SIDS has been associated with parental cigarette smoking and bedsharing.
3. You have a poor sleeping surface. Sharing sleep with your baby should not be done on a couch, a recliner, a water bed, or any location where the infant could become wedged between the surface and the parent.
4. Your baby is premature, is of low birth weight, or has a high fever.
5. There are other children or animals in the bed. The family bed should not include older children, who may not be as aware of the baby in bed.

Establishing Nighttime Routines

Regardless of which sleeping arrangement a family chooses, nighttime routines help everyone unwind from a busy day and help establish healthier sleep habits. Remember that especially for working parents, this is a "high attachment" part of the day! In the early weeks, the main routine is likely to be holding, rocking, and feeding. As mentioned earlier, your baby will sleep a lot at first and will have his own routine for a while, which is sure to be very different from yours. As he becomes a little more mature, his sleep routines will become a little more predictable, but they are guaranteed not to stay that way. Some infants are easily overstimulated by the environment, whether that environment includes television noise, playful siblings, car travel, or the general busyness of the day.

Sometimes babies will get fussy and cry and seem to fight sleep because they are overstimulated. What they may need is calming down by slowing

Risk factors found to be related to infant deaths in an adult bed are a smoking parent, prone sleeping position, parents affected by alcohol or drugs, use of heavy comforters or blankets that can cause overheating, and inappropriate sleep locations, such as a couch or waterbed.[19]

down the home environment. A pleasant bedtime routine may include playing soft music, giving the child a warm bath or a massage, rocking, reading, or singing to the child, and reducing stimulation in the period before sleep. You'll soon learn what quiet activities your baby enjoys, and it will serve to deepen your connection. Ignore any well-intentioned advice that by doing this you will "spoil" the baby. These kinds of routines, while seemingly tedious at times, can create lasting, loving memories.

The Magic of Lullabies

For many generations, mothers and fathers around the world have enjoyed rocking and singing to their babies. Today's parents are relearning long-forgotten lullabies from their own mothers, or learning new ones as they listen to lullabies on CDs. Researchers have found that mothers who sing to their babies every day have babies who are more advanced in their language and early communication skills, and they found an unexpected benefit to the mother. A recent study found "a number of parents who said [that] when they'd had post-natal depression, or feelings like that after the birth of their child, [singing] not only relaxed the child but relaxed them as well."[20]

No matter what the stresses of the day have been, one of the most relaxing things you can do is rock and sing to your baby. There are obvious benefits to the baby, who has been hearing her mother's voice in the womb for many months, and it has an immediate calming effect. The rocking motion is also important for the baby's vestibular system in the brain, which is responsible for balance, spatial perception, movement, and motor coordination. Several lullaby CDs are listed in Appendix C.

Developing Healthy Sleep Habits for the Older Child

Parents can experiment to find the routine that works best for their child, and remember that any bedtime routine is likely to take from thirty minutes to an hour or more. Some parents find it helpful to begin quieting down the environment up to two hours before bedtime. Recommendations for older children include eliminating food or drinks with caffeine or a lot of sugar (for some children, food dyes can create hyperactivity) from their diet, turning off the TV, dimming the lights, or reducing noisy activities before bedtime. If you are breastfeeding a toddler, continue to watch your diet, avoiding caffeine in drinks or chocolate and spicy or gassy foods—even foods with citric acid can be culprits. Also avoid sweeteners such as aspartame if you suspect they could be bothering your baby.

As bedtime approaches, many children calm down easily with a predictable nighttime routine; others experience a high-energy spurt just before bedtime and may need high-energy play before they can relax. Some children are relaxed by a bath, while others are excited by it. Do what works to help each individual child prepare for sleep, and remember the importance of a regular bedtime that is early enough to allow sufficient sleep—eight to ten hours—if the child must wake early for school or other activities.

A Father's Story

It may be a "different" arrangement, but I can't imagine it being any other way. I am awake and leaving the house before anyone else begins to stir. Some mornings it takes every ounce of self-restraint to keep from climbing back into bed and snuggling up to my loved ones in our big family bed. There is something surreal about sharing space, time, and warmth and listening to one another breathe in synchronicity for a moment, splinter into our own rhythms, and then find one another again.

We were already sharing a family bed when we heard about "cosleeping." Neither my wife nor I came from cosleeping families, but when our first son was born, it simply felt right to continue to have him right next to us. He had shared our bed while in utero; why should it change after he was born? Of course we had well-meaning friends and relatives express concern when they heard about our sleeping arrangement. We read other people's thoughts about it, both those for and against it. Even after we learned more about cosleeping, continuing to have our son in our bed simply worked for us.

Our oldest son knows that there is an option to sleep in his own bed in our room or in a separate room, but the choice and the change will be one that is based on his needs. When I wake up in the morning to see my little family cuddled together, nestled in against the coldest mornings, it's just what I need to go on.

—Dax L.

Keep in mind that sleep routines change as the child grows and matures. Try not to get stressed out; keep a sense of humor and remain flexible.

[WITH] FOUR KIDS . . . BEDTIME IS A CRISIS . . .
THEY ACT LIKE THEY'VE NEVER BEEN TO SLEEP BEFORE. "BEEEDDD?
WHAT'S THAT? NAW, I DON'T WANT TO DO THAT!" THEN IT
BECOMES SOME HOSTAGE NEGOTIATION BUT IN REVERSE. "LOOK, IF
YOU WILL STAY IN THERE I WILL GIVE YOU WHATEVER YOU WANT!
I WILL MEET YOUR DEMANDS. . . . [W]HAT DO YOU WANT, A
HELICOPTER TO CUBA? ANYTHING! STAY IN THERE!"

—Jim Gaffigan, stand-up comedian, Mr. Universe

Bedtimes may shift earlier or later as nap schedules and sleep needs change, and the total amount of sleep that a child needs decreases as he gets older. When a child transitions out of a nap or starts school, the sleep cycle can become erratic for a while. Illness and growth spurts can also contribute to changing sleep patterns. Through all of these changes, parents can help the child learn to trust his body and recognize the signs of tiredness without forcing him to go to sleep when he is not tired or keeping him awake when he needs sleep, just for the sake of a routine. Parents can be proactive in teaching their child ways to calm down to prepare his mind and body for sleep.

Transitioning Out of the Family Bed

When the time comes for a child to transition to her own bed, parents need to make sure that the transition is gentle and respectful of any feelings of fear or upset experienced by the child. This is especially true when a child is transitioning because of the birth of a sibling, since the child may already have some anxiety related to the birth. Young children who have their own beds often go to sleep more willingly when parents lie down with them in their beds until they are very drowsy or until they go to sleep—usually after reading a few stories. Children outgrow this need when they are developmentally ready and will happily go to sleep on their own, although older children may still enjoy a brief snuggle time with parents before bed.

Communicating with Your Partner

Since no set rules govern nighttime parenting, considering the needs of each family member will help you make the best choice for the family. Some parents do not feel comfortable with the idea of having a baby sleep in their bed, or one parent may want to cosleep and the other might not. It's not unusual for fathers to be a little more reluctant and resistant to cosleeping, but fathers have reported that they found bedsharing "more enjoyable than disruptive." Bedsharing helps fathers feel more quickly bonded to their babies.[21]

It's important to discuss individual feelings and to resolve any concerns in a way that is respectful to each parent while still meeting the baby's nighttime needs. When considering the different possible sleeping arrangements, some parents are concerned about how cosleeping will affect intimacy with the partner. Neither parenthood nor cosleeping has to put a damper on intimacy; a little creativity and preplanning can ensure that intimacy doesn't wither on the vine. (See Chapter 9 for more information about keeping intimacy and balance in your relationship.)

Parents need to discuss the idea of bedsharing as soon as possible—if not before the baby is born, then again shortly afterward to prevent any misunderstandings. For the family bed to work best, both parents need to be on board with the decision. If the mother is planning on nursing, she will find that bedsharing, or having the baby within arm's reach, will help her sleep and stay rested while better facilitating the breastfeeding relationship. If Mom is breastfeeding, it usually works out well for Dad, because he doesn't have to get up to get the baby.

The main priority is for both parents to be on the same page, so that the family bed doesn't create a wedge in the relationship. Frank, open communication is key in any relationship, so if problems arise, talk about them. If you don't know the answers, find information that can help you. An endless amount of information can be found on the Internet and in books. You can feel confident about any information that you find through API's website as well.

Night Waking

As they grow, many babies will go through a phase in which they sleep for longer periods, only to begin waking at night during different developmental stages. They may wake during nightmares (some actually experience "night terrors"), teething, illness, growth spurts, or times of family stress or transition in their lives. Babies are very sensitive to their parents' stress or when parents are simply trying to steal a few minutes of time to do something else, all of which can affect their sleep-wake patterns. It's possible that occasionally some babies may be overstimulated by sleeping with the parents. The only way to know is to try having the baby sleep on a separate surface near the adult bed. The key is tuning in to what the baby is trying to communicate and finding the sleep arrangement that works best for the family and in which everyone gets the best sleep. Recent research indicates that some babies do better if their sleep arrangements are consistently in the same place, whether bedsharing or sleeping separately. Just about any parent can tell you that babies seem to have built-in radar for when Mom and Dad want time to themselves. Don't take it personally! Baby is just trying to keep a connection with Mommy.

After thirty years of caring for children and counseling parents, the Searses has found that most infants wake up several times during the night. He reassures parents that it is not because of anything they have done. "Every baby is different, and sleep behavior has more to do with inborn temperament than with any 'bad habits' caused by Mom and Dad," say the Searses.[22]

Gentle Ways to Get Your Baby to Sleep

Dr. Jay Gordon is a pediatrician who knows firsthand from working with hundreds of families that sleep deprivation can become a big issue for many parents. He describes himself as one of the strongest proponents of attachment parenting and the family bed, but he understands that when parents become unhappy with the arrangement, largely because of frequent nursing and night-waking, then it is time to make some changes. However, Dr. Gordon is adamant that both parents be in agreement and feel good about the decision to gently change their child's sleep habits. He first warns parents:

> I don't recommend any forced sleep changes during the first year of life. Probably the only exception to this would be an emergency involving a nursing mom's health. There are many suggestions in books and magazines for pushing "sleeping through the night" during a baby's early months or during the first year. I don't think this is the best thing to do, and I am quite sure that the earlier a baby gets "nonresponse" from parents, the more likely he is to close down at least a little.[23]

In his books and on his website, Dr. Gordon provides parents with gentle, sensitive ways of teaching toddlers to sleep without nursing. He feels that parents are the best judges of whether his techniques work, and he encourages them to follow their instincts.

Other pediatricians, such as Dr. Paul Fleiss, raise concerns about the crying-it-out method of sleep training. He warns parents:

> Don't ignore your children's cries. After all, they may be sick, in danger, or in pain. Babies and young children are emotional rather than rational creatures. They can't comprehend why their cries for help are being ignored. Even with the best of intentions, ignoring children leads them to feel abandoned. The result will be insecure, unhappy children. You cannot "spoil" children by responding to their cries. "Spoiled" children are those who don't know what to expect from their parents. They are often alternately punished or praised for the same activity at different times.[24]

The Problem with Sleep Training

Parents who are frustrated by frequent night waking or who are sleep-deprived may be tempted to try sleep-training techniques that recommend letting a baby "cry it out." It was once believed to be healthy to teach a baby to "self-soothe." New research suggests that these techniques can have detrimental physiological effects on the baby by increasing the stress hormone cortisol in the brain.[25] The increase in cortisol can have long-term effects on emotional regulation, sleep patterns, and behavior. In *The Science of Parenting*, Margot Sunderland describes the physiological processes that occur when a baby is allowed to cry himself to sleep: "His stress levels will have gone up, not down. Studies show that after being left to cry, babies move into a primitive defense mode. This results in an irregularity in breathing and heart rate, both of which can fluctuate wildly, and high levels of cortisol."[26]

An infant is not neurologically or developmentally capable of calming or soothing herself to sleep in ways that are healthy. The part of the brain that allows her to begin the process of learning to regulate her own emotions, or self-soothe, isn't well developed until she is two and a half to three years of age. Babies and young children depend on their parents to help them calm down and learn to regulate their intense feelings—they are the child's "emotional regulators."

Sleep training involves placing the baby alone in a crib before he is fully asleep. When the baby cries, parents are taught to comfort the child verbally or with pats on his back only after waiting increasing amounts of time to respond and then leaving the room. The child finally falls asleep from exhaustion. After a few nights of this, some children will learn to fall asleep quickly and without crying.

"A popular childrearing standard encourages parents to allow little babies to cry themselves to sleep, with the presumption that this is the best course for family homeostasis as well as development of independent attitudes. The emphasis behind this practice is on learning to self-soothe at an early age, rather than gradual acquisition of these skills through mutual regulation with a caregiver. A host of reasons both psychological and neurochemical suggest that such practices may be directly or indirectly linked to the ongoing epidemic of depression."[27]

While sleep training has become extremely popular in Western cultures, it is not without controversy, because no evidence has shown that it is really beneficial in the long run, and, in fact, it may be detrimental to emotional and psychological development. Why is it so popular? In an effort to help parents get more sleep, this kind of advice is dispensed in popular parenting books, by pediatricians and sleep researchers who most often have little knowledge of children's normal emotional, cognitive, or neurological development. Such advice is often based on the premise that infants are neurologically ready to be "taught" when to go to sleep at night and that they should be able to sleep throughout the night uninterrupted.

Leaving infants to cry it out in order to learn to sleep on their own, Dr. McKenna has observed, deprives babies of oxygen and creates a situation in which the baby must redirect her energies away from growing and fighting disease. He states that "the baby is burning energy and calories needlessly that could have been put into other more beneficial processes."

McKenna offers powerful advice to parents on sleep training:

> I think sometimes parents are under the mistaken impression that if they don't sleep train their babies, somehow some developmental or social skill or competency later in life will be kept from them or that their babies will never exhibit good sleep patterns later in life.
>
> If they think this, then they really ought to know that there has never been a scientific study anywhere that has shown any benefit for babies whatsoever in sleeping through the night at young ages, or even sleeping through the night at any particular time. What is important is the nature of social relationships and support within which babies develop all kinds of skills pertaining to independence.
>
> One of the most important things I am hoping to do is remind parents that no one can tell them what they should do with their babies. They have to learn to trust their own judgment, look at the research that is now available on these issues of sleep behavior, and see that there are major critiques about this solitary sleep-training model.[28]

It's very likely that your baby's pediatrician will discourage you from bed-sharing, but he or she should be supportive of the baby sleeping in close proximity in accordance with the AAP guidelines, which state, "Room-sharing but not bed-sharing is recommended—there is evidence that [room-sharing] decreases the risk of SIDS by as much as 50%." In addition, the AAP recommends that bedsharing should be avoided with a baby younger than three months, and never to bedshare if either parent is a smoker or takes prescription medication, alcohol, or illicit drugs. Babies should never bed-share with anyone other than a parent.[29] You are not obligated to share information about your child's sleeping arrangements with your pediatrician, but you are obligated to be informed and to provide a safe sleeping environment wherever your child sleeps. For that reason, API has launched the Safe Sleep Campaign to help educate parents and professionals about how to create a safe environment. A brochure entitled Safe Infant Sleep Guidelines is available for free at http://attachmentparenting.org/infantsleepsafety. This brochure can be downloaded and used by any parent, professional, and agency. Be skeptical of any advice that goes against your instincts, and listen to your baby! As the parent, you have the right to make informed decisions for your child; when it comes to sleeping, keep it safe!

A sleep training program for infants looked at the physiological and behavioral dynamics of infants and their mothers. Saliva samples that measure levels of cortisol (a hormone that registers stress) were taken when the babies were left to "cry it out" for the night. Both mothers and babies had high cortisol levels when the babies were crying. After three days of sleep training the babies no longer cried for their mothers, resulting in the mother's cortisol levels being reduced, however the babies' levels remained high. The researchers were concerned that this "disconnect" could disrupt maternal-infant attunement which is essential for optimum child development.[30]

CHAPTER SEVEN

PRINCIPLE 6:
Provide Consistent, Loving Care

Keeping Baby's Attachment Secure

> The notion that relationships are essential for regulating
> our behavior and moods and feelings as well as for intellectual
> development is one that needs greater emphasis as we think about
> the kinds of settings and priorities we want for our children.
> The interactions that are necessary can take place in full measure only
> with a loving caregiver who has lots of time to devote to a child.
>
> —T. Berry Brazelton, MD, and Stanley I. Greenspan, MD,
> *The Irreducible Needs of Children*

Perhaps the most critical decision parents face in their parenting journey is who will be the primary caregiver of their cherished and vulnerable new baby. For most parents over the centuries, this has been the role of the biological mother, but, in the last fifty years, we have seen a huge cultural shift in the United States, with a larger percentage of mothers reentering the workforce with very young children. In 2011, 63.9 percent of mothers with children under the age of six were employed outside the home (compared to 11.9 percent in 1950).[1]

This chapter is about giving parents information about their baby's need for consistent loving care, why this is so important to a baby's development, and resources and creative solutions to help make this happen. We begin with the premise that all parents love their children and want what is best for their physical, emotional, and spiritual development, and when given the facts, parents can then make better decisions and come up with wonderfully resourceful ideas for their child's care. An important note to this chapter: When studies refer to "nonmaternal care," they are referring to care other than the baby's primary attachment figure, which is not necessarily always the mother. A growing number of fathers are taking on the role of the primary caregiver for their young children. When we speak of the primary caregiver, it can refer to the mother, the father, or any person who is the primary person caring for the baby or child during waking hours and to whom the baby has the most secure attachment. This could also be a grandparent, an adult sibling, other extended family members, or a nanny.

Dr. Stanley Greenspan, clinical professor of psychiatry and pediatrics at George Washington University Medical School, and T. Berry Brazelton, clinical professor of pediatrics emeritus at Harvard Medical School, have written movingly about the critical necessity for a stable, loving caregiver in the early years of a child's life. In their book *The Irreducible Needs of Children*, they advocate for parents to understand their essential roles in protecting the precious attachment process, which is the foundation of their child's future psychological, intellectual, and moral well-being.

Dr. Greenspan, one of the world's foremost authorities on infants and young children with developmental and emotional problems, conveys some of his ideas for child care in his book *The Four-Thirds Solution*. First, he gives parents insight about the critical emotional needs in a child's first three years: "Our society doesn't tell parents that the most important gift they can give their children is not a good education, elaborate educational toys, or summer camps, but time—regular, substantial chunks of it—spent together doing things that are emotionally and developmentally meaningful for the child."[2] The book describes how different families have adjusted their work schedules to make it possible for each parent to spend at least two-thirds of the day with the baby, not necessarily at the same time, giving a "four-thirds" solution for the child's care. This is one of many ideas for parents to consider if one parent cannot be the primary caregiver in the early years.

Attachment theory has been described in Chapter 1 of this book, and reviewing this introductory chapter lays an excellent foundation for understanding the attachment needs of a baby and young child. Exciting research in the field of neurobiology (the mechanisms by which human relationships shape brain structure and function) is confirming what attachment theorists have been seeing for more than fifty years: a baby's brain and even his DNA is shaped by relationships. This was a stunning discovery made possible only with the modern technology of brain imaging, the mapping of the genetic code, and the relatively new field of quantum physics. Ironically, mapping the genetic code only led to more questions, since the human body has far fewer genes than was theorized. Research in the field of cellular biology is showing us that the key to understanding our biology and psychology does lies not within our DNA but rather within the mechanisms of our cell membrane. Each cell membrane has receptors that pick up various environmental signals, and this mechanism controls the "reading" of the genes inside our cells. Our cells can choose to read or not read the genetic blueprint depending on the signals being received from the environment.

How Stress Affects a Baby's Brain

Cortisol is a stress hormone that is released by the adrenal glands when we are in a state of fear. Babies who are left to cry for long periods or who are afraid in a strange situation release massive amounts of cortisol, potentially creating a dangerous level in the brain. If released at toxic levels, it can damage key structures in the brain. Elevated cortisol levels are seen in the brains of depressed people and those with post-traumatic stress disorder: "Researchers at the National Institutes of Health have found a link between depression and traumas experienced in early childhood. Studies have shown that abused, neglected, or otherwise unnurtured infants and children are more likely to be depressed as adults, and now we have a way to understand the link between experience and the biology. It all relates to something called the hypothalamic-pituitary-adrenal axis."[3]

In other words, a baby who is stressed produces hormones that make the synapses and neurons more vulnerable to an injury. The longer they remain elevated, the more likely it is that the functioning of many emotional and biological systems is affected. Even in very young babies, the amount of stress has a profound effect on what is called the baby's "intrinsic memory." We cannot consciously recall events stored in our intrinsic memory; these memories are deeply encoded, creating generalizations from experience. The processing of these memories and emotional reactions takes place in the amygdala, which is an almond-shaped group of neurons located deep within the medial temporal lobes of the brain. This exciting research is where attachment theory and biology intersect. Dr. Daniel Siegel describes it this way:

> An infant who has a healthy, secure attachment has had the repeated experience of nurturing, perceptive, sensitive, and predictable caregiving responses, . . . which have been encoded implicitly in her brain. She has developed a generalized representation of that relationship—a mental model of attachment—which helps her know what to expect. . . . Given that these repeated experiences have been predictable, and that when there have been disruptions in mother-infant communication, the mother has been relatively quick and effective at repairing the ruptures, this fortunate infant has been able to develop a secure, organized model of their emotional relationship.[4]

Now more than ever before, we understand the vital role the parent-child relationship plays in shaping the template of the baby's emotional, intellectual, and biological life. It is critical that parents do everything they can to ensure that the primary caregiver in their baby's life be nurturing, predictable, and responsive.

Studies on Child Care

Studies done on the long-term effects of nonmaternal care of infants and young children have been controversial and confusing, with mixed conclusions. However, emerging data clearly sound warnings to parents. Some research indicates that babies under the age of one year who spend more than thirty hours in day care (some studies say twenty hours) may develop behavioral problems as they get older, such as excessively aggressive behavior. Boys seem to be particularly vulnerable to long hours in day care.[5]

Center care, in and of itself, adversely increased the likelihood of infants developing insecure attachment to their mothers, compared with infants who were in maternal care, individual non-parental care with a relative, individual non-parental care with a paid caregiver, or family day care. The results suggest that it is the poor quality of center care and the high infant-caregiver ratio that accounted for this increased level of attachment insecurity among center-care infants.[6]

Another key factor that emerges from this research is the importance of continuity of care in the early months and years of a child's life. Until the child is old enough to verbalize his needs to his caregiver, it is critical for the caregiver to be in attunement with the baby so that his needs are met consistently and sensitively. Try to imagine what it must be like for a baby who is crying to be fed or picked up when the caregiver is overwhelmed with several babies needing the same thing. A mother of triplets, or especially quadruplets, is given tremendous sympathy and often offered help in caring for her babies, yet in the best day-care situation, a four-to-one ratio is considered a manageable standard. Adding to this the low salaries day-care providers typically earn, is it any wonder that day-care employees have one of the highest turnover rates of any occupation? Dr. Isabelle Fox, in her book, *Being There: The Benefits of a Stay-at-Home Parent*, coined the phrase "caregiver roulette" to describe the high turnover rate of care providers in American day-care facilities. When a baby adjusts to the smells and voice of one care provider and then a new person comes in, she has no frame of reference and no comprehension of this new person, the new smells, or the new voice. When an infant experiences the frequent loss of caregivers, especially in the preverbal years, it can be emotionally devastating, and as a result she may become insecurely attached or learn not to attach to anyone.

The stress of caring for several babies all day long takes a tremendous toll, especially when the caregiver is not emotionally invested in the babies. Dr. Greenspan has found that even the most dedicated child-care providers often "hold back" emotionally because separating from their tiny charges would otherwise be "too emotionally wrenching."[7] He warns that even in the best centers, the ratio of infants to caregiver is four to one, and the toddler ratios can rise as high as ten to one.[8] "We are expecting [the day-care system] to operate the way very well-functioning families do. . . . As a result, children aren't getting the consistent one-on-one nurturing with the same caregiver . . . that almost all of us who study and work with children agree they need. Furthermore, many highly motivated caregivers don't receive the training, support, and pay they need to work with children on a sustained basis."[9]

Academic Warns Child Care Can Lead to Aggression

Professor Jay Belsky, director of the Institute for the Study of Children, Families, and Social Issues at Birkbeck University of London, revealed that U.S. research showed children who spent long periods in day care were more likely to have poor behavior. Researchers found that 17 percent of the children who were in care for more than thirty hours a week were regarded by teachers, mothers, and caregivers as being aggressive toward other children. That compared with 6 percent for the group of children in child care for less than ten hours a week.[10]

Working and Alternate Caregivers

Mothers who plan to return to work shortly after the birth of their baby sometimes tell their doctors or friends that they are afraid to get "too attached" to their babies. They are worried that this will make separation too painful when they must return to work. However, it is detrimental for parents to distance themselves emotionally from their babies, because it can permanently affect their growing relationships with their children. Instead, parents should treasure those early weeks of bonding with the baby and get to know her personality, feeding patterns, and what makes her unique. This will help a mother make better decisions about her baby's care and create better communication with the caregiver.

Pediatrician and author T. Berry Brazelton made this observation more than twenty years ago at a public talk in Denver, Colorado:

> I've had young [pregnant] women sitting in my office and they . . . don't want to get into the subject (of their babies) in depth anymore. I began to realize that what they were saying to me, when they were not willing to share the deeper emotional feelings about the turmoil of pregnancy or not wanting to talk about nursing, was that they had to return to work too soon. They were already guarding themselves, in pregnancy, from too deep an attachment. Now, that scares the hell out of me. . . . These young women are grieving for what they might have had at a time when they ought to be investing themselves so emotionally and passionately that, of course, it is going to hurt to leave. . . . If you can guard yourself like that, then what kind of a nurturing person are you going to be?[11]

Dr. Brazelton is one of many professionals who continually challenge parents to take very seriously their children's needs for consistent care. Parents must face the reality of the challenges of the child-care situation, and, if both parents must work (or in the case of a single parent), creative strategies can be used. If you live in a country that offers paid maternity leave, then consider yourself very fortunate. If not, find out if your employer offers a family leave of absence; a parent may be able to return to work after a year or two without sacrificing his or her career path. Parents can explore a variety of economic and work-arrangement options that permit their children to be cared for by one or both parents at all times. For example, parents can consider ideas for cutting expenses, or they may be able to use financial assets they already have so that one parent can be home. Today's workplace is increasingly flexible and family-friendly, providing employees with the opportunity to explore different work situations that best fit their families' needs. Some places of employment are getting creative and helping new parents with on-site day care, or even allowing the baby to stay with Mom or Dad at the workstation. Recently, an article in *USA Today* reported that an advertising firm in Austin, Texas, allows its employees to bring their babies to work until they are old enough to crawl. The article said that the Parenting in the Workplace Institute in Framingham, Massachusetts, reports that the number of companies allowing children at work on an occasional basis climbed to 29 percent last year, up from 22 percent in 2006, according to the Society for Human Resource Management. Some of these progressive companies include Marriott International, Microsoft, and J.C. Penney.[12]

The Parenting in the Workplace Institute (www.parentingatwork.org) promotes baby-friendly workplace programs, and it has identified more than eighty organizations (and it says this number is probably very low) in which employees can bring their babies to work every day. They have found that babies at work tend to be overwhelmingly content, primarily because their needs are met quickly and they are held much of the time by parents and coworkers. Mothers who take their babies to work are more likely to continue breastfeeding, and nursing on cue also keeps the babies happy and healthy. The institute is devoted to expanding the adoption of these baby programs as well as explaining and promoting the attachment care principles that lead to success for businesses and for babies.

Some companies allow parents to telecommute (work from home); this can allow both parents to interact with the baby during the day. Some employers allow parents to bring the baby to the workplace for breastfeeding or checking in. Working part-time, working as a

Poor-quality care can result in:

- Substantial amounts of unoccupied time spent tuned out and unengaged in social interactions.
- Delays in cognitive and language development, prereading skills, and other age-appropriate behaviors.
- Insecure attachment to caregivers.
- More frequent displays of aggression toward other children and adults.[13]

A four-state survey of one hundred randomly chosen child-care centers found that the vast majority of children who spent their days in child-care centers were receiving less than adequate care.[14]

Infants exposed to twenty or more hours a week of day care were more likely to be classified as insecurely attached than those in maternal or paternal care. Boys in particular showed vulnerability in attachment to both parents when in day care more than thirty-five hours a week.[15]

consultant, working on limited projects, or participating in a job share can all allow parents more access to their infant during the critical first year of life and beyond.

Parents who attend API support groups often share their solutions for how they found ways for one parent to be the primary caregiver. Here is one family's story:

> When I had my first baby, my husband was a struggling musician play-ing five nights a week at a nightclub, and I was teaching school. We decided to try to make it on one salary but soon realized that we could not pay our bills and were faced with me going back to teaching and putting the baby in day care. When we started looking at the costs, it almost didn't seem worth going back, so we got creative. We got a loan from the Teacher's Union to help us when money got short each month. I learned how to get very frugal with money, like clipping coupons and going to yard sales. In fact, my friends and I made a game of bargain hunting, and we helped each other when we saw a good sale or found a new recipe. We got by with one car, and I learned I was able to qualify for supplemental food through the WIC program in our community. When I look back on those years, I have no regrets about the sacrifices we made as a family—it was so worth it to be with my baby and not have the worry of whether he was crying and needing to be picked up or was taking his first step and one of us was not there for him. I went back to teaching school when he was a toddler, and my husband and his mother were able to share child-care duties for him during the day, so it was amazing what a little creativity and determination did to help us find a plan that worked for us.

Making the Transition to Work

Parents whose work situation does not lend itself to this type of flexibility have even more reason to practice attachment parenting. Being sensitive and responsive to the child's needs and feelings, holding, and cuddling can help parents and babies reconnect after being apart. For instance, parents that share sleep with their baby can have the extra touch time that they missed out on during the day. Infant massage is another way to reconnect in the evenings, and breastfeeding mothers find that pumping their milk while separated keeps up their supply so they can continue the nursing relationship when they are together in the evenings and on weekends.

It is also important to realize that the caregiver will be an incredibly important attachment figure in the child's life, and the parents may experience some jealousy. Keeping the lines of communication open is critical, and finding ways to keep the connection strong with your child while sharing this attachment with another caregiver is important to the health of your child and the success of this arrangement.

Here are some helpful tips when a parent is returning to work:

- It is extremely important to have continuity of care with a consistent, loving caregiver. The parent needs to make sure the caregiver is someone who makes the baby's needs the top priority. Ideally, the caregiver will be someone who already understands the importance of attachment-promoting practices. When possible, choosing a family member, close friend, or someone with whom parents have an ongoing relationship will reduce the incidence of caregiver turnover. In the case of a paid nanny, offer incentives up front to keep her for at least the first three years, if possible—perhaps a raise each year or other perks. Ideally, the care will take place in the baby's home environment.
- Parents should expect and encourage their child to form an attachment to the caregiver. They may consider introducing the caregiver to the Eight Principles of Parenting and explaining to the caregiver how they want the baby to be responded to and cared for. Parents may want to consider providing the caregiver with a sling to carry the baby.
- Ideally, the parent will give the child time to get to know a new caregiver in the parent's presence. Parents should begin the transition well in advance of any separation so that it is a gradual process and is comfortable for the child.
- Avoid "caregiver roulette." Frequent turnover of caregivers can be very damaging to the attachment process, so if you are looking at day-care arrangements, try to find a program where the caregivers are stable and

move up with the babies as they progress to the next age group. Minimize the number of hours in nonparental care as much as possible to provide the best opportunity for a child to build secure attachments with parents.

- Parents can find ways to reconnect with their children when separated because of employment. Try to spend some quiet time with your child at the end of the day rather than rushing to fix dinner or shopping. Planning ahead, perhaps cooking meals and freezing them, may give you more downtime with your child at the end of the day. Parents can include a child in day-to-day tasks, and babies enjoy being in a sling and watching Mom or Dad do tasks around the house.

The books listed in Appendix C go into much more detail about the pros and cons of substitute care, how to find and interview a potential caregiver, and how parents can find creative solutions to staying home, working part-time, or splitting care with parents and caregivers.

SOME PARENTS MAY SEE ANY CRITICISM ABOUT
CHILD CARE AS AN ATTACK ON THEIR PARTICULAR DECISIONS. . . .
THE ASSUMPTION IS THAT CRITICS OF DAY CARE ARE REALLY
ADVOCATING A RETURN TO AN ERA WHEN WOMEN STAYED AT HOME
AND CARED FOR CHILDREN INSTEAD OF PURSUING CAREERS.
THESE AGENDAS . . . ARE PREVENTING US FROM HAVING A COHERENT
DISCUSSION ABOUT THE ACTUAL QUALITY OF DAY CARE TODAY. . . .
IF WE CLEAR AWAY THE SMOKE . . . THIS IS WHAT WE SEE:
MUCH OF THE CHILD CARE AVAILABLE FOR INFANTS AND TODDLERS
IN THIS COUNTRY SIMPLY ISN'T GOOD FOR THEM.

—Stanley Greenspan, MD,
The Four-Thirds Solution: Solving the Child-Care Crisis in America Today

Separations Because of Shared Custody

Some families find themselves in a difficult situation because of work schedules, divorce, or shared custody. In their book, *The Unexpected Legacy of Divorce: A 25-Year Landmark Study*, Judith Wallerstein, Julia Lewis, and

Sandra Blakeslee give guidance to parents, attorneys, and judges in considering the attachment needs of babies and very young children:

> When a baby doesn't see her primary caregiver for several days, the
> child suffers a lot because she is likely to assume that the caregiver has
> disappeared and that she's been abandoned. But our knowledge about
> how much absence the infant can tolerate without severe suffering is
> still insufficient to build regular disappearances of a parent into the
> child's schedule. Putting the child's best interests forward and honoring
> what is best for the child is extremely hard to do. . . . It requires parents to
> stand apart from their raw, hurt, jealous, competitive feelings and take an
> objective, compassionate look at what life will be like for their child. . . .
> Surely the job of the court is to give priority to the helpless child over the
> demands of the parent.[16]

The U.S. court system obviously has an enormous need to receive education on the attachment needs of children whose parents are going through a
separation or divorce. Of particular
importance are custody decisions
that are based on the developmental
needs of the child. Usually a schedule
based on a baby's gradual abilities to
tolerate longer separations from his
primary caregiver is the ideal. Information on providing consistent and
loving care during these difficult situations is available through resources
listed on the API website, www. attachmentparenting.org.

The data from several studies suggest
that repeated overnight separations present
a greater challenge to the development
of organized primary attachments than
do daytime separations. Furthermore, it
is known that especially in high-conflict
separations, frequent transitions can
exacerbate interparental conflict.[17]

Short-Term Child-Care Choices

The first few weeks and months of parenting, your newborn will quickly
teach you what flexibility and "going with the flow" truly mean. Instead of
trying to fit a new baby into the existing prebaby schedule, parents can come
up with creative ways to design new routines that include the baby. This may

mean taking a sleeping newborn out on date night, getting exercise by taking walks with the baby in a sling, or working with employers to customize a schedule that maximizes parents' time with their children. Parents can take a trusted caregiver with them if they go out for a long evening or special event; many babies are happy to stroll around a restaurant or other interesting environment with a caregiver, allowing parents some time to be alone. This technique also works well for family vacations or business trips.

Being together as a family in the first months of a baby's life allows parents to solidify parenting views and ensure that the baby is receiving consistent care. A baby thrives when she knows what to expect and when her needs are met in a responsive and loving manner by caregivers (remember that babies love predictability). In the early months, a baby's natural attachment-promoting behaviors, along with a parent's instinctual drive for caregiving, work together to develop a strong bond. Families can support the breast-feeding relationship of mother and baby by helping them to stay close during infancy, thus making breastfeeding success more likely.

Practical Tips for Short Separations

Although having one or both parents or loving family members to provide consistent, loving care at all times is certainly the ideal, it is not always possible. If parents need to be separated from an infant or a young child for a short time, the following tips may help minimize stress and fear:

- Leave the child with a trusted care provider to whom the child is attached and who is familiar with, supportive of, and willing to use attachment parenting principles. A good option is family members or friends with whom your child has developed a trusting relationship.
- Respect the child's feelings and follow his lead about his readiness to separate. Being empathetic, understanding, and patient allows the child to adjust to separations according to his own timetable.
- Talk to older children about the separation. Parents should let the children know they are leaving, call to check in, and let them know when they can expect to see their parents again.

- Accept that even older children have occasional difficulties with separation from one or both parents. Toddlers and older children naturally like to be with their parents, and some level of separation anxiety is perfectly normal and age-appropriate. Parents know their child better than anyone and can judge when his anxiety is unusually problematic. If this is the case, it is necessary to evaluate other factors in the child's life that need special attention.
- Use creativity to help avoid unnecessary anxiety-producing experiences. For example, some parents have found that it is easier for a young child to separate if the child is picked up for an outing with a caregiver rather than the parent(s) leaving the child at the caregiver's home.
- When the child becomes verbal, she will be better able to handle separation, especially if she has a solidly attached relationship with her parents as a foundation. She will be better able to communicate her feelings, signaling her parents that she is ready for short separations, and also allowing parents to check in with her during those separations.

A Mother's Story: An Unexpected Evening Out with Our Five-Year-Old

You never know when a precious family memory will start out as a seeming disaster! Many years ago, my husband and I had been planning a special evening out with his boss. I bought a new dress and carefully arranged child care with a trusted family friend. The plan was that I would drop off our boys (ages seven, five, and two), come home, and have a leisurely bath, so we'd have plenty of time to get ready. For some reason, our five-year-old son did not want to be left that night—he worried about it all day, but I kept reassuring him that he'd have so much fun, we'd only be gone a few hours, and that Mommy and Daddy would spend some special time with him the next day. I finally got them all in the car, but as I was pulling away from the curb, I looked back to see that he was still very distressed, and he begged me to let him stay home. Impulsively, he ran back into the house and I followed, asking my husband to talk to him, since I had no choice but to take the other boys to the sitter. I dreaded the scene when I returned home, thinking that they would both be upset and my husband would be stressed about what to do. We were going to a very exclusive restaurant that did not cater to children, so I wondered if we'd have to cancel.

I will never forget the joy on my son's face when I came back in the house. My husband had dressed him in his Sunday best suit, and they were both looking so handsome. They had talked through the problem and decided that if it was this traumatic to be left, and if he was willing to go to a grown-up event and sit quietly in the restaurant, we would let him go with us. Of course, he was an angel that night and all the guests couldn't get over his maturity and sweetness. I remember how it felt so right to listen to him and find a positive solution that kept all of our dignity intact. And I will always be grateful to my husband for trusting that our son's needs came above a dinner out with the boss!

—Barbara N.

Parents must avoid using shame, fear, threats, or intimidation to force the separation or to attempt to prevent children from crying about it. This can prolong and exacerbate a child's fears of separation. Be especially aware of the preverbal child's reaction and behavior both when the parent leaves and when parent and child are reunited. The child may cry, be extremely clingy, or may suddenly revert to a less mature behavior. Parents must take into account their child's personality and developmental stage in assessing whether the separation or child-care situation is causing anxiety or stress.

Some children seem to accept separations that are not their choice, only to later display negative behavior or sadness caused by the stress they have experienced. Therefore, it is important to be aware of the child's reactions and sensitive to his feelings. Parents may acknowledge a child's feelings by articulating what he must be feeling: "You feel sad because Mommy left, don't you?" Long separations can cause a baby to go through feelings of grief and loss and can affect his attachment to his parents. Therefore, it is critically important that parents who are separated from their children spend focused and intentional time reconnecting with their child after separation.

Children are ready for separation at different ages, and sensitive parents will know what their child's tolerance levels are, depending on who the caregiver is and the length of time they will be away. Being in attunement with your child will give you the knowledge and insight of what is best for keeping strong the security of attachment you have nurtured.

CHAPTER EIGHT

PRINCIPLE 7:
Practice Positive Discipline
Be the Change You Wish to See

When we use punishment, our children are robbed of the
opportunity to develop their own inner discipline—the ability to act with
integrity, wisdom, compassion, and mercy when there is no external
force holding them accountable for what they do.

—Barbara Coloroso,
Kids Are Worth It!

From the attachment-parenting perspective, positive
discipline embodies the "golden rule" of parenting; in other words, treat
children the way you would want to be treated if you were the child. Positive
discipline is an overarching concept based on the understanding that when
a child is treated respectfully within loving, age-appropriate boundaries, he
will develop a conscience guided by his own internal discipline and empathy
for others. Positive discipline is rooted in a secure, trusting, and loving relationship between parent and child. With a strong foundation of trust, positive discipline incorporates empathetic and respectful strategies that over
time will strengthen the connection between parent and child, while harsh
or overly punitive discipline weakens the connection.

A New Way of Seeing Children

The concept of positive discipline is very different from what is generally practiced in Western cultures and calls for nothing less than a paradigm shift in the way we view and treat children. Adults have a tendency to project their own perspectives or reasons to explain a child's behavior, often to justify spanking or other harsh punishment: "She's doing that just to make me mad!"; "If I don't stop my two-year-old from talking back to me now, just wait until she's a teenager!" These responses generally reflect the parents' lack of understanding of appropriate child development or a repetition of what they learned from their own early childhood experiences. Without a conscious effort to be open to new information and a willingness to change, we are destined to parent the way we were parented, which, in many cases, continues to perpetuate myths and misunderstandings about children.

Becoming a Conscious Parent

In their book *Giving the Love That Heals*, Harville Hendrix and Helen Hunt describe conscious parenting this way:

> The conscious parent meets the needs of the child by providing safety, support, and structure for the child as she moves through each developmental stage. He is attuned to the unique personality and temperament of his child and able to see what his child needs as she grows and changes. He is educated about the developmental stages of children and is able to stay alert and flexible in interactions with her.[1]

Every day new child development and neuroscience research provides deeper insights about children, how they think, and why their behavior changes during childhood. So much of their behavior corresponds to brain development. For instance, brain researchers have found that the part of the brain that controls impulsive behavior, the prefrontal cortex, is the last part of a child's brain to develop; this occurs during the fourth to fifth year of life. The prefrontal cortex, located in the forehead above the eyes, is considered to be the seat of the conscience, where the capacities of empathy and compassion are developed. Through the use of new brain-imaging techniques, researchers have found that the brain of a child who was abused and neglected is considerably smaller, with an underdeveloped prefrontal cortex, than the brain of a healthy child. When the prefrontal cortex is damaged, these children are less likely to be able to develop a conscience and will not be able to feel empathy for anyone. Scientists call this "adaptive behavior," which the child develops for his own survival. Brain research is providing amazing new information about babies and children that helps us understand them more fully, especially in the realm of prevention and how we can encourage healthy development. If you are interested in brain research, we strongly recommend books and materials written by Drs. Bruce Perry, Dan Siegel, and Allen Schore.

Your empathetic care will create the "hardwiring" in your baby's brain and allow for the healthy development of the baby's capacities for trust, empathy, and affection, which are the building blocks for your child's growing conscience. According to neuroscientist Bruce Perry, "The simple and unavoidable conclusion of these neurodevelopmental principles is that the organizing, sensitive brain of an infant or young child is more malleable to experience than a mature brain. While experience may alter the behavior of an adult, experience literally provides the organizing framework for an infant and child. Because the brain is most plastic (receptive to environmental input) in early childhood, the child is most vulnerable to variance of experience during this time."[2]

While principles of attachment parenting encourage parents to trust their own instincts, many lack confidence and feel the need to rely on science to validate and substantiate what they already know on an intuitive level, if only to quiet the doubts of family or friends.

What Is Positive Discipline, and Why Is It Important?

At the heart of positive discipline is a secure attachment relationship with your child. Gordon Neufeld and Gabor Maté write in their book *Hold On to Your Kids* that "for purposes of childrearing, the crowning achievement of a working attachment is to instill in a child the desire to be good." In other words, they say when a child feels secure in her connection (attachment) to her mother and father, she will want to be good, and she will be a child who is easy to parent.[3]

The word *discipline* is derived from the word *disciple*, meaning one who follows another's teachings. Children learn by example, so it's important that parents strive to model positive actions and relationships within a family and with others—strive to be the kind of adults you would like your children to be. If you consider that the act of disciplining is actually teaching through modeling behavior and keeping your connection strong, then the very first lessons of inner discipline begin with consistently responding with empathy to your baby's feelings and needs.

Your presence and responsiveness, as discussed in Chapter 7, are critical components for forming a trusting bond. As babies learn to communicate their needs more effectively, and as parents begin to develop their intuitive sense of interpreting their babies' signals, babies learn that their needs will be met, and soon a reciprocal relationship of attunement is formed. This strong bond, if maintained, will continue to fulfill the child's innate needs for trust, safety, and protection while fostering his capacities for trust, empathy, and affection.

Positive discipline involves creating a positive home environment that not only allows but also encourages children to learn and explore. Does that mean putting away breakable items for a while? Absolutely! The more relaxed, safe, and secure a child feels in her own environment, the more she will explore and learn. After all, child's play is learning. An environment that is more child-friendly helps minimize stress for you, too.

> [T]HE CROWNING ACHIEVEMENT OF A WORKING
> ATTACHMENT IS TO INSTILL IN A CHILD THE DESIRE TO BE GOOD. . . .
> WHAT WE DON'T SEE IS THAT IT'S THE CHILD'S ATTACHMENT
> TO THE ADULT THAT FOSTERS THAT GOODNESS.
>
> —Gordon Neufeld, PhD, and Gabor Maté, MD,
> *Hold On to Your Kids*

Positive discipline requires a shift in thinking and a new understanding about children. Seeing the world through the eyes of your child will enhance both you and your child's empathy skills. This is where it is critical that you learn as much as you can about child development through books and other resources. Once you learn what the cognitive and behavioral expectations are for different ages and phases, it is much easier to be patient and respond appropriately to redirect and guide the child's behavior. One of the primary factors that contributes to parents' overreacting or becoming abusive to their children is inappropriate developmental expectations.[5] When you see your child in this way, respect, understanding, and compassion, rather than yelling, threatening, and the use of physical punishment, will come naturally. In this process, you will begin to uncover his unmet needs (and sometimes your own). For example, when your toddler has an emotional meltdown, you can learn not to take his behavior personally and recognize that it could possibly be due to lack of sleep, hunger, feeling sick, or the need for one-to-one time. Positive discipline involves positive communication and, with older children, crafting solutions together while keeping everyone's dignity intact.

> There are six triggers for bad behavior: tiredness and hunger; an immature brain; unmet psychological needs; intense emotions; parental stress; and a parenting style that activates the alarm systems in a child's lower brain.[4]

The Goal of Positive Discipline

The goal of positive discipline is to help your child develop her own conscience and self-discipline. In doing so, we hope to raise cooperative, happy, joyful, and compassionate children who not only care about others but who also do what is right because it is the right thing to do, rather than because they are afraid of punishment.

What does positive discipline look like in day-to-day life? Some see it as proactive—using strategies to prevent unnecessary problems or challenges with children. Such preventive strategies include anticipating and preparing for foreseeable problems in order to eliminate stress, frustration, and tantrums. Strategies include substituting a toy or an object rather than forcing a toddler to share when she doesn't yet understand the concept of sharing or using redirection to gently guide toddlers and young children away from harm by getting them interested in something else.

Parents are instrumental in helping their children explore safely by seeing the world through their children's eyes, modeling respect and empathy, and, when appropriate, allowing children to experience the natural consequences of their actions. For example, when your baby is crawling around and decides to touch something you don't want him to touch, recognize that he is fulfilling his need to explore and learn. Quickly move the object or get his attention, then redirect him toward something else. As he gets older, you can use words to explain what you want him to do rather than getting in the habit of saying, "No" or "Because I said so!" Few of us would like anyone to talk to us that way. We want to model respect to our children so they in turn will learn respect for us. Parents who practice positive discipline have a general understanding of developmentally appropriate behavior and tailor loving guidance to the capabilities, needs, and temperaments of their children.

Learning to practice positive discipline takes time and a lot of trial and error, so don't be discouraged when you make mistakes. Most people weren't raised with positive discipline; it can be very hard to change old ways of thinking. We live in a culture where this type of parenting goes against the cultural norm, so it's very important that parents surround themselves with other parents who share the same values, if at all possible. If that isn't possible, the two parents can support each other and use books, websites, and parenting chat lists for resources.

Most parents wish they could handle every situation perfectly, but no parents are perfect; we were trained on the job like everyone else. At times, tempers will flare and patience will be lost. When parents react in a way that creates tension, anger, or hurt feelings, they can help repair any damage to the parent-child relationship by taking time to reconnect, talk about what happened, and apologize after everyone has calmed down. Think about how it happened and what you can do the next time a similar situation occurs. Having a mental plan will help redirect your anger and frustration. Try using these three reflective questions to guide you in how you determine your course of action:

1. Am I treating my child the way I would want to be treated?
2. Will my words or actions strengthen my connection with my child?
3. Will my actions give my child an opportunity to learn from this experience?

> ADULTS TEACH CHILDREN IN THREE IMPORTANT WAYS:
> THE FIRST IS BY EXAMPLE, THE SECOND IS BY EXAMPLE,
> THE THIRD IS BY EXAMPLE.
>
> —Albert Schweitzer,
> physician, philanthropist, and
> Nobel Peace Prize recipient

Establishing Boundaries

The big question in every parent's mind is, "What about boundaries?" Every healthy family has clear guidelines for acceptable and unacceptable behavior. For instance, some families make it clear that "in our house, we do not hit." As we mentioned earlier, children have an intrinsic need for predictability, which, as the child grows, takes the form of structure, routine, and learning the boundaries of others. Part of that structure involves understanding your personal limitations and values and the limitations within the household that incorporate the needs, feelings, and values of other family members.

Your developing connection and knowledge of child development will guide you in establishing boundaries. There is nothing wrong with explaining to your child why she can't do a certain activity or why she has to do something she really doesn't want to do. Some will say that children should be obedient regardless and that adults shouldn't have to explain anything to children. However, research has found that children who were more empathetic and able to avoid conflict had parents, particularly mothers, who were more empathetic themselves, were not critical of the child, and took the time to explain the consequences of their child's actions and offered suggestions for how to effectively deal with the situation or person.[6] Again, it goes back to simply treating your children the way you would want to be treated.

Also, know when to "pick your battles." Too often, we adults become rigid in our thinking and can become unreasonable in our expectations. The key to parenting (and life) is being flexible (within reason). Make sure your expectations and boundaries are developmentally appropriate by referencing trusted resources such as books or websites.

The Dangers of Traditional Discipline

Using shame, humiliation, guilt, manipulation, coercion, or physical forms of discipline can interfere with the connection between parent and child. Instilling fear in children serves no purpose and creates feelings of shame and humiliation. Dr. Neufeld strongly warns against using these tactics for getting children to behave: "We must never intentionally make a child feel bad, guilty, or ashamed in order to get him to be good. Abusing the attachment conscience evokes deep insecurities in the child and may reduce him to shut it down for fear of being hurt. The consequences are not worth any short-term gains in behavioral goals."[7]

Physical forms of discipline have been shown to lead to an increased risk of future antisocial behavior, including crime and substance abuse.[8, 9] Children raised with the fear of being hurt learn to behave positively because they are in sight of their parents or another authority figure. They may fear punishment, or they may fear a loss of parental love and affection. Although physical discipline and fear may change behavior in the short run, it will not have the desired effects in the long run.

> Children raised in homes dominated by punitive parenting styles are more likely to exhibit aggressive behavior.[10] Coercive, harsh, inconsistent discipline and poor parent involvement and monitoring are predictors of children's antisocial behavior.[11]

In 2002, research scientist Elizabeth Thompson Gershoff, PhD, working at Columbia University's National Center for Children in Poverty, conducted a meta-analysis on the use of corporal punishment that covered more than three hundred studies and spanned sixty-two years. She found that ten of the eleven studies in the meta-analysis indicate parental corporal punishment is associated with the following undesirable behaviors and experiences:

- decreased moral internalization
- increased child aggression
- increased child delinquent and antisocial behavior
- decreased quality of relationship between parent and child
- decreased child mental health
- increased risk of being a victim of physical abuse
- increased adult aggression
- increased adult criminal and antisocial behavior
- decreased adult mental health
- increased risk of abusing own child or spouse

Corporal punishment was associated with only one desirable behavior; namely, increased immediate compliance. Gershoff summarizes: "For one, corporal punishment on its own does not teach children right from wrong. Secondly, although it makes children afraid to disobey when parents are present, when parents are not present to administer the punishment, those same children will misbehave."[12]

Likewise, spanking a child or using other physical discipline techniques may temporarily stop a behavior, but it does not teach the child appropriate self-discipline. Instead, studies show that it can create ongoing behavioral and emotional problems.[13] Harsh, physical discipline teaches children that violence is the only way to solve problems. Controlling or manipulative discipline compromises the trust between parent and child and harms the attachment bond.

In *Beating the Devil Out of Them*, researcher Dr. Murray Straus writes of our culture's "conspiracy of silence" on the subject of corporal punishment:

> The universal and chronic use of corporal punishment and its potentially harmful effects on children is the best-kept secret of American child psychology. It is almost as though there is a conspiracy of silence among those who do research on children or write about childrearing. The discrepancy is so glaring that it is worth considering some of the reasons for the silence."[14]

What About "Spare the Rod and Spoil the Child"?

While we strongly believe that attachment parenting practices are fully compatible with the beliefs of all major religions, we realize that the beliefs of some readers may conflict. We want to briefly touch on a couple of points that have helped families feel comfortable practicing positive discipline. Dr. William Sears and Martha Sears cowrote *The Complete Book of Christian Parenting and Child Care*, which goes into much more depth about the applications of Christian teachings to attachment parenting. Here is some information from their website, AskDrSears.com:

Why Spanking Doesn't Work

- It increases the risk for abuse by parents.[15]
- It increases impulsive behavior in children.[16]
- It increases aggression and antisocial behavior.[17]
- It is a risk factor for depression, suicide, and violent behavior later in life.[18]
- It models aggressive behavior as a solution to conflict, and increases risk of substance abuse.[19]
- It increases the risk of disease (such as cancer and heart disease) because of the relationship of stress to pathogenic effects.[20]

Some believe that it is the duty of a God-fearing parent to spank, citing specific "rod verses" to support this belief. "Spare the rod and spoil the child" is a misquote of "he who spares the rod hates his son, but he who loves him is careful to discipline him" (Prov. 13:24).

At first glance, these rod verses may sound pro-spanking. But we ask you to consider a different interpretation of these teachings. "Rod" (*shevet*) can mean several different things. The Hebrew dictionary gives this word various [shades of] meanings: a stick (for punishment, writing, fighting, ruling, walking, etc.). While the rod could be used for hitting, it was more frequently used for guiding wandering sheep. Shepherds didn't use the rod to beat their sheep—and children are certainly more valuable than sheep. As shepherd-author Philip Keller teaches so well in *A Shepherd Looks at Psalm 23*, the shepherd's rod was used to fight off prey, and the staff was used to gently guide sheep along the right path ("Your rod and your staff, they comfort me" Psalm 23:4).

The book of Proverbs is one of poetry. It is logical that the writer would have used a well-known tool to form an image of authority. We believe that this is the point that God makes about the rod in the Bible—parents take charge of your children.

When you reread the "rod verses," use the concept of parental authority when you come to the word "rod," rather than the concept of beating or spanking. It rings true in every instance.[21]

In *Spare the Child: The Religious Roots of Punishment and the Psychological Impact of Physical Abuse*, author Philip Greven found the term "spare the rod, spoil the child" cannot be attributed to the Bible. The origin of the phrase came from a poem by Samuel Butler written in 1664 entitled "Hudibras."[22]

A Look at Discipline Through the World's Religions

When we have talked to parents from many different religious backgrounds, it has been affirming to learn that we have more in common than not, especially when it comes to the core teachings of their religions. All the major world religions have what has been called "the Golden Rule" for guiding humanity in how to treat our fellow human beings. It is also the guiding principle of attachment parenting philosophy as it applies to children. Here are some quotations from several of the major religious texts:

- Christianity: "And as ye would that men should do to you, do ye also to them likewise" (Luke 6:31, King James Version).
- Islam: "None of you [truly] believes until he wishes for his brother what he wishes for himself" (Number 13 of Imam Al-Nawawi's Forty Hadith).
- Hinduism: "This is the sum of Dharma [duty]: Do naught unto others which would cause you pain if done to you" (Mahabharata 5:1517).
- Judaism: "Thou shalt love thy neighbor as thyself" (Leviticus 19:18).
- Buddhism: "Hurt not others in ways that you yourself would find hurtful" (Udana-Varga 5:18).
- Baha'i: "Blessed is he who preferreth his brother before himself" (Tablets of Baháæ 'u' lláh).
- Confucianism: "Do not do to others what you do not want them to do to you" (Analects 15:23).

Every one of these statements is an excellent expression of the word *empathy*. If one word could encapsulate the parenting philosophy described in this book, *empathy* would be that word. All over the world, people have been taught to love and treat their neighbors as they love themselves, yet we struggle with this teaching when it comes to our children. If we truly put ourselves in their place, if we imagine what our needs were as an infant or as a teenager, we have the most profound parenting strategy ever given. However, we must remember an important part of this philosophy: we must first learn to love and understand ourselves to be able to love our children. Reflecting on our own childhood histories, taking care of our own emotional, physical, and spiritual needs, and filling our own "love tank" gives us the ability to care for others. Just like the analogy of the flight attendant's instructions to "put your oxygen mask on first" and then tend to your little ones, it is critical that we take time every day to love and nurture ourselves.

> Responsive, nonpunitive, and nonauthoritarian parenting results in children with higher levels of empathy and prosocial behavior.[23]

Rewards and Punishments

Rewards and punishments are other ways that we as parents manipulate and coerce our children. This is a topic that will probably stimulate much discussion and doubt, but remember that the main focus of positive discipline is connection and cooperation. You may be thinking that taking away rewards and punishments leaves you no tools for effectively disciplining your children, but many alternatives exist. We have listed our top twenty-five tips for positive discipline in this chapter, as well as some of our favorite resources in Appendix C. Our intent is to change the consciousness of child-rearing attitudes; this means looking at the root causes of the behavior and working on the attachment relationship rather than reacting to the behavior itself. We realize that change is gradual, and even in our own families we have had to adjust our thinking and strategies over the years. Many wonderful resources available today offer parents a variety of ways to begin this change and communicate more effectively.

Alfie Kohn, father, educator, and author, sheds new light on the use of rewards in his book, *Unconditional Parenting: Moving from Rewards and Punishments to Love and Reason*:

> The first thing to understand is that rewards are remarkably ineffective at improving the quality of people's work or learning. A considerable number of studies have found that children and adults alike are less successful at many tasks when they're offered a reward for doing them—or doing them well. In fact, the first scientists to discover this result were caught off-guard. They expected that some sort of incentive for high achievement would motivate people to do better, but they kept finding that the opposite was true.[24]

Gordon Neufeld and Gabor Maté agree that the use of rewards and punishments can "destroy the precious internal motivation to be good," and then it becomes necessary to use them in order to control a child's behavior.[25] They strongly advise parents to carefully nurture a child's desire to be good and protect their connection, warning parents, "It is a violation of the relationship not to believe in the child's desire when it actually exists, for example, to accuse the child of harboring ill intentions when we disapprove of behavior. Such accusations can easily trigger defenses in the child, harm the relationship, and make her feel like being bad." For instance, a one-year-old child is not developmentally capable of understanding the concept of sharing. When young children are together playing with toys and another child decides he wants the very toy that the other child is playing with, it often leads to frustration, hitting, and tears. Rather than understanding the child's intent of fulfilling his natural drive for curiosity, exploration, and play, parents sometimes assume their child's intent is selfishness because they don't understand his emotional and cognitive abilities. Rather than punishing the child, it's so much easier and healthier to quickly intervene, using a soft, kind voice, offering another attractive toy. If that doesn't work, then the parent of the child with the toy can try to interest her in another toy and make an exchange. These strategies work much of the time, but, barring those, changing the child's environment altogether will provide a major distraction while using empathy and a caring voice to redirect his attention.

As your children grow older, many teachable moments can be used to help guide behavior that promotes the development of your child's conscience in healthy ways. When a child feels remorse for something she has done, this is a good sign and provides the opportunity to talk to your child about the feelings of others (empathy) and to discuss ways to make amends for the behavior, if it seems appropriate. Feelings of remorse are indications of a healthy developing conscience, and, as most of us have experienced, we are usually quite harsh with ourselves when we feel this way. However, when parents disregard a child's remorse and use harsh punishments (spanking, grounding, removal of favorite toys, etc.), then the child's remorse turns to anger toward the parent, and the child becomes motivated to misbehave. Over time, children learn not to care anymore—they can become detached from the pain of spankings, detached from their possessions and caring about others. Their behavior becomes driven by external rather than internal factors; they behave out of fear of punishment rather than a moral sense of what is right and wrong. Rewarding a child's behavior is just as detrimental as punishing; it may temporarily stop the behavior, but in the long run it denies children opportunities to develop desirable intrinsically motivated qualities and behavior.

Parenting promises intense and challenging moments, despite our best intentions to develop and maintain a strongly connected relationship. Parents who want to practice positive discipline may sometimes have difficulty communicating with, understanding, or feeling empathy toward their child. In the "perfect storm" of fatigue, stress, and frustration, some parents will react harshly or feel like hitting their child. This is not uncommon, and it is important that parents realize that anyone can snap under the "right" circumstances. It is a sign of strength and personal growth for a parent to examine his or her own childhood experiences, to explore how these may negatively influence parenting, and to seek professional help if needed. When your connection with your child breaks, always take the time to repair it, whether that means apologizing or making amends to your child. By doing so, you are modeling the very behavior you want to instill in your child.

The Words We Say

There once was a little boy who had a bad temper. His father gave him a bag of nails and told him that every time he lost his temper, he must hammer a nail into the back of the fence.

The first day the boy had driven thirty-seven nails into the fence. Over the next few weeks, as he learned to control his anger, the number of nails hammered daily gradually dwindled. Eventually he discovered it was easier to hold his temper than to drive those nails into the fence.

Finally, the day came when the boy didn't lose his temper at all. He told his father about it and the father suggested that the boy now pull out one nail for each day that he was able to hold his temper. The days passed and the young boy was finally able to tell his father that all the nails were gone.

The father took his son by the hand and led him to the fence. He said, "You have done well, my son, but look at the holes in the fence. The fence will never be the same. When you say things in anger, they leave a scar just like this one. You can put a knife in a man and draw it out. It won't matter how many times you say 'I'm sorry,' the wound is still there."

The little boy then understood how powerful his words were. He looked up at his father and said, "I hope you can forgive me, Father, for the holes I put in you."

"Of course I can," said the father.

—AUTHOR UNKNOWN

Compassionate Communication

Who of us hasn't hurt others with our words out of ignorance, anger, or frustration? Who of us hasn't been hurt by harsh words or felt like we weren't being heard by others? In all human relationships, the ability to communicate effectively and compassionately is one of the most important skills we can learn. The words we use, the way in which we speak to others (especially our children), and our ability to listen have profound, lasting effects. We live in a world where we commonly use our words as weapons to manipulate others, to get our needs met, or to express our emotions, and we learn them from the day we are born. Along with compassionate communication, empathetic listening is a skill that must be taught. We live in such a fast-paced culture that it's "normal" to be only partially tuned-in to what the other person is saying. Often our minds are zoning out on other matters or racing ahead, thinking about what we want to say next. We have never learned how to be conscious in our conversations with others, and this has led to misunderstandings, misperceptions, hurt feelings, anger, frustration, the breakup of relationships, and war. Just like parenting, we learn to communicate from our parents and other adults. It takes a conscious effort to let go of old habits and learn new ways, but it is definitely possible and, in a real sense, necessary to help develop strong emotional connections and strengthen relationships, whether with your child or your spouse. Teaching your children how to communicate compassionately becomes an opportunity for you to learn new ways of communicating with other adults.

Marshall Rosenberg, the developer of a program called Nonviolent Communication (NVC), believes that we humans are not very good at identifying or expressing our needs to others, nor are we very good at listening empathetically to the needs of others. The NVC program is so effective that Dr. Rosenberg has been asked to use it in foreign political peace negotiations and warring tribes, with great success. A primary goal of NVC is to "create human connections that empower compassionate giving and receiving." NVC fits hand in glove with the principles of attachment parenting because of its focus on respecting the needs of adults and children while developing empathy and creating emotional connections. As stated on the NVC website, "This approach to communication emphasizes compassion as the motivation for action rather than fear, guilt, shame, blame, coercion, threat, or justification for punishment. In other words, it is about getting what you want for reasons you will not regret later. NVC is not about getting people to do what we want. It is about creating a quality of connection that gets everyone's needs met through compassionate giving." [26]

Learning to Express Our Needs

The NVC program offers many resources through its website, www.cnvc
.org, including on-site training, CDs, and DVDs. The four basic steps in following NVC are stating (1) observations, (2) feelings, (3) needs, and (4)
requests.

Step 1—**Observations:** Descriptions of what is seen or heard without
added interpretations. For example, instead of saying, "She's having a
temper tantrum," say "She is lying on the floor crying and kicking."

Step 2—**Feelings:** Our emotions rather than our story or thoughts about
what others are doing. For example, instead of saying, "I feel like
you're irresponsible," which includes an interpretation of another's
behavior, say "I feel worried."

Step 3—**Needs:** Feelings are caused by needs, which are universal and
ongoing and not dependent on the actions of particular individuals.
State your need rather than the other person's actions as the cause.
For example, say "I feel annoyed because I need support" rather than
"I feel annoyed because you didn't do the dishes."

Step 4—**Requests:** Doable, immediate, and stated in positive action
language (what you want instead of what you don't want). For
example, "Would you be willing to come back tonight at the time
we've agreed?" rather than "Would you make sure not to be late
again?" By definition, when we make requests, we are open to hearing
"No" and taking it as an opportunity for further dialogue.[27]

Positive Discipline Leads To . . .

- increased moral judgment[28]
- increased empathetic behavior[29]
- more competence[30]
- more positive behavior[31]
- better grades[32]

- positive attitude[33]
- lower risk of smoking[34]
- lower risk of drug use[35]
- cooperation and respect[36]

Our Top Twenty-Five Tips
for Practicing Positive Discipline

The following tips are a compilation of ideas from a variety of sources, many of which fall closely in line with the NVC model of communication. No one-size-fits-all approach can cover discipline; positive discipline takes into consideration the child's age, personality, and temperament. We strongly encourage you to continue to educate yourself about alternatives to harsh discipline and seek support from like-minded friends or an API support group. This area of child rearing can be the most difficult as a result of one's own lack of experience and the lack of support from our culture. Additional resources can be found in Appendix C.

Tip No. 1: Maintain a positive relationship. Refrain from projecting your own perceptions of your child's intentions. Neufeld and Maté warn, "It is a violation of the relationship not to believe in the child's desire [to be good] when it actually exists," and accusing a child of bad intentions when they didn't exist can harm your relationship and actually create within the child the desire to be bad.[37] Resolve to maintain a positive relationship with the child, even in the most difficult situations. Stay focused on identifying needs and exploring solutions. Through all stages of development, children are observing their parents and internalizing parental behaviors as appropriate. It is important for parents to model the kind of adult they would like their child to become.

Tip No. 2: Use empathy and respect. Be empathetic and respectful by acknowledging a child's feelings; keeping his needs, abilities, and developmental level in mind; and using a win-win attitude that seeks to meet as many needs as possible.

Tip No. 3: Research positive discipline. Read books or watch DVDs that focus on positive communication and discipline, and talk to like-minded parents with children of similar ages. These resources offer reassurance and helpful parenting suggestions.

Tip No. 4: Seek to understand the unmet need. What is your child trying to communicate? Children often communicate their feelings through their behavior. By looking at the world through their eyes, parents model the first lesson of empathy. Helping the child think about and understand what others are feeling also fosters this empathy. Recognize and meet the child's need for nutrition, rest, and comfort. When children are cranky and not behaving their best, it's often because they are hungry, tired, or feeling a lack of connection, and they need their "emotional tank" to be refilled.

Tip No. 5: Work out a solution together. Propose a solution, or ask an older child to propose one. Be open to creative solutions that meet both the parent's and the child's needs. This negotiation of simple conflicts teaches the child valuable conflict-resolution skills.

Tip No. 6: Be proactive. Try to monitor the child and watch for the early signs of a problem or unmet need. Get involved quickly before major issues arise. It takes only a second for a situation to get out of control. It's much easier to avoid a situation than it is to deal with it after the fact.

Tip No. 7: Understand your child's developmental abilities. Preverbal children often cannot understand concepts such as sharing, and developmentally they have little or no impulse control. Therefore, creating lots of rules and restrictions is likely to be an exercise in frustration for both parent and child. Use redirection to guide babies or toddlers away from dangerous areas or to divert their attention to something else. Understand basic child development and develop appropriate expectations based on the child's age and abilities.

Tip No. 8: Create a "Yes" environment. Before saying "No," stop to think, "Why not?" If the activity is inconvenient rather than dangerous, consider allowing it. If a toddler can attempt to navigate a desired path or activity with parental assistance, provide it. If you can't jointly complete the activity safely, try substituting something similar. Rather than saying no, try telling the child what he can do instead.

Tip No. 9: Teach discipline through play. Turn power struggles into playful games. Use imaginative play to work through conflicts. If a child cannot have what she wants, help her to create an imaginary scene where she can. Find the fun in everyday tasks and transitions.

Tip No. 10: Change the environment by breastfeeding, cuddling, singing, dancing, or being silly. A change of pace can be very helpful in relieving the stress of a situation, giving parents and children a mental break and allowing them to reconnect in a fun way without parents feeling the need to resort to more punitive discipline.

Tip No. 11: State a fact rather than making a demand. For example, saying, "You are close to the edge of the stairs" or "That vase is glass and will break very easily" allows the child to internalize the danger and decide for himself what action is needed to mitigate it. For younger toddlers, or in areas where the child has no experience, tell the child exactly what is expected of him. For example, "Let Mommy help you set it on the table very slowly and softly, like this, so that it won't break."

Tip No. 12: Avoid labeling children and focus instead on the behavior and the need that it is not meeting. For example, instead of calling a child "aggressive" or "clumsy," describe and demonstrate the preferred behavior for the child to understand. "This is how we pet the kitty so he feels safe," or "Hold the cup with both hands, like this, and it won't spill."

Tip No. 13: Use affirmative language. Make requests in the affirmative: "You're standing in the chair. I need to feel you are safe. Sit on the chair, please," rather than the negative "Don't stand on the chair!" Provide a need-based reason whenever possible. Tell your child what you want her to do rather than what you don't want her to do.

Tip No. 14: Allow your child to experience some natural consequences. Natural consequences can be excellent teachers. Parents should intervene if a natural consequence would be harmful or too scary or if the child is cognitively unable to connect the action and the consequence. Parents should also be prepared to assist when a natural consequence occurs, especially when that consequence is not one the child expected. For example, if a child goes out without a coat, bring one along for when he realizes that he is cold.

Empathize with the child about his feelings (that he's cold) rather than say-ing, "I told you so!"

Tip No. 15: Be sensitive to strong emotions. Be sensitive to crying and tan-trums, which can be a child's way of communicating or releasing strong emo-tions. Keeping the child safe (which may require relocating the child) while being calm and empathetic to the child's immediate needs communicates unconditional understanding, love, and acceptance. It may not be helpful to try to stop the crying or tantrum if the child is working through strong feel-ings. A parent's empathetic presence may be all that is needed. It may help the child if an adult can help her put her feelings into words or fantasize with her about what she wished had happened.

Tip No. 16: Redefine "time-out." Time-out is a term used to describe a variety of discipline techniques. One popular version involves putting a child on a chair or in a room, separated from his parent, for a given amount of time. We would like to take back this term, remembering its original inten-tion: stopping the activity, taking a break, and coming back with renewed perspective. Keeping this in mind helps parents work on their relationship with their child, rather than focus on the child's behavior, and make efforts that strengthen the parent-child connection. Positive discipline replaces the punitive use of time-out with another version of the technique. Some parents prefer to use the term "time-in" and some choose not to use these terms at all. Time-out or time-in then becomes an opportunity to reconnect and work through the underlying problem that your child is having. To help an older toddler or child regain composure and perspective, explain to the child that both of you need to take some time away from the activity. If he is ready and willing, you can sit with your child and discuss his emotions and needs in a calm, compassionate way. In some cases, snuggle time without talking may be all that a child needs. When both you and your child are calm and ready, he can return to the activity.

Consider implementing a "meeting on the couch" policy, where any mem-ber of the family (including the child) can call a "time-out" when tensions begin to arise or when he or she feels the need for a period of reconnection.

Tip No. 17: Parents' "time-out" is also an effective way for parents to regain composure and perspective. Parents can explain to the child that they are going to sit quietly for a bit and think. They can use this time to examine their expectations both of themselves and their child. If a child resists the parent taking a time-out or the child is too young to be out of the sight of the parent, the parent can sit calmly in the same room, close his or her eyes, take a few deep breaths, and have an internal "time-out." If parents feel at risk for harming a child, they must take the steps necessary to ensure the child is in a safe location and separate themselves rather than reaching the breaking point—don't hesitate to call a friend or neighbor for help. For more information on how to deal with anger toward a child, see www.stophitting.com.

Tip No. 18: Talk to your child. If a child is having a conflict with a peer, talk to the child before directly intervening, whenever possible. In circumstances where someone could get hurt, swift action may be required to ensure everyone's safety, but many times asking the child how she's feeling and why she did a particular thing yields better results than immediately intervening. Keep in mind the age of your child; with very young children, keep language short and simple.

Tip No. 19: Apologies should come from the heart. Many parents remember being forced to apologize to another as a child, whether it was a sincere apology or not. It probably made the parents feel better, but it did nothing to make the hurt child feel better, nor did it teach the children anything about resolving conflicts in a positive way. Apologies should come from a child's heart and be a genuine expression of his feelings.

Allow the child to apologize in his own way, understanding that if he does not verbally apologize, he has witnessed appropriate role modeling and will begin to apologize to others when he is developmentally ready and feels genuine remorse. Children raised with empathy are much more likely to feel compassion and spontaneously apologize.

Tip No. 20: Comfort the hurt child first. Although it is difficult for a parent to see their child hurt by another, it is important for parents to go immediately to their own child when she is hurt and comfort her, letting the parents of the aggressor deal with the other child in their own way. However, note that it may be necessary to separate the hurt child from the aggressor if the aggressive child's parents are unavailable or not immediately responding to the situation. After comforting the hurt child, attention can turn to the aggressive child if this child is also in your care. Talk to the child about what happened and how it made the other child feel, and explore with him other ways of solving the conflict or expressing his feelings.

Tip No. 21: Offer choices. When offering choices, avoid masking a threat as one of the choices. If the child does not wish to comply with your request, use reflective wording. "I know that you want to stay here and play, because you're having so much fun! But we must go now because we need to pick up your brother from soccer practice." Then offer two choices that would be appealing, such as "Would you like to race me to the car, or would you prefer to ride the tricycle there?"

Tip No. 22: Develop cooperation. Cooperation comes from working together. It is possible as your children grow to enlist their help in working out solutions to any problem. For example, if a four-year-old child is coloring on the wall, using the steps of NVC, the parent might say, "I see you are coloring on the wall. I feel frustrated because I need your help in keeping the wall clean. Would you help Mommy by coloring on the paper?" If the child insists on coloring on the wall, it's a good time to take time out together to explore potential solutions. Restate the problem, find out why the child has a need to color on the wall, express your needs, discuss how to solve this together, and be open to creativity from the child. When children contribute to the solution, they are more likely to follow it. Needless to say, it won't necessarily work if parent and child are upset with each other. Wait until you both are calm and feeling connected.

What about "logical consequences"? This is a term that has been used for decades that refers to the parents imposing a consequence for a behavior of the child. For example, taking privileges away if a child breaks a rule or acts inappropriately is what most people regard as a logical consequence. We want to redefine and clarify a more positive use of the term that eliminates blaming, criticism, shame, and punishment. Instead, consider using the opportunity to craft solutions together: "What can we do to solve this problem together?" The point is to create logical consequences that are not disguised as punishments. For instance, you might agree that the crayons need to stay in the kitchen and ask for permission from Mom or Dad to use them next time.

When your are in doubt about a consequence, Barbara Coloroso offers a simple technique to help you determine if the logical consequences are appropriate:

R: Is it reasonable?
S: Is it simple?
V: Is it valuable as a learning tool?
P: Is it purposeful?

She says, "If it isn't all four of these, it probably won't be effective, and it could be punishment disguised as a reasonable consequence."[38]

Tip No. 23: Use praise conservatively. In the last thirty years, many well-intentioned parents may have gone a bit overboard with praise and rewards to make sure their child developed healthy self-esteem. Thanking your child for helping out or doing something nice is more meaningful than just saying, "Good job." The overuse of praise, rewards, and value judgments may be experienced by a child as disingenuous or manipulative. Of course, everyone loves to be praised and acknowledged occasionally, but overdoing it can place an inappropriate value on a child's activities, interfering with the child's intrinsic motivation, decision-making skills, and his ability to self-evaluate; inadvertently encouraging the child to constantly seek approval; or stifling his motivation. As with other types of discipline, parents are in the best position to evaluate how to use praise and rewards and their effects on the child. Sharing feelings and describing what the child has accomplished with genuine enthusiasm—separate from the desire to change or shape a child's behavior—can build an authentic, straightforward relationship. For example, say, "Your toys are all in the toy bin!" in an excited voice. Consider celebrating the effort rather than the result, such as "You worked very hard on that puzzle," so that children know their efforts are worthwhile even if they don't always succeed.

Tip No. 24: Use incentives creatively. As children grow, they may recognize habits in themselves that they would like to change. Incentives are most effective when the child genuinely desires to change a behavior such as thumb sucking and has input into developing the incentive. The incentive should be something small and fun but not something that would be seen as a punishment if it were not received. This is an opportunity for the child to talk with the parent as to whether this is a strategy that she would like to try and to reevaluate if it doesn't seem to be working. In other words, this technique is not something the parent would arbitrarily use without the child's input and consent. If at any point the child chooses not to, for example, stop sucking her thumb, a parent should accept this decision without shame or humiliation.

If, over time, the child consistently chooses not to change the behavior, then the parent should explore whether the child has an underlying unmet need and discuss the situation with the child.

Tip No. 25: Consider carefully before forcing your will on your child. Remember, your goal is not to break a young child's will but to help instill the desire to be "good" and develop his own will to make good decisions. This will mean that he can feel good about having some control in his life that can lead to better cooperation. First, make reasonable attempts to find an agreeable solution that will satisfy both your needs, such as your need to leave and his need to play. You might try to use playfulness, such as turning a task into a game, by offering a couple of choices—not too many—or with a toddler, redirect the child to another activity. If nothing works, lovingly intervene in a way that acknowledges and demonstrates respect for your child's feelings and desires.

Taking the First Steps

Learning to use positive discipline may not come easily for many parents, especially if they were raised in a more traditional, authoritarian environment. The intent of this chapter is to open hearts and minds to a new way of thinking about training children: to seek out and try positive alternatives. Some will embrace this information without question, while others will need time and small steps of change. Some will have skepticism and doubt because they have never known a person who wasn't raised without being spanked, and it can be very unnerving to think that it is even possible. Many of us were spanked as children and feel that we turned out okay; we may have turned out okay in spite of the spankings or because of the unconditional love of others. That's why it's so important to attend API support group meetings to talk with other parents. Many resources are available in books and on the Internet, such as parent forums on the API website, to provide the support you may need.

We need to be patient with ourselves as we learn new ways of thinking and behaving with children—it isn't easy! Alfie Kohn reminds us in a lighthearted way of the challenges we face as parents:

> The bottom line is that raising kids is not for wimps. My wife says it's a test of your capacity to deal with disorder and unpredictability—a test you can't study for, and one whose results aren't always reassuring. Forget "rocket science" or "brain surgery": When we want to make the point that something isn't really all that difficult, we ought to say, "Hey, it's not parenting."[39]

The process of discipline does four things that the act of punishment cannot do. The steps are:

1. Show children what they have done wrong.
2. Give them ownership of the problem.
3. Give them options for solving the problem.
4. Leave their dignity intact.[40]

Never Violence

In 1978, Astrid Lindgren author of Pippi Longstocking received the German Book Trade Peace Prize for her literary contributions. In her acceptance speech, she told the following story:

> When I was about twenty years old, I met an old pastor's wife who told me that when she was young and had her first child, she didn't believe in striking children, although spanking kids with a switch pulled from a

tree was standard punishment at the time. But one day when her son was four or five, he did something that she felt warranted a spanking—the first in his life. And she told him that he would have to go outside and find a switch for her to hit him with. The boy was gone a long time. And when he came back in, he was crying. He said to her, "Mama, I couldn't find a switch, but here's a rock that you can throw at me." All of a sudden, the mother understood how the situation felt from the child's point of view: that if my mother wants to hurt me, then it makes no difference what she does it with; she might as well do it with a stone. The mother took the boy onto her lap and they both cried. Then she laid the rock on a shelf in the kitchen to remind herself forever: never violence. Because violence begins in the nursery—one can raise children into violence.[41]

A Mother's Story: Meeting on the Couch

In our family, we use a tool called "meeting on the couch." We started this when Sophia was about two, and we were finding that our attempts to negotiate solutions to disagreements were ending in a lot of frustration. We needed a way to stop the action and talk about it.

The couch had always been a place of connection and snuggles for us, so this is the spot we picked for our meetings. An important component of our agreement is that anyone in the family can call a meeting on the couch, and then everyone must stop whatever they are doing and go to the couch. Sophia calls them at least as much as we do, and, while sometimes it's frustrating to stop and go to the couch, we always do.

First, we just snuggle. Especially if emotions are running high, we don't talk right away. Sometimes I tell Sophia that I need a few minutes to calm down, and sometimes she says she does. We take deep breaths, look at each other, and practice nurturing touch. If I'm really, really having a hard time calming down, sometimes we'll turn on the TV just for a few minutes to distract us from the emotion. We try to let Sophia talk first. When she's ready, she'll tell us why she's upset. We empathize and help her put words to her emotions. We ask questions so that we really understand why it is she feels she needs to do something. Then we try to communicate our feelings and our reasons for reacting the way we do. We set boundaries where they need to be set, in the context of which need of ours needs to be met. Then there is some negotiation—a component that has gotten more advanced as she's gotten older.

When she was a toddler, it was mostly about us offering suggestions and alternatives. Now, as she approaches age five, she often amazes us with her insight and creative suggestions. It isn't about "winning" or getting her to do anything specific. For example, if she can suggest a way to do what she wants to do while meeting the need that was causing us to say no, then we're open to that. Sometimes the negotiation takes two minutes, sometimes it takes twenty. Once we come to an agreement, we "shake on it" and give hugs. Then we go back to what we were doing. If the same issue comes up again, we can often just say, "Remember our agreement!" (Or sometimes she says it to us!) If anyone in the family is having a hard time keeping the agreement, then we call another meeting on the couch and try again to come up with a solution to which everyone can agree. Sometimes it's the same solution, just reaffirmed.

When we come to an agreement, it isn't a rule imposed by us on her; it is something we've discussed and agreed to together. It's a relationship. It's touching when Sophia calls "meeting on the couch" with her dolls or tries to call them with the cat (which doesn't always go over so well!). We believe we are teaching her to approach conflict by seeking [to solve it through] connection and understanding, rather than coercion or bullying, and we think that's a wonderful thing she will carry with her throughout her life.

—Pam S.

CHAPTER NINE

PRINCIPLE 8:
Strive for Balance in Your Personal and Family Life

Peace Within Creates Peace at Home

This style of parenting is for a short season in a marriage—
or in your own personal life—and when you devote yourselves fully to
that season and find the fulfillment that it brings, the season passes
soon enough. You are left with no regrets over how you met the
needs of your little ones and no regrets about distance between you
and your partner because you didn't allow that distance to happen to
the point that you couldn't reconnect. . . . Remember that what your
kids need most are parents in a stable relationship, or, in the case
of a single-parent home, a mother or father who is emotionally healthy.
You can't give out what you don't have inside yourself, even though
sometimes it feels like we have to dig awfully deep to find it.
Getting a rich spiritual life, one where we are connected to God,
is probably the most important thing we do as parents.

—Martha Sears, RN and mother of eight,
in "Mothering Maven Martha Sears on Balance,"
in *Attachment Parenting: The Journal of API*

Balance, like the principle of responding with sensitivity, permeates all of the Eight Principles of Parenting. When there is balance, parents are better able to be emotionally available and responsive to their children and to others. In turn, family members feel more loving, more nurturing, and more supportive of one another.

Why would "striving for balance" be a principle? Finding balance in your personal and family life often seems as ellusive as finding happiness, but it needs to be part of your everyday routine—a principle of life. It may help to know that, like happiness, balance isn't an event but a journey that everyone struggles with on a daily basis. Balance requires focusing on nurturing all aspects of oneself—physical, emotional, intellectual, and spiritual— although not necessarily all at the same time. You can easily recognize when you are feeling out of balance when you are impatient, irritable, angry, tearful, anxious, or depressed.

Some people are really good at balancing their lives, but most are not, especially in our fast-paced culture that creates so many unrealistic expectations. One of the most common parental stresses is the fact that parents feel social and cultural pressures that do not support children and families.[1] Take the myth of the "supermom" as an example: the mother who can do it all—work full-time, keep a clean and organized house, have happy and well-mannered kids, and have enough emotional reserves to give focused attention to her husband! Another hot topic about cultural expectations concerns the overly hyped "mommy wars" that put even more pressure on mothers to perform outside the home as well as in the home. Whether you work outside the home or not, balance is the key to being a happy, successful person and parent.

As a mother, it becomes that much harder to find balance when little, helpless human beings require your constant attention; it's easy to lose yourself in the care of the child. In the early weeks and months after the birth of your baby, you have to meet all of his needs, which are all-consuming most days. Remember the saying "You can't give what you don't have"? If you deplete your emotional resources, you cannot be emotionally available to your children or your spouse.

No matter how many times you hear "Your life is going to change when you have a baby" or "Being a parent is hard work," it doesn't really sink in until you become sleep-deprived and totally exhausted. Try not to wait until you have the baby before thinking about how you will juggle the immense responsibilities of parenthood and day-to-day life. During pregnancy is the optimum time to talk to your spouse or partner about what to expect; discuss how he and others can provide support for you and ways to share the workload.

At the Relationship Research Institute in Seattle, Washington, researchers John Gottman and Julie Schwartz Gottman studied couples in their transitions to parenthood and found that the secret to parents transitioning successfully has to do with learning to nurture their own relationship. According to John Gottman, "The secret to Dad's involvement with the baby is his relationship with the mother. She is able to be a better mother if he is involved with her."

We believe this principle is critical not only to your emotional health and well-being but also to your relationship with your spouse and your children. In this chapter, we will give you tips to help you find balance.

Balance Is the Foundation on Which Attachment Grows

In the United States, many families live a good distance from extended family members, which is a relatively new phenomenon in the history of humankind. In generations past, new parents had grandparents, siblings, aunts, and uncles to help with the care of children and household tasks. They mentored the young family and provided much-needed support when a new baby was born. It certainly wasn't perfect, but everyone had to rely on one another for basic survival and had a deep sense of responsibility and connectedness, which is very rare today. New parents find themselves living away from their families and isolated within their own communities. Since most parents were never really prepared to be parents in the first place, it's no wonder so many families are in crisis.

I KNOW ONE THING FOR SURE: IT IS IMPOSSIBLE TO FIND
ONE'S OWN BALANCE FROM THE OUTSIDE IN. I NOW KNOW BEYOND
A DOUBT THAT FINDING—AND MAINTAINING—
OUR BALANCE IS AN INSIDE JOB.

—Lu Hanessian, "Chaos Theory," in
Attachment Parenting: The Journal of API

The best way to prevent the feeling of isolation is to look outward to create a support network within your local community. If you don't have an extended family nearby, you can create one from your circle of friends and other parents who share similar child-rearing values. You can meet other parents through online parenting message boards, childbirth classes, breastfeeding support groups, and API parent support groups. Finding like-minded friends is critical support for meeting the challenges of the myriad decisions parents face. Your personal network can provide emotional support for its members, especially when parents don't feel supported by the greater community. Don't be afraid to ask for help once your "village" or community is established, especially if a new baby is in the family. Parents can ask friends to bring over some prepared meals, to help with household chores such as cleaning, laundry, or dishes, or to simply answer the phone or door while the

Mothers who received support from spouses and other social support networks before giving birth tended to be more sensitive to their infants.[2]

exhausted new parents enjoy some solitude—resting, reading, or even taking a bath. Give a helper a grocery list and send him to the store or have her run an errand. Need to relax? Ask a friend for a shoulder or foot massage. Sometimes it can be comforting just having one good friend who is willing to help, even if that simply means listening.

Even with ample support from the outside, parents must look inward for family and individual balance. They must take into consideration the needs of each family member; when one person is out of balance, everyone else is affected. Certainly, the infant's needs must be a priority, as they are the most intense and immediate. Even so, she is one piece of the complete family picture that also includes the needs of the parents as individuals and as a couple, siblings, and the family as a whole; it can be overwhelming to juggle. When you are prioritizing the tasks of the day, don't forget to make yourself a priority. We're not talking about carving out hours within a day. Start small and give yourself fifteen minutes a day. You may not be able to meet all of your needs each and every day, but start with one—whatever gives you a feeling of satisfaction, relief, or happiness. Remember that some days, all you may get to fully appreciate is the delicious peace that happens when you sit and nurse or go for a stroll with your baby in the evening.

If you are single or have a spouse who is away for long periods, creating balance will be even more challenging. In these situations, it is extremely important to seek out a support network so that you can attend to your own self-care, not just your child's. Parents should not let pride interfere with asking for help; healthy and happy parents are better able to respond to their children.

When you do get it right and have a great day, don't forget to acknowledge that to yourself. It's too easy to focus on the negative things that happen, so try to focus on the positive and make a point of expressing gratitude each day. If you write these things down, you will be surprised how many positive things occur each day that are taken for granted. The end of the day is a good time to reflect on the incredible work you are doing for your child and how you as a person are growing in so many wonderful ways.

The biggest stress reported by single mothers is that of isolation.[3]

Daily Self-Assessment Checklist

"Check in" with yourself first thing each day or before you go to sleep at night. To make sure you're getting your own needs met, ask yourself these questions:

- What small thing can I do to satisfy my physical needs?
- What small thing can I do to satisfy my emotional needs?
- What small thing can I do to satisfy my spiritual needs?
- What small thing can I do to satisfy my intellectual needs?
- What small thing can I do to satisfy a need of my spouse or partner?

Musings from a Mother of Multiples *(Conclusion)*

Balance was slow to return after the birth of twins. The babies' needs were so intense. Holding one baby rather than two was a "break." I stole a few minutes whenever I could. I meditated in the shower and at night while I was lying with them in bed. I think with all infants the parent's less-pressing needs take a backseat for a while. But with twins it was amplified exponentially. Eating, drinking, and peeing were hard to accomplish. Anything higher than that on Maslow's hierarchy was impossible for about two years. It was hard, and it felt like it was lasting forever. But just as other moms of twins told me it would, it got so much easier when they were approaching two. Suddenly they were entertaining each other, and it was in some ways easier than having a single two-year-old. The older they get, the truer this becomes. I tell new moms of twins to try to keep perspective. It's such a short time in the grand scheme of things, and a balanced life will return. We reached a real equilibrium when the boys were about three. Their dad was able to easily watch them for several hours at a time, and I had returned to old hobbies and even started new ones. They would go off and play for short periods by themselves so that I could read or enjoy a slow cup of coffee. It *does* get better!

—PAM S., MOTHER OF FOUR

Focus on Your Relationship

"No matter how much they love each other, no two people share the same values or feelings or have the same perspective on life, and few things highlight these personal differences as pointedly as the birth of a child," writes Jay Belsky in *The Transition to Parenthood*.[5] Belsky and his research colleagues conducted one of the largest, most extensive studies ever done in the early 1990s on the transition to parenthood from birth through the first three years. They found that what new parents argue about most is categorized into five basic areas:

> Studies have found that a happy marriage provides the strongest foundation for the first line of support.[4]

- division of labor (care of baby and household chores)
- money
- work
- their relationship
- social life[6]

In their study, the Gottmans found that between "forty to seventy percent of couples experience stress, profound conflict, and drops in marital satisfaction during this time, all of which affect their baby's care."[7] A long-term study at the Relationship Research Institute in Seattle, Washington, showed that the level of relationship satisfaction dropped significantly in two-thirds of couples after the birth of their baby. "Conflict and hostility toward each other dramatically increased," and "their emotional intimacy deteriorated," said the researchers.[8] Fatigue and exhaustion can also lead to a significant increase in postpartum depression. On the other hand, attending parenting classes can minimize unrealistic expectations and enhance the couple's relationship. An important factor in maintaining a positive marital relationship is expressing or demonstrating appreciation to each other, such as "Thank you for giving the baby a bath" or "Thank you for cooking dinner and washing the dishes," and complimenting each other, such as "You are such a loving mother to our baby" or "You look really sexy in that shirt."

Dads especially like to feel that they are desired by their wives, and they need intimate time with them to feel connected.[9] Making time for intimacy should be a priority, and it doesn't always have to be about having sex. Having time alone and doing things together that you enjoy are ways to reconnect. You can do this in creative ways, with the realization that you now have to plan ahead, making sure the needs of your baby are being met, and schedule your time together. You can do several simple things to eliminate potential stressors that really strain a relationship after a baby arrives:

- Simplify, simplify, simplify! Sit down and seriously talk about what you can do as a couple to simplify your life, to reduce everyday stressors such as cutting your commuting time by moving closer to work, buying a smaller house (or lowering your rent), or cutting out unnecessary expenses to reduce the strain of money. Eliminate unnecessary commitments to others, such as volunteer work, coaching, and meetings.

- Discuss ways in which you can divide the household chores. This takes out the guesswork and eliminates the need to be a "mind reader." Express what your needs are and how you can help each other. "I need to have a clean kitchen before I go to bed. Will you help me by making sure it's cleaned up each night?"

- In the early weeks and months, your time together is likely to be moments when baby is with you, asleep in a sling or carrier, such as while taking walks in the park or around your neighborhood.

- When the baby is sleeping or napping at home, it's a good time to talk, watch movies together, have a picnic dinner on the floor in front of the fireplace, or play games together. When you feel your baby is ready, you can introduce a "mother's helper," who can be a trusted friend, neighbor, or responsible teenager, to play with the baby so you can have time together—either in another room or another part of the house.

- If you plan an evening out while your baby is still an infant-in-arms, consider having a mother's helper go with you and care for the baby out of sight, allowing Mother to be nearby and available when needed, especially if breastfeeding. Some may wonder, "Why not just ask a babysitter to feed the baby breast milk or formula in a bottle?" Remember, the intention is more about maintaining the attachment relationship than it is about how the baby will be fed.

- Show appreciation and love by surprising your spouse with a special meal or dessert, a gift, or a letter expressing your love. It's the little things in life, the thoughtful gestures, that will help keep you emotionally connected.

As these studies have shown, it is critically important to consciously work on your relationship with your partner and keep communication open and honest. The first two to three years can be intense (with just one child), but realize you are investing in your child's emotional health and investing in your relationship. Be patient and understanding with each other. Know that seeking balance in your relationship and in your life is most important. If you need help, and many parents do, look for parenting classes in your area such as "Bringing Baby Home," a program developed by the Gottmans, or API parent support groups.

A primary hierarchy of needs on the part of mothers is that of spousal support, followed by social support from family of origin and friendship or community.[10]

Children Need Both Parents

Children need loving, committed parents who are willing to make their relationship a priority and help each other recognize when things get out of balance. It may help to know that mothers and fathers are wired differently; unspoken expectations of each other may create unnecessary stress. For instance, a survey found that 70 percent of fathers took weeks and months to form a strong attachment to their babies, most likely because of the other finding of the survey: fathers, on average, spend ten to fifteen minutes a day interacting with their babies. Once a baby is born, it's common for fathers to feel the need to ratchet up their work ethic because they are thrust into being the primary breadwinner for the family. When they get home, many fathers say they are ready to relax, and yet mothers are hoping the father will give them a reprieve (the "six o'clock savior"), which sets the stage for conflict. Mothers, on the other hand, spend so much time with the baby that they feel isolated, out of touch, and lonely, while fathers can feel left out, unappreciated, and unloved.

It is all too common in the transition into parenthood, but it doesn't have to be that way. If you find your relationship falling into the symptoms of constant criticism of one or the other, feeling defensive, or just shut down—and you quit talking to your spouse—these may be warning signs that you might need relationship therapy.[11]

Not only do these behaviors break down relationships, they also affect the emotional health and development of the children. Dr. Gottman and his colleagues found that children in these kinds of stressful marriages had difficulty regulating their emotions and paying attention. Mothers in the study reported that their children were sick more often with colds and coughs, with higher levels of stress-related hormones in their urine.[12]

Dispite the best of intentions, many parents end up getting a divorce. If you are yourself a child of divorce, then you know all too well the lasting psychological harm it can create. At API, we hear from parents on a weekly basis about a divorce situation and how the attachment relationship with their baby or young child is being compromised. These parents have a very difficult road ahead, not only in terms of dealing with an ex-spouse who may resent the close attachment relationship, but also in terms of dealing with attorneys and judges. Most court systems are not informed about the attachment needs of children. They are overwhelmed with divorce cases and must make very tough decisions that usually don't consider the attachment needs of the child but consider only the needs of the parents. You have read in Chapter 7 about the detrimental effects of separation because of custody arrangements. Equally important is the degree to which both parents are able to subdue their own feelings for the best interests of their child. In the book *The Unexpected Legacy of Divorce: A 25-Year Landmark Study*, research showed that when parents divorce, their children are "exquisitely sensitive."[13] Children may have disorganized attachments to both parents if the parents are angry and unable to cooperate with each other. This may also affect their security of attachment to others in their lives as well. If, however, the parents learn to cooperate and have peaceful interactions when they exchange their child, there is a much better chance that the baby or child will thrive.

> Partners who provide each other with strong emotional and cognitive support are strongly predictive of parental competence in healthy full-term and preterm babies.[14]

When Parents Are Not Together

Whether or not their parents are married, children thrive best when both parents are involved in their lives. All children long to have a relationship with both parents, whether the parents are together or not. Barring problems such as the potential for emotional and physical abuse by a parent, every effort should be made to help children nurture relationships with both. If the father is absent from the child's life, it is important that the child be allowed to develop a loving, trusting relationship with another male role model, such as an uncle or grandfather. The same would, of course, hold true if the mother was absent in the child's life: a female role model would be needed with whom the child could build an affectionate relationship. The characteristics and qualities that both sexes provide create balanced experiences for the child that will develop a stable emotional foundation affecting all future relationships.

When Parents Disagree About Parenting Practices

Parents who are having difficulties in their relationship will find parenting to be an added stressor, not necessarily the blessing that solves all their problems. One conflict that can be a great challenge is disagreement on the AP principles. Sometimes parents may disagree on only one issue, like whether the baby will sleep in their bed. For these problems, it's relatively easy to find a compromise solution. For instance, Mom may have the baby sleep next to her side of the bed in a cosleeper, giving Dad plenty of room in the bed to stretch out. It is more serious when one parent disagrees with the entire AP philosophy and wants a more rigid, authoritarian approach to parenting. This is when a tremendous amount of dialogue, empathetic listening, and perhaps compromises on both sides can be key in keeping the marriage intact. Relationship experts have found that one of the most influential determining factors of a parent's ideas and beliefs about discipline and child care is their own childhood history, influencing their general psychological and mental health.[15] Couples need to take the time to discuss the deeper issues from their pasts to be able to understand and work through these conflicts. Books like *And Baby Makes Three* by John and Julie Gottman, *Giving the Love That Heals* by Harville Hendrix and Helen Hunt, and *Nonviolent Communication* by Marshall Rosenberg are excellent resources. These books may also give you the insight to determine if your conversations would be helped by employing a professional counselor to learn skills in communication and compromise.

Many parents have told us that reading parenting books and attending support-group meetings have actually made their marriage relationships stronger. The same tools that they use to talk positively to their children work beautifully with adults, too! We can all use improvement in communication skills, and the parenting journey forces us like no other form of therapy to either improve and grow or to stay stuck in the past, repeating old tapes like an outdated recorder. For the most part, the loving, nurturing skills we learn through attachment parenting have a profoundly positive effect on the entire family.

Q   What can we do to help create a harmonious home life when the mother is an attachment parent and the father is not?

A   First, I would suggest being curious about the possibility that the father's lack of participation is rooted in not feeling needed and feeling criticized for not caring for the infant as well as (or the same as) Mom. I would also challenge this couple to become aware of its power struggle and the underlying dynamics surrounding other relationship issues. If these issues are unconscious, not addressed, and unresolved, the spouses may be creating an oppositional parenting relationship.

Another idea is to listen to each other's childhood stories and memories to see if their experiences of attachment might be influencing their parenting style. An insecurely attached adult with clinging energy can use attachment parenting to compensate for her unmet childhood needs in ways that use the baby in unhealthy ways and promote hyperdependency. Often her husband, who also grew up insecurely attached and has an avoidance attachment style, would be fostering a hyperindependence. It is easy to see how a couple in which both individuals come from insecure attachments could be fighting in the present over how to parent a child, when in reality the energy of this fight is rooted in the indiviuduals' own insecure childhood attachments. Becoming conscious of their childhood patterns could help them listen, understand each other, and cocreate a joint parenting plan, providing a healthy, stable environment for their child.[16]

—Rod Kochtitzky, MDiv,
IMAGO relationship counselor

Practical Tips for Maintaining Balance

Try to enjoy today by being mentally and emotionally present! Children grow up so quickly. The intense newborn stage passes in the blink of an eye; the infant stage is gone in two blinks. If you can, learn to accept—even embrace—your new unpredictable life as a parent. Simply allowing yourself to be flexible can often make the daily challenges easier to manage. You may have heard the warning, "After you have a baby, your life will never be the same." Some parents try to "disprove" this by attempting to maintain a lifestyle similar to life before kids but often quickly learn that it is too stressful for everyone.

No doubt about it, life changes when children join the family, and, while some things may change or be on hold, you stand to gain so much more. A proactive approach to balance can help parents avoid crisis situations in which they feel burned out and exhausted.

The following tips come from years of experience from many mothers and fathers. By following these tips, you will have some tools to help keep you on the right track for your own mental health and the emotional health of your family.

- **Set realistic goals.** Evaluate balance over a full day or week, not every single moment. Instead of wanting to be the "best" parent who has to do everything right, choose to be a "very good" parent who sometimes makes mistakes and learns from them. Parents have to learn "on the job" and should give themselves a break (figuratively and literally). Parenting is hard work!

- **Get organized and establish routines.** We don't mean create a rigid schedule, but rather, prioritize what has to be done each day. Delegate when possible, even if that means calling in reinforcements such as family members or friends. This is not the time to be independent—that strong spirit of being independent and not needing anyone contributes to isolation and burnout. Get better at asking for help and accepting help when it is offered.

- **Put people before things.** When feeling overwhelmed by household duties, parents can take a little time to reexamine and reassign chores in a more balanced way. Changing expectations around them may help also. If your sink is full of dishes, but you had a great day with your kids, you're doing okay.
- **Don't be afraid to say no.** Unfortunately, some people perceive at-home parents as "not working." Don't be afraid to say no when asked for a favor that would compromise individual or family needs. Ask these questions before committing to any new activity: Why do I want to do this? How will it affect our family life? Is it worth it?
- **Turn "unpleasant" parental duties into enjoyable ones.** This can be done by consciously making a change of attitude and making a point to look at the positive aspects of daily tasks. For example, changing diapers can be enjoyable because it's an opportunity to look into the adoring eyes of the little person who loves you more than anyone else in the whole world. Sing songs, whistle, or hum while performing less savory duties!
- **Be creative in finding ways to spend time as a couple.** Find ways to be together without compromising the needs of the infant. Try changing things around a bit. Have a candlelit dinner or a picnic in the living room. Something as simple as taking a walk together while wearing baby in a sling can be fun and can help a couple reconnect or venture farther abroad—many new infants can sleep through an entire dinner out in a restaurant.
- **Take time for yourself.** Each parent should try to find some time each day to do something he or she enjoys or that helps him or her relax. It is not always easy to do, but taking this time while the other parent enjoys some one-to-one time with the baby will help everyone involved. A parent who doesn't have a partner to provide some break time might arrange for a close friend, relative, or neighbor to come over at a certain time each day (or every few days) to provide support. If possible, use this time to read, walk, meditate, take a long bath, or do something else that helps you unwind.

- **Use a "mother's helper."** Have someone that the child knows well come over to play and entertain baby while the parents have some quiet time together somewhere else in the house. This allows parents to focus on their relationship while keeping baby close by. Babies, especially newborns, are more content when they have access to their mothers.

- **Eat healthy foods.** Healthy eating is important to keep parents healthy and balanced. Prepare ahead to have good meals. Make large batches of food on the weekends, and freeze the extras for use during the week. A soft carrier allows baby to be with parents during food preparation and meals; however, safety precautions should be used when working near a hot stove.

- **Get regular exercise.** Include baby in your exercise routine. Walks and outings, yoga exercises, and other light activity can all be done with baby along.

- **Take naps when baby sleeps during the day.** Don't be tempted to get all of your household chores done while the baby is napping. You need rest, too! Many people find they actually sleep better at night when they have napped or rested during the day.

- **Take care of yourself.** Get regular physicals and attend to self-care. Consider whether a physical problem could be contributing to feeling out of balance. For example, insomnia or low blood sugar can lead to feelings of fatigue and may prevent parents from achieving balance.

- **Avoid overscheduling.** As a matter of fact, it may be wise not to schedule anything at all when you have a newborn!

- **Look for ways to make routine tasks easier.** For instance, baby's diaper or clothes need to be changed several times a day, so choose baby clothing that is easy to put on and take off, and have changing stations and extra clothing in the most-used areas of the house (and the latter in the diaper bag).

- **Get out of the house.** Breastfeeding makes it easier to get out of the house for time as a couple, exercise, or errands since the baby's food is always packaged and ready to go. Many states have laws protecting a mother's right to breastfeed her child in public. Parents should be informed about the laws in their state so that they can rest assured that mother and baby can enjoy breastfeeding while out and about.

- **Follow your heart and listen to your baby.** Some days your mantra will be "This too shall pass" and "I must put my baby's needs first. The house may not be clean, the dishes may be piled in the sink, but I'm putting people before things, and tomorrow is another day!"

A major risk factor for child maltreatment occurs when parental isolation is combined with the lack of social networks and poor psychological well-being of the parents.[17]

Tips for Supporting New Mothers

If you are a spouse, professional, friend, or relative, you can support a new mother and family in many ways. A new mother can become so involved in the care of her infant that she doesn't recognize her own needs until she is in emotional or physical trouble. Mothers need frequent rest, fluids, and food just as infants do. As the mother's partner or support person, you can best help her by:

- Being patient and sensitive to her feelings and needs.
- Advocating for her need to rest and for quiet bonding time with her baby by limiting visitors.
- Saying something appreciative about each other every day: "You are such a loving mother and wife," "Our baby adores you, and so do I," "I appreciate all you are doing for our family."
- Taking initiative and doing the needed chores around the house or hiring outside help.
- Asking if you aren't sure what to do.
- If reinforcements are needed, making calls to family or friends to ask them to pitch in, or being a support person for Mom.
- Being grateful. Giving her the benefit of the doubt and treating her as an ally. Imagine what it would be like to parent solo!
- Seeking to become a more empathetic listener. Read *Nonviolent Communication: A Language of Life* by Marshall B. Rosenberg, PhD, or *Giving the Love That Heals* by Harville Hendrix, PhD, and Helen Hunt, PhD, for tips on how to achieve this.

Finding Balance While
Parenting the Older Child

As babies grow into toddlerhood and beyond, they bring a new set of challenges. The following tips will help the family maintain balance with an older child:

- Bring a friend or mother's helper along to entertain an older baby or toddler while Mom enjoys an activity. Baby will be comforted by

  > Mothers reported lower stress levels when they had support from the baby's father.[18]

  his mother's close proximity, and Mother will feel more relaxed knowing her baby is nearby and not feeling stressed.
- Don't overdo extracurricular activities. Allow the child some free time instead of scheduling every minute of the child's day. Children love to have time to hang around the house, read, have their friends over, talk, play games, or be creative.
- Remember to spend time together, getting to know each other and just being together. Spend time talking with each other about each family member's personal interests; this helps family members relate and improves communication. Develop family traditions together.
- Individual children need individual time with one or both parents. Parents can make a "date" on a regular basis with each of their children for special time together.
- Create family traditions with special nights, like "game night," "movie night," or "music night." Most young children look forward to special times like these and love to help with the planning.
- Parents need to nurture themselves and their relationship. As children get older and develop trusting relationships with friends and family outside the immediate family, parents can find more opportunities to have time alone together. Parents can also develop their own hobbies, interests, or do volunteer work they may have put "on hold" when their children were younger. Set an example for the children and include them when possible.

Dealing with Parent Burnout

When families get out of balance, parents can feel burned out and out of touch from the demands of parenting. Recognize the symptoms of burnout. Burnout is a physical, emotional, and mental response to high levels of stress. Parents may feel relentlessly fatigued, strained, and physically, emotionally, and mentally exhausted. They may also feel overworked, underappreciated, angry, resentful, powerless, hopeless, drained, frustrated, detached, antisocial, unsatisfied, resentful, like a failure, indifferent, and unmotivated. Parents who feel their emotions are taking over should get help immediately!

> EATING A VARIED, BALANCED, NUTRITIOUS DIET IS IMPORTANT FOR EVERYONE, ESPECIALLY BUSY PARENTS. CERTAIN FOODS ARE ESSENTIAL FOR THE PRODUCTION OF KEY BRAIN CHEMICALS, AND WITHOUT THEM, YOU MAY FEEL MISERABLE AND TIRED.
>
> —Margot Sunderland, *The Science of Parenting*

Regain balance and heal burnout by trying the following:

- Make regaining balance a priority today. It's easy to forget everything except the needs of the child, but what a child needs most of all is healthy, balanced parents. Parents should not feel guilty about taking some time for themselves to regain balance.
- Parents can take time for themselves while remaining sensitive to the needs of their children.
- Cultivate friendships with other parents who practice attachment parenting. Better yet, join (or start!) an API support group. Parents of older children can share ideas and tips, while parents of similarly aged children can empathize.
- Make time to prioritize the family's needs, and don't be afraid to simplify and let unnecessary things go. A spotless house doesn't do any good if the people who live in it are unhappy, out of touch, and out of balance.
- Every so often, take several deep breaths and slowly release them. Use yoga, meditation, visualization, or other techniques to regain calm and let go of stressful feelings.

- Professional counseling can be beneficial in helping families regain balance and in linking them to resources or other services in the community.
- When all else fails, remember those words of wisdom, "This too shall pass," and try to focus more on any positive aspects of your life's circumstances and write them down.

Lu Hanessian, mother, author, and TV show host, has intimately experienced how difficult it is to balance family and a career. She writes, "Finding balance is no cakewalk. There are the voices. People all around you are convinced about what's right for you and your children, what you should be doing with your life, your toddler, your breasts, your heart, your time, your aspirations, your groceries, your money. . . . A sense of balance comes naturally when we can let go of worry, not let anger fester, find ways to be proactive instead of reactive, befriend and forgive ourselves. With no boundaries, we invite resentment, over-exhaustion, depression, self-pity, self-loathing, guilt, shame, hopelessness."[19]

Perfecting the Balancing Act

In *The Hidden Feelings of Motherhood*, Dr. Kathleen Kendall-Tackett offers seven wise ways to perfect the balancing act:

1. Stop describing yourself as too busy. Your thoughts are powerful. Viewing a situation as negative releases the stress hormone cortisol. This is not good for you!
2. Guard your mind. Be careful what you allow in your mind. Pay attention to what you watch, listen to, and read. Even art, books, or films can be excessively negative.
3. Take care of your body. You cannot strike a balance between your needs and the needs of your family if you are constantly run-down. Make it a priority to eat well, exercise, sleep, and get regular physicals. Stop getting up early or going to bed late so you can catch up on a few extra chores.

4. Unplug and unwind. If you want to de-stress, it is important that you have time every day, or most days, when you are not available. That means turn off your cell phone, ignore the fax, and don't check e-mail.

5. Practice being in the present. It is amazing how much time we devote to thinking about the past or the future. Make a conscious effort to be present for at least a few minutes a day and see if it doesn't refresh your spirit. Practice paying attention and enjoying what's going on now.

6. Plan restorative vacations. To make vacations more enjoyable, (a) stay within your budget, (b) try traveling someplace closer to home, and (c) gradually reenter your life, giving yourself a day or two to prepare and unpack.

7. Be grateful for what you have. The difficulty of the stressed lifestyle is that it keeps us looking to what we don't have, what we haven't accomplished, and what's wrong with our lives. By standing back and looking at your life, you may start to see the things that are really going well for you and that can also help you reduce stress. [20]

A Mother's Story: The Mommy Marathon

A few weeks ago, my husband and I watched the Eco-Challenge on the Discovery Channel, a five-day, 200-mile race over impossible terrain. For me, parenting feels an awful lot like an endurance sport. My children require a lot from me. Their play is loud; their fights are even louder. There are no small events and no quiet moments in my house.

All of this upheaval takes a serious toll on my emotional stamina. To remain present, centered, and fair in the midst of all this chaos is a Herculean task. I want to be their emotional anchor, but for whatever reason serenity escapes me. I either expend tremendous amounts of energy trying to keep it together amid the storm, or I get swept up with my children in their emotional hurricane and we are all lost in it.

The only possible balance that I see for my life would be if my children were somehow "less"—less intense, less strong-willed, less, well . . . loud. But that, unfortunately, is not an option and so it is up to me to grow and stretch *far* beyond my comfort level. I am required to go much farther than I thought I would have to, for much longer, and with much less sleep. Sometimes I hate all this growing.

There have been dark times when I surely thought my body would crack open from fatigue and grief and desperation. It is so much like labor; yet, unlike labor, I'm never sure when it will be "over." There is no monitor or measurement to tell me where I am in the process. It's like the Eco-Challenge, except there's no map, no finish line, and no emergency helicopter to get you the heck out of the race because you simply cannot take one more step. The course that I'm on has few stops and even fewer pieces of level ground. I'd love to have the space and the energy to enjoy the view, but the difficulty of my course doesn't often allow for that.

The best I can do some days is to keep focused on putting one foot in front of the other and pray for some easier road ahead.

I'm coming to understand two things: that selflessness does not mean being "without self," and that taking care of ourselves is not as simple as taking a darned bubble bath. Filling our energy reserves requires us to work on many different levels and to know that if we want to spare our children from the screaming harpies we can become, we must do what we can to keep our reserves from running dry.

Here are a few things that, in retrospect, I wish I had known when the road was long, steep, and really, really rocky.

- Know yourself. It's important to understand your own temperament and the ways in which your energy gets both drained and replenished. When are you likely to get tired? Do you get drained by too many people or stimulation?
- Recognize and identify your needs and validate your right to have them. To get our needs met, we first need to know what those needs are and what we need in order to refuel. We also need to know that needing a break does not mean we're a bad or lazy parent. Don't wait until it's too late. Don't wait until the rough days to take a break. A little break each

day, over time, may prevent total breakdowns because you keep your reserves from completely drying up.

- Actively cultivate a sense of inner calm (without falling asleep). When the world feels chaotic, we need an inner safe place, an eye of the storm. Some sense of peace can give us a place to ride it out.
- Actively seek out a supportive community. It really is impossible to parent without some kind of support, believe me. I tried to tough it out, and I would not recommend it. Do what it takes to find others who can support you. I could go on about how I wish society would make it easier for moms to have access to the things that would help give us balance. But it's really about making our sanity and stamina a priority and doing just a little of what it takes to get it.[21]

—MACALL GORDON, *API News*

This mother's story is a deeply honest description of what so many of us have felt at one time or another in our parenting journey. It's really hard. Without support and other resources, we are taking a big risk for our children and ourselves. Margot Sunderland addresses the critical issue of stress and balance from a brain chemistry perspective in her powerful book *The Science of Parenting*. She describes the positive effects of the hormone oxytocin and its role in helping all human beings be calm. We are designed to help provide emotional regulation for children and each other. When a parent is alone most of the time without other caring adults to talk to, stress hormones rise, feelings get out of balance, and irritability and anger lash out. All of us have an "emotional tank" that needs constant refueling, and it's important to be able to recognize when you are running low.

"Hugs and warm, affectionate touches with your partner trigger the release of oxytocin. This gives you a warm, calm feeling."[22] If your partner isn't available, caring friends can provide much-needed relief by providing an outlet for stress through talking and empathetic concern.

Research has shown that the following activities can stimulate oxytocin:

- Meditation
- Acupuncture
- Massage or physical affection
- Yoga
- A warm bath
- Daylight or good artificial lighting[23]

> AN ENORMOUS BODY OF RESEARCH REVEALS
> THAT THE ROOT OF STRESS AND ULTIMATELY ILLNESS
> IS A SENSE OF ISOLATION, AND MOST TOXIC OF ALL
> APPEARS TO BE OUR CURRENT TENDENCY TO PIT
> OURSELVES AGAINST EACH OTHER
>
> —Lynn McTaggart, *The Bond*

One of the best ways to find relief and emotional regulation is by attending parent groups. API parent support groups have been successful because they provide the friendship, information sharing, problem solving, and empathetic support that so many parents are seeking. Talking to other like-minded parents who have "been there" can provide a wealth of knowledge and relief through simple conversations. If you are new in an area and the only friend you have is 2,000 miles away, she can still be a support system for you. Often the simplest of ideas can have a profound positive effect on your relationship with your child or spouse or on stress at home. As a culture, we are finally beginning to accept that we are relational beings and need one another for connection and support, whether we are parents or not. If you believe that you need more than a parent support group can provide, then by all means get professional help.

Balance begins within, and that includes not worrying so much. When you are a first-time parent, it is natural that you want to do it right; after all, you are responsible for a helpless human being that you created. William and Martha Sears emphasize that attachment parenting doesn't mean that mothers must be anxious about the baby's every move or that they have to personally respond to the baby every time; rather, involve Dad as much as possible.

Don't strive for perfection, but do your best to be "good enough." Attachment parenting will give you the gift of love, empathy, and connection that will last a lifetime. "It will give you more confidence in yourself and in your ability to be not a perfect mother, but a good one."[24]

CHAPTER TEN

Nurturing Children for a Compassionate World

There is a lot of talk about world peace—peace between nations, peace between religions, peace among races. There are many theories about why we don't have peace and what we can do to bring it about. We blame other countries. We blame the president. We blame congressional leaders. We blame the newspeople. We blame this political party or that. . . . We think that if we could be more politically active or influential we could help solve the world's problems. . . . But let's take a look at our own family. How much peace do we have in our own homes? Do we like our children? Do we see our spouse as our equal friend and partner? Do our children like us and feel good about being with us? Do our children like each other? Where is the peace in our own families? If we can't create peace in our families, how can we create peace in the world? Peace in our families is what creates peace in the world.

—David and Lee Stewart, cofounders of
the InterNational Association of Parents and Professionals
for Safe Alternatives in Childbirth (NAPSAC)

This book has been written as a guidepost, not only for parents looking for practical parenting advice, but also for anyone with a vision for a more compassionate world. For some parents, the Eight Principles of Parenting are a comfortable affirmation of how they were raised themselves and want to parent their own children. For others, it may be a transformative new philosophy that connects on a deep spiritual level. We have a vision for the world that is even broader than a mere parenting program. We hope that this book will be used as a tool for opening the doors of empowerment for parents, that they will see that their role is the fundamental underpinning of civilization. The Dalai Lama has observed that the only hope for a peaceful society is learning how to access the wisdom of our hearts: "The question of world peace, the question of family peace, the question of peace between husband and wife, or peace between parents and children, everything is dependent on that feeling of love and warm-heartedness."[1] We know that for some parents becoming more conscious about their parenting choices brings up many challenges. Perhaps they were not raised in a very nurturing home and are conflicted about trying a different path with their own children. Most parents in the United States were raised in families that used some form of reward and punishment. Behavior modification is still a common tool used by classroom teachers, and it will probably be many decades before we incorporate other classroom methodologies. Unfortunately, in many states in the United States, corporal punishment is still sanctioned in the schools as a legitimate way to punish even special-needs children in the classroom. In the meantime, each family has the unique opportunity to change the paradigm in its own home. You may decide to make choices in raising your children that are different from the choices your own parents made, but it does not mean you are rejecting them personally. We all try to do the best we can with the knowledge we have at the time.

Most mothers and fathers improve in their parenting from the previous generation to some degree, and healthy families recognize and hope that this will happen. If grandparents put strict conditions on their love and support, that may be a red flag of deeper issues in the family that need to be addressed; it is not necessarily a reason to doubt that what your heart is telling you is best for you and your children.

THE PRESSURES OF BEING A PARENT ARE EQUAL TO
ANY PRESSURE ON EARTH. TO BE A CONSCIOUS PARENT, AND
REALLY LOOK TO THAT LITTLE BEING'S MENTAL AND PHYSICAL HEALTH,
IS A RESPONSIBILITY WHICH MOST OF US, INCLUDING ME,
AVOID MOST OF THE TIME BECAUSE IT IS TOO HARD.

—John Lennon,
musician, songwriter, and peace activist

The Joys of Attachment Parenting: Being in Attunement with Your Children

A common theme that we hear from many parents is the relief, joy, and peace that comes from parenting in a more empathetic and positive way. Even in the most challenging circumstances, when you have the tools to step back from the situation, assess what the child is experiencing, and act with a foundation of empathy and trust, most crises can be avoided. We hope that after reading this book, you will feel you have the guidance you need to make more positive choices in parenting your children. The confidence that comes from seeing these solutions actually work can be thrilling, especially if we started our parenting journey with very limited strategies. We like the metaphor of "tuning in" to our children. We know that when the radio is not quite on the station, all we hear is static. Our home life can be like that sometimes—the children are whining or fighting, and we just can't seem to figure out what's wrong. Fine-tuning the dial to get a clear, beautiful song may look like this in the home: take some deep breaths; limit the distractions; turn off the TV, computer, or telephone; and really give focused attention to the children. Then when calm returns, our family is back in attunement.

Another benefit of AP, including the support many AP parents receive from parent groups and other networking channels, is empowerment. Most of us were raised to trust authority figures—such as medical professionals, government leaders, and teachers—without question. When we become parents, we have a responsibility to look objectively at all our decisions and advocate for our children, many times in the process learning how to advocate for ourselves. We know from personal experience that in the process of raising our own children, we learned how to take more responsibility for many lifestyle changes in our adult lives as well. It is almost impossible to practice AP without doing a tremendous amount of soul-searching. We can't expect our children to be healthy human beings, lifelong learners, and caring adults if we don't set the example.

As we stated in the introduction, real change in society only happens from the "bottom up"; that is to say that all of us are the critical component in this paradigm shift to a more compassionate world. When we see even our toddlers reaching out with love and care to their friends or family members, we are witnessing the seeds of change that will blossom in future generations.

The greatest joy comes from seeing our children grow up into compassionate adults. Just as they taught us all along our journey to learn, listen, and trust, we continue to learn from them as we watch them interact with their friends, teachers, and coworkers. It would be an interesting study to follow adult children of AP families! From our experience, we know so many of these young adults are very confident to make choices based not on fear or distrust but on consideration of the facts and an empathetic viewpoint. An example of this comes from a parent whose daughter was volunteering with her church in an orphanage in Russia. She knew that the care providers were overworked, but what the children needed were hugs and touch. Even though she was

Study on the Intergenerational Transmission of Positive Parenting

Researchers used a sample of 228 New Zealanders who were parents of young children. Information on how the parents were themselves reared when they were between the ages of three and fifteen had been obtained from repeated interviews with their mothers when they were growing up. The now-grown children were videotaped interacting with their children in a variety of situations when their children were three to five years old. Their findings concluded that "if a mother was raised in a positive, nurturing environment, she was more likely to engage in a warm, sensitive, stimulating parenting style herself when raising the next generation."[2]

a teenager, she was able to set an example of loving care for the children and encouraged the workers to use infant slings rather than leave the babies alone in their cribs.

Many of us have great hope when we see our grown children taking an interest in their communities, either through volunteering in their churches, making more conscious choices like recycling in their homes, or getting involved in mentoring programs or political action groups. And of course the greatest joy is seeing how they interact with children, becoming empathetic parents themselves! This ripple effect will have a profound effect on entire communities and ultimately society as a whole. When we look at the challenges different nations of the world face in establishing a more democratic way of government, we can reflect on the words of Australian psychotherapist and author Robin Grille, who has written eloquently on the subject of what makes a democracy possible:

> The temperament and maturity required to be one's own authority, to feel the equal of all others, to be a responsible and active participator in public life and decisions, the inner strength to refuse tyranny or autocracy; all these qualities are second nature to those in whom they have been fostered from youth. . . . Individuals who have never been exposed to democratic notions of personal responsibility and egalitarianism in their upbringing cannot be expected to automatically immerse themselves in democratic living as soon as democracy is foisted upon them. Time and again, history teaches us that the first lessons in democracy must be delivered, through example, in the family home.[3]

In countless ways, we teach our children the values of liberty and freedom. From the first time we offer our baby solid food and trust his ability to let us know he's ready, to the most mundane choices like giving him an option in what outfit to wear to school, we are planting the seeds of social equality. When we give our children the opportunity to help with tasks around the house, when we include them in discussions about everyday family decisions, they learn that as a family we must all help one another. When we model involved citizenship, community service, and ethical principles, our children learn our values by witnessing the best tool we have available: our example.

Challenges Parents Face

A PERFECT PARENT IS A PERSON WITH EXCELLENT CHILD-REARING
THEORIES AND NO ACTUAL CHILDREN.

—Dave Barry, humorist

Throughout this book, we have discussed the importance for new mothers and fathers to go into parenting with a fierce determination to meet the needs of their babies. We hope that this book has given you the confidence, information, and resources you need to begin your parenting journey. However, we also know from years of talking with and counseling parents that many challenges occur along the way. Being aware and giving this some consideration may diffuse some of these concerns and give you the assurance that these are common problems that most parents experience. None are insurmountable, and we all have the capabilities to overcome whatever curves life may bring us.

More than twenty years ago, Dr. Montagu observed that forces seemed to be conspiring to deprive parents and babies of their rights to basic human connection. Here's an example from his book *Touching*:

> All through pregnancy, the mother has been elaborately prepared to minister to the dependent needs of her child . . . an indispensability that . . . is generally not understood by the very persons who have been elected the experts or authorities. . . . It is as if there was a conspiracy against both mother and child to deprive them of their . . . constitutional rights to human development.[4]

Whether we think of these issues as a conspiracy or merely a challenge that any conscious parent can overcome, let us always remember to look at our choices through the eyes of our babies and children and do our best to advocate for healthy attachment. The following section provides some examples to heighten our awareness and propose some solutions.

Receiving Criticism for Parenting Choices

Attachment-parenting practices are sometimes seen as a "new style of parenting," even though the basic principles of natural childbirth and breastfeeding, responsiveness, and respectful discipline have been practiced around the world since recorded history! We hear stories from some grandparents who are pleased to see parents who are going back to the "old ways" of keeping babies close and finding more natural solutions to common problems. However, parents may find that they receive criticism for practices that are unfamiliar in their own families or communities.

Mothers can be particularly vulnerable to criticism right after giving birth or adopting a newborn and adjusting to motherhood for the first time. This is when the husband or partner can be particularly indispensable in protecting the mother-baby dyad. When grandmother wants to come in and take over with the newborn, for instance, Dad can gently suggest she help him with the cooking and cleaning so Mom and the baby can nap together. Holidays can sometimes be a challenge when going to homes of relatives who might not approve of breastfeeding or the baby sleeping in close proximity to the parents. It's good to think ahead and rehearse some clever comebacks. Some parents bring books with them that explain their choices in medical terms. Often, if the grandparents or other relatives know that the pediatrician recommends and encourages these methods, they are relieved and supportive.

A sense of humor is always a great way to deal with criticism, too. Some parents shared that if they handled any concerns with a funny anecdote, it seemed to break the ice and defuse any stress they might be feeling from relatives or friends. When a mother of a six-month-old was asked how long she was going to nurse, she laughingly said, "Oh, I'm thinking about all the money we'll save if I keep it up until he goes to college!" Or when asked if his baby would be "too attached" or developmentally delayed from being carried in a sling, a dad replied, "I figure once he goes to kindergarten, he'll just have to learn to walk on his own!"

Your greatest advertisement for attachment parenting will be your healthy, happy babies and children. Over and over again, we have seen criticism dissolve when families and friends see the joyful, caring children that are a product of such loving care. It is very gratifying when we hear the grandparents brag to their friends about their loving grandchildren!

> ALTHOUGH OUR INTELLECT-DRIVEN SOCIETY LEADS US
> TO BELIEVE THE OPPOSITE, THE INTELLECT EXISTS TO SERVE THE
> WISDOM OF THE HEART—NOT VICE VERSA. ALL THE DRUGS
> AND TECHNOLOGY IN THE WORLD CAN'T MEND A BROKEN HEART OR
> HEAL SOMEONE WHOSE HEART IS NO LONGER IN THE GAME OF LIFE.
> THE EKG SIGNAL COMING FROM THE HEART IS 60 TIMES STRONGER
> THAN THE EEG SIGNAL FROM BRAIN WAVES. SO WHEN THERE'S
> A CONFLICT BETWEEN THE INTELLECT AND THE HEART, THE HEART
> ALWAYS WINS. AND THE ONLY WAY TO HEAL THE TRUE DISCOMFORTS OF
> THE HEART IS TO FEEL THEM FULLY, HAVE FAITH IN A POWER GREATER
> THAN YOURSELF, AND THEN LIVE YOUR LIFE ROBUSTLY.
>
> —Christiane Northrup, MD

Handling Unwanted Advice

"Help! I'm getting so frustrated with the endless stream of advice I get from my mother-in-law and brother! No matter what I do, I'm doing it wrong. I love them both, but how do I get them to stop dispensing all this unwanted advice?" Just as your baby is an important part of your life, she is also important to others. People who care about your baby are bonded to you and your child in a special way that invites their counsel. Knowing this may give you a reason to handle the interference gently, in a way that leaves everyone's feelings intact.

Regardless of the advice, it is your baby, and, in the end, you will raise your child the way that you think best. So it's rarely worth creating a war over a well-meaning person's comments. You can respond to unwanted advice in a variety of ways:

Listen first: It's natural to be defensive if you feel that someone is judging you, but chances are you are not being criticized; rather, the other person is sharing what he feels to be valuable insight. Try to listen—you may just learn something valuable.

Disregard: If you know that there is no convincing the other person to change her mind, simply smile, nod, and make a noncommittal response, such as, "Interesting!" Then go about your own business—your way.

Agree: You might find one part of the advice that you agree with. If you can, provide wholehearted agreement on that topic.

Pick your battles: If your mother-in-law insists that baby wear a hat on your walk to the park, go ahead and pop one on his head. This won't have any long-term effects except that of placating her. However, don't capitulate on issues that are important to you or the health or well-being of your child.

Steer clear of the topic: If your brother is pressuring you to let your baby cry to sleep, but you would never do that, then don't complain to him about your baby getting you up five times the night before. If he brings up the topic, then distraction is definitely in order, such as, "Would you like a cup of coffee?"

Educate yourself: Knowledge is power; protect yourself and your sanity by reading up on your parenting choices. Rely on the confidence that you are doing your best for your baby.

Educate the other person: If your "teacher" is imparting information that you know to be outdated or wrong, share what you've learned on the topic. You may be able to open the other person's mind. Refer to a study, book, or report that you have read. Quote a doctor—many people accept a point of view if a professional has validated it. If your own pediatrician agrees with your position, say, "My doctor said to wait until she's at least six months before starting solids." If your own doctor doesn't back your view on that issue, then refer to another doctor—perhaps the author of a baby care book.

Be vague: You can avoid confrontation with an elusive response. For example, if your sister asks if you've started potty training yet (but you are many months away from even starting the process), you can answer with, "We're moving in that direction."

Ask for advice: Your friendly counselor is possibly an expert on a few issues that you can agree on. Search for these points and invite guidance. She'll be happy that she is helping you, and you'll be happy you have a way to avoid a showdown about topics that you don't agree on.

Memorize a standard response: Here's a comment that can be said in response to almost any piece of advice: "This may not be the right way for you, but it's the right way for me."

Be honest: Try being honest about your feelings. Pick a time free of distractions and choose your words carefully, such as "I know how much you love Harry, and I'm glad you spend so much time with him. I know you think you're helping me when you give me advice about this, but I'm comfortable with my own approach, and I'd really appreciate if you'd understand that."

Find a mediator: If the situation is putting a strain on your relationship with the advice giver, you may want to ask another person to step in for you.

Search out like-minded friends: Join a support group or online club with people who share your parenting philosophies. Talking with others who are raising their babies in a way that is similar to your own can give you the strength to face people who don't understand your viewpoints.[5]

—Elizabeth Pantley,
Gentle Baby Care

The Challenge of Consumerism and Overuse of Technology

There's something that's so engrossing about
the kind of interactions people do with screens that
they wall out the world. . . . I've talked to children who

TRY TO GET THEIR PARENTS TO STOP TEXTING WHILE DRIVING
AND THEY GET RESISTANCE, "OH, JUST ONE, JUST ONE MORE
QUICK ONE, HONEY." IT'S LIKE "ONE MORE DRINK."

—Sherry Turkle, author of *Alone Together,*
in "The Risks of Parenting While Plugged In," *New York Times*

Our culture of consumerism is another enormous challenge parents face when trying to raise their children with the values of empathy and compassion. Young families are bombarded with an overwhelming array of choices: the latest cribs, strollers, swings, clothes, and electronic toys. Many are convinced that these are all must-haves to raise a happy, smart, and healthy child. Our media's focus on celebrity, wealth, sensational crimes, and other extreme behavior enters our homes via television, newspapers, magazines, and the Internet every day. As soon as a baby is old enough to understand language, products are being directly marketed to this age group, with child psychologists acting as consultants! As noted in Chapter 9, it is all about balance. Some of the products advertised can be of help to an overwhelmed mom who may need to occasionally put the baby in a swing while she's cooking or attending to other children. Educational videos or beautiful music can of course enhance family life in ways our grandparents could have never imagined. AP parents learn to ask themselves whether a "convenient" device will further separate them from a strong connection with their baby or enhance their relationship with their child. We must realize that allowing our children to view something on the Internet or TV is like inviting a guest into our homes—our kids look to us to protect them from inappropriate products and developmentally unsuitable programs.

The National Institute on Media and the Family reports that many children are spending most of their waking hours in front of an "ever expanding number of screens."[6] For too many children, screen time has replaced time with parents or caregivers engaging in more nurturing or educational activities like reading, imaginative play, and storytelling. Thirty-nine percent of children ages two to three have televisions in their bedrooms!

Twelve Tips to Tame the Tube

Here are ideas to give you control over television:

1. **Avoid using TV as a babysitter.** Think of how careful you are about choosing a babysitter and day care. Try to be just as careful about what your children watch on TV every day.

2. **Know what your kids are watching.** It is important to be aware of program content as well as the content of the daily news. The younger the child, the more impressionable he or she is, and the less experienced in evaluating content against the values of family and community. Additionally, emotional images may intrude upon and interrupt sleep.

3. **Keep TV out of kids' bedrooms.** It is difficult to monitor what your children are watching when they are watching TV in their own rooms. Having a TV in a child's room discourages participation in family activities and encourages him or her to watch TV when he or her could be studying, reading, or sleeping.

4. **Set some guidelines about when and what children watch.** This can be done in conversation with your children, but the final call belongs to the adults. The clearer the rules (e.g., no TV before school, or until homework is completed), the better. Setting new limits may be upsetting to your children at first, but consistency is very important.

5. **Practice "appointment" TV.** Decide in advance what's good and watch it as a family. Go through the TV guide in the paper on Sunday, and make family decisions on shows to watch for the week. Discuss reasons for the decisions with your children. If in doubt, get more information. In choosing TV shows or videos, make use of independent evaluations, such as KidScore, TV and movie guides, and articles in magazines. Discuss issues and ideas with other adults, friends, and parents of your children's playmates.

6. **Talk to your child about what he or she is watching.** Discuss what you are watching and ask specific questions. Ask what they see, because it may be very different from what you see. Ask them to tell you what

things mean to them. Ask them why they watch specific shows, which characters they like and don't like. Discuss the commercials and their perception of toys, cereals, and so on, and the people who sell them.

7. **Turn the TV off during meals.** Catch up with one another. Focus on one another. Share stories and activities from each family member's day.

8. **Use the DVR or DVD player to your advantage.** Record a good show and schedule a special family viewing—complete with popcorn. If a show is on at an inconvenient time, such as mealtime, homework time, or family time, record it to watch later.

9. **Put the family on a TV diet.** Schedule some fun alternative activities. When you do watch television, watch it with your children.

10. **Create a TV coupon system.** Kids get coupons and turn them in when they watch a program. Unused coupons can be "cashed in" for a special family activity.

11. **Don't make the television the focal point of the room.** Make your children the focus of your attention, not the TV. Research shows that people watch less TV if it is not in the most prominent location in the room.

12. **Patronize good programs and demand more of them.** Express your opinions to TV and radio stations, network executives, and advertisers. Tell them not only what you do not like but also what you like. Addresses for networks and local stations are in your TV guide. Also, remember that your money has a voice of its own.[7]

The Canadian Society for the Prevention of Cruelty to Children (CSPCC) has been on the forefront of the issue of TV and advertising for decades. Its journal, *Empathic Parenting*, can be accessed on the website (www.empathicparenting.org), with well-researched and documented articles on the challenges parents face from a corporate culture of mass advertising to children. Dr. Elliott Barker, the founder of CSPCC, writes, "That happiness is to be attained through limitless material acquisition is denied by every religion and philosophy known to man but is preached incessantly by every American television set. Market-driven forces have usurped the role once assumed by family, home, and community. Few societies could imagine themselves surviving very long when one of their central institutions was advocating unrestrained greed."[8] Children are also a captive audience at many public schools. Some school systems partner with commercial companies that give them revenue in exchange for closed-circuit TV news and educational programs and (more important to them) the advertising of products directly to this vulnerable population. Can we swim against this tidal wave of consumer goods and protect our children from society's onslaught of materialism and unhealthy values? Parents and schools need to be vigilant about exposing their children to such blatant commercialism and create an environment conducive to learning—not only academic subjects, but, more important, the values of living in a humane and compassionate society.

The good news is that many parents are actively seeking alternatives to such strongly negative cultural influences. When families experience the simple joys of just spending more time together, turning off the TV, reading, walking, and eating meals together, they can recapture the connection that so often becomes lost in their busy lives. These simple ideas don't cost any money, either! The beauty of attachment parenting is that it encourages us to look at the most basic values in life—love, connection, and simple living.

WE MAY BE BOUNCING BETWEEN THE FUTURE AND
THE PAST, YET OUR CHILDREN—THE LITTLE ZEN MASTERS—
LONG TO STAY SUSPENDED, FULLY ENGAGED, IN THE MOMENT.
OUR VERY BEST HOPE IS THAT THEY'LL DEVELOP THEIR OWN VOICES,
THEIR OWN INSTINCTS AND RESILIENCY, AT THEIR OWN PACE.
AND DESPITE HOW MANY TIMES WE FORGET—SOMETIMES
IN A SINGLE DAY—WE ABSOLUTELY KNOW
THIS WILL TAKE TIME.

—Kim John Payne,
Simplicity Parenting

Marketing to Infants and Toddlers

Did You Know?

- By six months, babies are forming mental images of corporate logos and mascots.
- According to market research, babies are requesting brands as soon as they can speak.
- Baby paraphernalia is routinely festooned with licensed characters—these same icons will sell them media, food, toys, and other products throughout childhood.
- In their quest for "cradle-to-grave brand loyalty," companies that manufacture products for adults also target babies.

Screen-Saturated Infants and Toddlers

- By the age of three months, 40 percent of infants are watching screen media regularly. By the time children are two, the number jumps to 90 percent.
- 19 percent of babies one year and under have a TV in their bedrooms.
- 14 percent of children under two spend more than two hours a day with screen media.
- Marketers urge parents to soothe fussy babies with cell phone videos.
- The American Academy of Pediatrics recommends no screen time for children under the age of two.

The Baby Media Scam

- Baby media companies routinely make unfounded educational claims to sell parents their products.
- 56 percent of parents of young children believe that baby videos are good for child development.
- While television can be an effective teaching tool for older children, there is no credible evidence that babies and toddlers learn anything useful from screens.[9]

Medical and Professional Advice

And now we come to the greatest challenge of all for many parents: To whom do we listen in the medical and professional world? This can be overwhelmingly difficult for new parents—as soon as they find out they're pregnant or wanting to adopt, they are immediately faced with many critical decisions. If you take only one important lesson from this book, we sincerely hope it will be that you have the power, as your child's greatest advocate, to make your own choices, based on what is best for your family.

A Mother's Story of Empowerment

I am not always graceful when it comes to defending myself from criticism. The toughest situations for me are when I encounter a medical professional who is giving out perhaps well-intentioned but biased non-AP advice. I find it frustrating when I know more than my child's healthcare provider about the science behind AP, or when the doctor or nurse is too conservative or traditional to see that there are other parenting styles than those promoted in the mainstream.

Once when I was at my oldest daughter's one-year checkup at a local clinic, I encountered a doctor who advised me to start disciplining my child. As a preemie, she was only nine months developmentally and couldn't even walk. That seemed a little young to me to begin disciplining. Then the doctor informed me that he expected me to spank her so that she would learn "no." I debated this issue with him for several minutes, but after he made it clear that he wasn't going to change his mind, I decided to switch to another medical clinic in search of a doctor who would allow me, as the parent, to make my own decisions and who would be more open to AP.

I think the key to being able to thwart criticism is being confident in my parenting decisions, which comes from experience, taking the time to do a little reading on the research behind AP, and having at least one person among my family and close friends who supports AP. I also rely heavily on API.

AP parents can also empower themselves by deciding to educate their crit-ics instead of staying silent when someone gives them unwanted advice con-tradicting their parenting choices. I try to educate my critics when I can, but, if my words fall on deaf ears, it's okay. I know that AP is working for me and my family, and that's all that matters.

—RITA B.

Doctors and other medical professionals are only human—they base their advice not only on what they learned in medical school but also, in the parenting arena, often on what they experienced in their own homes. Remember that doctors' experience and counsel varies widely from one to the next, depending on their training and their ability to read and digest mountains of the latest research and methodologies. Many patients have educated their doctors in the areas of healing and child rearing! Your job as the consumer is to ask a lot of questions—do your homework not only by reading and researching but also by talking to trusted friends, relatives, and parents. Ultimately, you should listen to your own common sense and decide what seems to be a good fit for you and your family. Networking can be your greatest tool and asset when looking to find a professional in your area. One of the reasons that we founded API (maybe the most important reason!) was to give parents a way to support one another in their parenting and to create a networking opportunity for finding all kinds of resources in the community. API groups often invite speakers to give talks on a variety of subjects—from birth options to educational options to medical professional choices in the community.

IF WE TRULY WANT PEACE IN THE WORLD,
LET US BEGIN BY LOVING ONE ANOTHER
IN OUR OWN FAMILIES.

—Mother Teresa

A Legacy of Love

Our children are living examples of what it means to fully embrace life with joy, passion, and enthusiasm by living in the moment and finding wonder in everything. The love, empathy, and affection our children learn from us and others in their lives will carry on into their adult relationships and with their children. Our children can be our greatest teachers in life if we allow it—they will challenge us to grow in ways we never believed possible, and, as a result, we will become better human beings and parents.

If we can truly be "the change we wish to see in the world," then we can provide a home rich with love, safety, protection, imagination, and joy. When children are carefully and consciously raised with empathy, they will naturally be more compassionate toward others.

Our children don't care if we have money, position, fame, or beauty. To them, we are the universe, and all they ask of us is our love, our time, and our nurturance. In return, they give us their unconditional love and joy and the promise of a lifetime of connection.

Afterword

· ·

We have touched on many issues in this book, and each of the eight principles deserves a volume of its own to give it the depth of coverage it deserves. Perhaps after reading this overview of the principles, you will find that one chapter is a particular "hot button" or one that you would like to research further. The API website has many resources, including forums and blogs where parents and professionals communicate, new books are discussed, and support groups blossom in communities all over the world. We sincerely hope that some of these resources will be of great help to you and your family.

Appendix A:
Myths and Facts About Attachment Parenting

Myth: I heard in the media that attachment parenting basically meant parents had to do three things: breastfeed, wear their baby, and bedshare. Is that true?

Fact: No, attachment parenting (AP) is much more than that. Breastfeeding, babywearing, and bedsharing are "tools" or strategies for parents who want to provide for their baby's emotional and physical needs as well as promote secure attachment. Attachment parenting is not a one-size-fits-all style of parenting; the goal is to develop an attuned, connected parent-child relationship, and that's not easy to do in today's world, which pushes detachment. There are no rules; parents aren't mandated to use all the strategies but are free to use what works best for their family situation and leave the rest. There are the Eight Principles of Parenting, not three, that are rooted in sound science and designed for the optimal physical and emotional development of infants and young children. They teach us how to get in touch with our instincts and allow us to have richer family relationships.

Myth: Attachment parenting (AP) means never putting your child down, right?

Fact: Attachment parenting encourages the use of slings or soft carriers that give a child access to the movement and closeness of the parent's body. Advocates do not suggest that an infant should never be put down. AP is about being responsive to a child's needs for closeness, not about thwarting their natural drive toward independence. Children need a firm foundation of closeness before authentic, age-appropriate independence can occur.

Myth: Is there a problem in using baby gadgets (plastic carriers, swings, playpens, etc.)?

Fact: Babies are born with a biological need for human closeness and interaction. The more parents rely on things like swings and infant seats, the less time they spend actually holding and interacting with the baby. Gadgets can be helpful when used sparingly, but the key is to avoid overusing them when a baby really wants you.

Myth: My child will be spoiled if I always respond to his cries and hold him a lot.

Fact: Responding to a baby's cries and holding him will not spoil him. A quick, appropriate response tells the child that the parent takes his needs seriously and will help him manage his distress. Responding to a child's cries lays a critical foundation of trust and communication.

Myth: If a child sleeps in our bed, she will never leave.

Fact: The experience of generations of bedsharing parents has not proved this to be true. Depending on the child's temperament, most children naturally leave the parents' bed around two or three years of age. You can adapt to the changing sleep needs of family members in many ways. Some families place an infant in a cosleeping device attached to the side of the bed or have a toddler in a crib nearby in the same room. The key is being responsive to a child's need for a parent's presence and not rushing her into self-reliance too soon.

Myth: Bedsharing is more dangerous than sleeping in a crib.

Fact: Bedsharing has not proved to be any more dangerous to infants than sleeping alone in a crib. If parents follow specific safety guidelines, cosleeping and bedsharing can be safe and beneficial for both infant and parent. Parents should never cosleep or bedshare with their infants if they smoke, drink, or take drugs (even prescription medications that may cause drowsiness), become overly fatigued, or use a water bed, very soft mattress, or a lot of fluffy bedding. For more information about safe cosleeping go to http://attachmentparenting.org/infantsleepsafety/.

Myth: Attachment parenting means nursing your child until he is four or five years old.

Fact: AP advocates believe that when to wean is a personal decision and a cooperative process between each mother and baby. Extended breastfeeding has many documented benefits, and current recommendations in the United States by the American Academy of Pediatrics are generally to breastfeed for the first twelve months and as long as is mutually desirable after that.

Myth: If you work outside the home, you can't adopt this style of parenting.

Reality: Working parents can certainly adopt this approach to parenting. Attachment-parenting principles suggest limiting the frequency and length of separations if possible when the baby is very young in order to maintain a healthy bond. Mothers can continue to breastfeed with the help of a part-time or flexible schedule and a breast pump. Both parents can still wear the baby in a soft carrier around the house and sleep near or with the baby at night. In fact, many working parents find attachment parenting an excellent way to create and maintain connections with the baby in spite of the daytime separation.

When you choose a caregiver for your baby, make sure to find a person or program that supports your philosophy. It's also important to pay attention to the rate of caregiver turnover. Frequent changes in caregivers (also known as "caregiver roulette") can cause the child to experience a continuous cycle of bonding and grieving.

Appendix B:
UNICEF's Ten Steps to Successful Breastfeeding
(Baby-Friendly Hospital Initiative)

Every facility providing maternity services and care for newborn infants should:

1. Have a written breastfeeding policy that is routinely communicated to all healthcare staff.
2. Train all healthcare staff in skills necessary to implement this policy.
3. Inform all pregnant women about the benefits and management of breastfeeding.
4. Help mothers initiate breastfeeding within a half hour of birth.
5. Show mothers how to breastfeed and how to maintain lactation, even if they should be separated from their infants.
6. Give newborn infants no food or drink other than breast milk, unless medically indicated.
7. Practice rooming-in—allow mothers and infants to remain together—twenty-four hours a day.
8. Encourage breastfeeding on demand.
9. Give no artificial teats or pacifiers (also called dummies or soothers) to breastfeeding infants.

10. Foster the establishment of breastfeeding support groups and refer
    mothers to them on discharge from the hospital or clinic.

Steps can be found at www.babyfriendlyusa.org/about-us/baby-friendly
-hospital-initiative/the-ten-steps.

Appendix C:
Additional Resources

Recommended Reading

- *The A.D.D. Book: New Approaches to Parenting Your Child* by William Sears, MD, and Lynda Thompson.
- *Adventures in Tandem Nursing: Breastfeeding During Pregnancy and Beyond* by Hilary Flowers.
- *Alone Together: Why We Expect More from Technology and Less from Each Other* by Sherry Turkle.
- *And Baby Makes Three: The Six-Step Plan for Preserving Marital Intimacy and Rekindling Romance After Baby Arrives* by John Gottman, PhD, and Julie Schwartz Gottman, PhD.
- *Attached: The New Science and How It Can Help You Find and Keep Love* by Amir Levine and Rachel Heller.
- *The Attachment Connection: Parenting a Secure and Confident Child Using the Science of Attachment Theory* by Ruth Newton, PhD.
- *The Attachment Parenting Book: A Commonsense Guide to Understanding and Nurturing Your Baby* by William Sears, MD, and Martha Sears, RN.
- *Baby Matters: What Your Doctor May Not Tell You About Caring for Your Baby* by Linda F. Palmer, DC.
- *The Baby Sleep Book: Guide to a Good Night's Rest for the Whole Family* by William Sears, MD, Martha Sears, RN, Robert Sears, MD, and James Sears, MD.
- *Beating the Devil Out of Them: Corporal Punishment in American Families* by Murray Straus, PhD.

- *Becoming Attached: First Relationships and How They Shape Our Capacity to Love* by Robert Karen, PhD.
- *Being There: The Benefits of a Stay-at-Home Parent* by Isabelle Fox, PhD.
- *The Biology of Belief: Unleashing the Power of Consciousness, Matter & Miracles* by Bruce Lipton, PhD.
- *Birth and Breastfeeding: Rediscovering the Needs of Women During Pregnancy and Childbirth* by Michel Odent, MD.
- *The Birth Book: Everything You Need to Know to Have a Safe and Satisfying Birth* by William Sears, MD, and Martha Sears, RN.
- *Birth Matters: A Midwife's Manifesta* by Ina May Gaskin and Ani DiFranco.
- *The Birth Partner: A Complete Guide to Childbirth for Dads, Doulas, and All Other Labor Companions* by Penny Simkin.
- *Birth Reborn* by Michel Odent, MD.
- *Birth Without Violence* by Frederick Leboyer, MD.
- *The Bond: How to Fix Your Falling-Down World* by Lynne McTaggart.
- *Bonding: Building the Foundations of Secure Attachment and Independence* by Marshall Klaus, MD, John Kennell, MD, and Phyllis Klaus.
- *Born in the USA: How a Broken Maternity System Must Be Fixed to Put Women and Children First* by Marsden Wagner, MD.
- *The Breastfeeding Book: Everything You Need to Know About Nursing Your Child from Birth Through Weaning* by William Sears, MD, and Martha Sears, RN.
- *Building Healthy Minds: The Six Experiences That Create Intelligence and Emotional Growth in Babies and Young Children* by Stanley Greenspan, MD.
- *Buy, Buy Baby: How Consumer Culture Manipulates Parents and Harms Young Minds* by Susan Gregory Thomas.
- *Calms: A Guide to Soothing Your Baby* by Carrie Coty, PhD, and Debby Takikawa, DC.
- *Child Honoring: How to Turn This World Around* edited by Raffi Cavoukian and Sharna Olfman.
- *The Complete Book of Pregnancy and Childbirth* by Sheila Kitzinger.

- *Connection Parenting: Parenting Through Connection Instead of Coercion, Through Love Instead of Fear* by Pam Leo.
- *Consciously Parenting: What It Really Takes to Raise Emotionally Healthy Families* by Rebecca Thompson.
- *The Continuum Concept: In Search of Happiness Lost* by Jean Liedloff.
- *Creating Effective Parenting Plans: A Developmental Approach for Lawyers and Divorce Professionals* by John Hartson, PhD, and Brenda Payne, PhD.
- *Creating the Capacity of Attachment: Treating Addictions and the Alienated Self* by Karen Walant, PhD.
- *The Crying Baby* by Sheila Kitzinger.
- *Depression and New Mothers: Causes, Consequences, and Treatment Alternatives* by Kathleen Kendall-Tackett, PhD.
- *The Developing Mind: How Relationships and the Brain Interact to Shape Who We Are* by Daniel Siegel, MD.
- *The Discipline Book: How to Have a Better-Behaved Child from Birth to Age Ten* by William Sears, MD, and Martha Sears, RN.
- *The Drama of the Gifted Child: The Search for the True Self* by Alice Miller, PhD.
- *Eat Healthy, Feel Great* by William Sears, MD, and Martha Sears, RN.
- *Eat Well and Lose Weight While Breastfeeding: The Complete Nutrition Book for Nursing Mothers* by Eileen Behan.
- *Eating Well for Optimum Health: The Essential Guide to Bringing Health and Pleasure Back to Eating* by Andrew Weil, MD.
- *Everyday Blessings: The Inner Work of Mindful Parenting* by Jon Kabat-Zinn, PhD, and Myla Kabat-Zinn.
- *Evolution, Early Experience and Human Development: From Research to Practice and Policy*, edited by Darcia Narvaez, PhD, Jaak Panksepp, PhD, Allan Schore, PhD, and Tracey R. Gleason, PhD.
- *The Family Nutrition Book: Everything You Need to Know About Feeding Your Children—From Birth Through Adolescence* by William Sears, MD, and Martha Sears, RN.
- *Feeding the Whole Family: Whole Recipes for Babies, Young Children, and Their Parents* by Cynthia Lair.

- *The Five Love Languages: How to Express Heartfelt Commitment to Your Mate* by Gary Chapman.
- *For Your Own Good: Hidden Cruelty in Child-Rearing and the Roots of Violence* by Alice Miller, PhD.
- *Forgive for Good: A Proven Prescription for Health and Happiness* by Dr. Fred Luskin.
- *The Four-Thirds Solution: Solving the Child-Care Crisis in America Today* by Dr. Stanley Greenspan, MD.
- *Fussy Baby Book: Parenting Your High-Need Child from Birth to Age Five* by William Sears, MD, and Martha Sears, RN.
- *A General Theory of Love* by Thomas Lewis, MD, Fari Amini, MD, and Richard Lannon, MD.
- *Ghosts from the Nursery: Tracing the Roots of Violence* by Robin Karr-Morse and Meredith Wiley.
- *Gifts: Mothers Reflect on How Children with Down Syndrome Enrich Their Lives* by Kathryn Lynard Soper.
- *Giving the Love That Heals: A Guide for Parents* by Harville Hendrix, PhD, and Helen Hunt, PhD.
- *A Good Birth, a Safe Birth: Choosing and Having the Childbirth Experience You Want* by Diana Korte and Roberta Scaer.
- *The Good Divorce: Keeping Your Family Together when Your Marriage Comes Apart* by Constance Ahrons, PhD.
- *Good Nights: The Happy Parents' Guide to the Family Bed (and a Peaceful Night's Sleep!)* by Jay Gordon, MD, and Maria Goodavage.
- *Great Expectations: Pregnancy and Childbirth* by Sandy Jones and Marcie Jones.
- *The Happiest Baby on the Block: The New Way to Calm Crying and Help Your Newborn Baby Sleep Longer* by Harvey Karp, MD.
- *The Healthiest Kid in the Neighborhood: Ten Ways to Get Your Family on the Right Nutritional Track* by William Sears, MD, Martha Sears, RN, James Sears, MD, and Robert Sears, MD.
- *Heart-to-Heart Parenting: Nurturing Your Child's Emotional Intelligence from Conception to School Age* by Robin Grille.
- *The Hidden Feelings of Motherhood: Coping with Stress, Depression, and Burnout* by Kathleen Kendall-Tackett, PhD.

- *High Risk: Children Without a Conscience* by Ken Magid and Carol McKelvey.
- *Hold On to Your Kids: Why Parents Need to Matter More Than Peers* by Gordon Neufeld, PhD, and Gabor Maté, MD.
- *How to Raise a Healthy Child in Spite of Your Doctor* by Robert Mendelsohn, MD.
- *How to Really Love Your Child* by Ross Campbell, MD.
- *How to Talk So Kids Listen & Listen So Kids Talk* by Adele Fabor and Elaine Mazlish.
- *How Weaning Happens* by Diane Bengson.
- *Husband-Coached Childbirth: The Bradley Method of Natural Childbirth* by Robert Bradley, MD.
- *Immaculate Deception: A New Look at Women and Childbirth* by Suzanne Arms.
- *In the Realm of Hungry Ghosts: Close Encounters with Addiction* by Gabor Maté, MD.
- *Ina May's Guide to Childbirth* by Ina May Gaskin.
- *Infant Massage: A Handbook for Loving Parents* by Vimala McClure.
- *Kangaroo Care: The Best You Can Do to Care for Your Preterm Infant* by Susan Luddington-Hoe, PhD.
- *Kids Are Worth It! Giving Your Child the Gift of Inner Discipline* by Barbara Coloroso.
- *Kids: How Biology and Culture Shape the Way We Raise Our Children* by Meredith Small, PhD.
- *Let the Baby Drive: Navigating the Road of New Motherhood* by Lu Hanessian.
- *Life Lessons for Busy Moms: 7 Essential Ingredients to Organize and Balance Your World* by Dorothy K. Breininger, Debby S. Bitticks, and Lynn Benson.

- *Magical Beginnings, Enchanted Lives* by Deepak Chopra, MD, David Simon, MD, and Vicki Abrams, IBCLC.
- *Magical Child* by Joseph Chilton Pearce.
- *Medication Madness: The Role of Psychiatric Drugs in Cases of Violence, Suicide, and Crime* by Peter R. Breggin, MD.
- *The Men They Will Become: The Nature and Nurture of Male Character* by Eli Newberger, MD.
- *The Milk Memos: How Real Moms Learned to Mix Business with Babies and How You Can, Too* by Cate Colburn-Smith and Andrea Serrette.
- *Mind over Labor: A Breakthrough Guide to Giving Birth* by Carl Jones, Marian Tompson, and Emmett E. Miller.
- *The Mindful Child: How to Help Your Kid Manage Stress and Become Happier, Kinder, and More Compassionate* by Susan Greenland.
- *Mindsight: The New Science of Personal Transformation* by Dan Siegel, MD.
- *Molecules of Emotion: The Science Behind Mind-Body Medicine* by Candace Pert, PhD.
- *Mom's House, Dad's House: Making Two Homes for Your Child* by Isolina Ricci.
- *Mom's House, Dad's House for Kids: Feeling at Home in One Home or Two* by Isolina Ricci.
- *Mother Nature: Maternal Instincts and How They Shape the Human Species* by Sarah Blaffer Hrdy, PhD.
- *The Mother's Guide to Self-Renewal: How to Reclaim, Rejuvenate and Re-Balance Your Life* by Renee Peterson Trudeau.
- *Mothering Magazine's Having a Baby Naturally: The Mothering Magazine Guide to Pregnancy and Childbirth* by Peggy O'Mara.
- *Mothering Multiples: Breastfeeding and Caring for Twins or More!* by Karen Kerkhoff Gromada.
- *Mothering the Mother: How a Doula Can Help You Have a Shorter, Easier, and Healthier Birth* by Marshall Klaus, MD, Phyllis Klaus, and John Kennell, MD.
- *Mothering Your Nursing Toddler* by Norma Jane Bumgarner.

- *My Child Won't Eat: How to Enjoy Mealtimes Without Worry* by Carlos Gonzalez, MD.
- *The Natural Child: Parenting from the Heart* by Jan Hunt.
- *Natural Family Living: The Mothering Magazine Guide to Parenting* by Peggy O'Mara.
- *Nighttime Parenting: How to Get Your Baby and Child to Sleep* by William Sears, MD.
- *The No-Cry Sleep Solution: Gentle Ways to Help Your Baby Sleep Through the Night* by Elizabeth Pantley.
- *Non-Violent Communication: A Language of Life* by Marshall Rosenberg, PhD, and Arun Gandhi.
- *Nurturing Yourself and Others* by Lee Schnelby.
- *The Official Lamaze Guide: Giving Birth with Confidence* by Judith Lothian and Charlotte De Vries.
- *Optimal Care in Childbirth: The Case for a Physiologic Approach* by Henci Goer and Amy Romano.
- *The Other Baby Book: A Natural Approach to Baby's First Year* by Megan McGrory Massaro and Miriam J. Katz.
- *Our Babies, Ourselves: How Biology and Culture Shape the Way We Parent* by Meredith Small, PhD.
- *Our Bodies, Ourselves: Pregnancy and Birth* by the Boston Women's Health Book Collective and Judy Norsigian.
- *A Parent's Guide to Autism: Answers to the Most Common Questions* by Charles A. Hart.
- *Parenting for a Peaceful World* by Robin Grille.
- *Parenting from the Inside Out* by Daniel Siegel, MD, and Mary Hartzell.
- *Parenting from Your Heart: Sharing the Gifts of Compassion, Connection, and Choice* by Inbal Kashtan.
- *Parenting Through Crisis: Helping Kids in Times of Loss, Grief, and Change* by Barbara Coloroso.
- *Parenting Without Power Struggles: Raising Joyful, Resilient Kids While Staying Cool, Calm, and Connected* by Susan Stiffelman.

- *Peaceful Parent, Happy Kids: How to Stop Yelling and Start Connecting* by Dr. Laura Markham.
- *Playful Parenting* by Lawrence Cohen, PhD.
- *Positive Discipline for Single Parents: Nurturing, Cooperation, Respect and Joy in Your Single-Parent Family* by Jane Nelsen, Cheryl Erwin, and Carol Delzer.
- *The Pregnancy Book: Month by Month, Everything You Need to Know from America's Baby Experts* by William Sears, MD, Martha Sears, RN, and Linda Hughey Holt.
- *Pregnancy, Childbirth, and the Newborn: The Complete Guide* by Penny Simkin, April Bolding, and Janelle Durham.
- *The Premature Baby Book: Everything You Need to Know About Your Premature Baby from Birth to Age One* by William Sears, MD, Robert Sears, MD, James Sears, MD, and Martha Sears, RN.
- *Prenatal Parenting: The Complete Psychological and Spiritual Guide to Loving Your Unborn Child* by Frederick Wirth, MD.
- *Pre-Parenting: Nurturing Your Child from Conception* by Thomas R. Verny, MD, and Pamela Weintraub.
- *Pushed: The Painful Truth About Childbirth and Modern Maternity Care* by Jennifer Block.
- *Raising America: Experts, Parents, and a Century of Advice About Children* by Ann Hulbert.
- *Raising an Emotionally Intelligent Child: The Heart of Parenting* by John Gottman, PhD, and Joan DeClaire.
- *Raising Children Compassionately* by Marshall Rosenberg, PhD.
- *Raising Our Children, Raising Ourselves: Transforming Parent-Child Relationships from Reaction and Struggle to Freedom, Power, and Joy* by Naomi Aldort.
- *Respectful Parents, Respectful Kids: 7 Keys to Turn Family Conflict into Cooperation* by Sura Hart and Victoria Kindle Hodson.
- *A Ride on Mother's Back: A Day of Baby Carrying Around the World* by Emery Bernhard.
- *Roots of Empathy: Changing the World Child by Child* by Mary Gordon.

- *Scared Sick: The Role of Childhood Trauma in Adult Disease* by Robin Karr-Morse with Meredith S. Wiley.
- *The Science of Parenting: How Today's Brain Research Can Help You Raise Happy, Emotionally Balanced Children* by Margot Sunderland.
- *Screamfree Parenting: The Revolutionary Approach to Raising Your Kids by Keeping Your Cool* by Hal Runkel.
- *The Secret of the Unborn Child: How You Can Prepare Your Baby for a Happy, Healthy Life* by Thomas R. Verny, MD, and John Kelly.
- *A Secure Base: Parent-Child Attachment and Human Development* by John Bowlby, MD.
- *Shelter for the Spirit: Create Your Own Haven in a Hectic World* by Victoria Moran.
- *Silent Knife: Cesarean Prevention and Vaginal Birth After Cesarean (VBAC)* by Nancy Wainer Cohen and Lois J. Estner.
- *Simplicity Parenting: Using the Extraordinary Power of Less to Raise Calmer, Happier, and More Secure Kids* by Kim John Payne.
- *Sleeping with Your Baby: A Parent's Guide to Cosleeping* by James J. McKenna.
- *Spare the Child: The Religious Roots of Punishment and the Psychological Impact of Physical Abuse* by Philip Greven, PhD.
- *Special Children, Challenged Parents: The Struggles and Rewards of Raising a Child with a Disability* by Robert Naseef.
- *Spiritual Midwifery* by Ina May Gaskin.
- *The Stay-at-Home Dad Handbook* by Peter Baylies and Jessica Toonkel.
- *The Thinking Woman's Guide to a Better Birth* by Henci Goer.
- *Three in a Bed: The Benefits of Sleeping with Your Baby* by Deborah Jackson.
- *To Touch Is to Live: The Need for Genuine Affection in an Impersonal World* by Mariana Caplan, PhD.
- *Touching: The Human Significance of the Skin* by Ashley Montagu, PhD.
- *Transition to Parenthood* by Jay Belsky, PhD.
- *The Truth About Children and Divorce: Dealing with the Emotions So You and Your Children Can Thrive* by Robert E. Emery.

- *The Ultimate Breastfeeding Book of Answers: The Most Comprehensive Problem-Solving Guide from the Foremost Expert in North America* by Jack Newman, MD, and Teresa Pitman.
- *Unconditional Parenting: Moving from Rewards and Punishments to Love and Reason* by Alfie Kohn.
- *The Unexpected Legacy of Divorce: A 25-Year Landmark Study* by Judith Wallerstein, PhD, Julia M. Lewis, and Sandra Blakeslee.
- *The Vaccine Book* by Dr. Robert Sears.
- *Vital Touch: How Intimate Contact with Your Baby Leads to Happier, Healthier Development* by Sharon Heller, PhD.
- *What About the Kids? Raising Your Children Before and After Divorce* by Judith Wallerstein, PhD.
- *When Children Push Your Buttons: And What You Can Do About It* by Bonnie Harris.
- *Wherever You Go, There You Are: Mindfulness Meditation in Everyday Life* by Jon Kabat-Zinn.
- *Whole Foods for Babies and Toddlers* by Margaret Kenda.
- *Whole Foods for the Whole Family* by La Leche League International.
- *Why Dads Leave: Insights and Resources for When Partners Become Parents* by Meryn Callander.
- *Why Love Matters: How Affection Shapes a Baby's Brain* by Sue Gerhardt.
- *Why Your Child Is Hyperactive: The Bestselling Book on How ADHD Is Caused* by Artificial Food Flavors and Colors by Ben Feingold, MD.
- *Wisdom for Parents: Key Ideas from Parent Educators* edited by Arminta Jacobson and Robert Klein.
- *The Womanly Art of Breastfeeding* by La Leche League International.
- *Your Amazing Newborn* by Marshall Klaus, MD and Phyllis Klaus, MD.
- *Your Best Birth: Know All Your Options, Discover the Natural Choices, and Take Back the Birth Experience* by Ricki Lake and Abby Epstein.

Books in the Sears Children's Library

- *Baby on the Way*
- *Eat Healthy, Feel Great*

- *What Baby Needs*
- *You Can Go to the Potty*

(All four of these children's books are authored by William Sears, MD, Martha Sears, RN, Christy Watts Kelly, and Renee Adriani)

Recommended DVDs

- *Baby Baby Oh Baby: Breastfeeding* and *Baby Baby Oh Baby: Infant Massage* produced by David Stark. Two videos that can be purchased at www.babybabyohbaby.com that help familiarize parents with the basics of breastfeeding and infant massage
- *The Benefits of Bedsharing* (2005), written by Dr. Helen Ball, Sally Inch, and Marion Copeland. Platypus Media, www.platypusmedia.com.
- *Birth Story: Ina May Gaskin and the Farm Midwives*, www.birthstorymovie.com.
- *The Business of Being Born*, Ricki Lake and Abbie Epstein's powerful documentary, www.thebusinessofbeingborn.com.
- *Creating Secure Infant Attachment: Helping Your Baby Get the Best Possible Start in Life*, by Jeanne Segal, PhD, www.helpguide.org/video/attachment_sd.htm.
- *The Happiest Baby on the Block* by Harvey Karp, MD.
- *It's My Body, My Baby, My Birth: A Film About Natural Childbirth*, www.itsmybodymybabymybirth.com/Home.html.
- *Laboring Under an Illusion: Mass Media Childbirth vs. The Real Thing*, birth-media.com/laboring-under-an-illusion/.
- *More Business of Being Born* (the sequel to the documentary *The Business of Being Born*) www.thebusinessofbeingborn.com.
- *Vaccinations? Assessing the Risks and Benefits* by Dr. Jay Gordon.
- *The Well-Loved Baby: Helping You Nurture and Care for Your Child*, Childcare Media, http://childcaremedia.com/.

Recommended CDs

- *Baby Beluga* by Raffi

- *Dream Big* by Roger Day
- *The Gift of Love: Songs for a Mother's Journey* by Lu Hanessian
- *Good Night, Sleep Tight* by Marylee and Nancy
- *Growing Minds with Music: Traditional Lullabies* by Twin Sisters Productions
- *The Happiest Baby on the Block: New "Super Soothing" Calming Sounds* by Harvey Karp, MD
- *Lullabies for Sleepy Eyes* by Susie Tallman
- *Quiet Time* by Raffi
- *Return to Pooh Corner* by Kenny Loggins
- *Singable Songs for the Very Young* by Raffi
- *Traditional Lullabies* by Growing Minds with Music.
- *Welcome Home, My Child: Songs for a Mother's Journey* by Lu Hanessian.

Useful Websites

Academy of Breastfeeding Medicine: www.bfmed.org.

Adoptive Families: www.adoptivefamilies.com

American Academy of Husband-Coached Childbirth: www.bradleybirth. com.

American Academy of Pediatrics Task Force's Policy Statement on Circumcision (the 2012 update on the American Academy of Pediatrics Task Force's Policy Statement on Circumcision): http://pediatrics. aappublications.org/content/130/3/585.abstract.

American Association of Birth Centers (provides a list of birth centers in the United States): www.birthcenters.org.

Association for Pre- and Perinatal Psychology and Health (focuses attention on human development from preparation for pregnancy through the postpartum period): www.birthpsychology.org.

Association for Treatment and Training in the Attachment of Children: http://attach.org.

Attachment Parenting (resources for families who need support/

information on blended families, divorce, and custody issues from an attachment perspective): www.attachmentparenting.org/parentingtopics/divorcecustodyblendedfamilies.php.

Attachment Parenting International: www.attachmentparenting.org.

Attachment Treatment & Training Institute: http://attachmentexperts.com

Babies at Work (information for parents and businesses who want to implement a policy for bringing baby to the workplace): www.babiesatwork.org.

Baby-Friendly Hospital Initiative of UNICEF (includes information on helping establish good feeding practices as soon as the baby is born): www.bfhi.org.

Birth Works International (childbirth preparation course): www.birthworks.org.

Breast Crawl (amazing footage of a baby crawling on his mother's body to her nipple and beginning to suckle immediately after birth): www.breastcrawl.org.

Breastfeeding Made Simple (information for breastfeeding mothers who may have questions about depression, medications that are safe for breastfeeding, and alternative therapies): www.breastfeedingmadesimple.com.

Dr. Peter Breggin (forensic psychiatrist and psychiatry reformist): www.breggin.org.

Bringing Baby Home: www.bbhonline.org/.

Campaign for a Commercial Free Childhood: www.commercialfreechildhood.org.

Canadian Society for the Prevention of Cruelty to Children (CSPCC) (founded by forensic psychiatrist Elliott Barker, MD): www.empathicparenting.org.

Canadian Society for the Prevention of Cruelty to Children: An Online Parenting Course (CSPCC) (online questionnaire provided by the CSPCC for new or prospective parents): www.parentingcourse.net.

Center for a New American Dream (includes information on parenting in a commercial culture): www.newdream.org.

Center for Divorce Education (providing resources to assist parents in helping children adjust through a difficult family transition): www .divorce-education.com.

Center for Effective Discipline (a great deal of information about spanking, discipline at home, and school and state laws): www.stophitting.com. For a list of states that still allow corporal punishment in the schools and information on how you can get involved in this issue, see www.stophitting. com/index.php?page=legalinformation.

Center for Nonviolent Communication: www.cnvc.org.

Child Trauma Academy (founded by Bruce Perry, PhD, MD): www.childtrauma.org.

Circumcision Information (provides resources and information on circumcision): www.cirp.org.

Coalition for Improving Maternity Services (CIMS): www.motherfriendly .com.

Barbara Coloroso (author, speaker, and educator): www.kidsareworthit.com.

Continuum Concept (concepts from the book by Jean Liedloff): www.continuum-concept.org.

Doctors Opposing Circumcision (discusses human rights law and the circumcision of children): www.doctorsopposingcircumcision.org/DOC/ statement09.html.

Doulas of North America (DONA International): www.dona.org.

Durham University Parent-Infant Sleep Laboratory (UK; director Dr. Helen Ball): www.dur.ac.uk/sleep.lab.

Family and Home Network (resources and support for stay-at-home parents): www.familyandhome.org.

Generation Rescue (information and research for parents and professionals on vaccinations and the possible link to autism): www.generationrescue. com/studies.html.

Jay Gordon, MD (specializes in pediatric nutrition): www.drjaygordon.com.

Lu Hanessian (author of *Let the Baby Drive: The Road of New Motherhood*): www.letthebabydrive.com.

The Happiest Baby (website for Harvey Karp, MD, nationally renowned pediatrician, child development specialist, and assistant professor of Pediatrics at the USC School of Medicine): www.happiestbaby.com/.

Hardwired to Connect Report (a report to the nation from the commission on children at risk): www.americanvalues.org/html/hardwired.html.

HealthConnectOne (a nationally recognized nonprofit training and technical assistance agency that uses innovative, community-based approaches to support direct-service providers in promoting the health of mothers, infants, and families): www.healthconnectone.org.

Hypnobabies Childbirth Hypnosis (hypnosis for childbirth, pregnancy, and motherhood): www.hypnobabies.com.

HypnoBirthing: The Mongan Method (information about using hypnosis for a relaxed birth): www.HypnoBirthing.com.

Imago Therapy (restoring relationships): www.gettingtheloveyouwant.com.

Infant Massage USA: www.infantmassageusa.org.

Infant-Parent Institute (specializes in clinical services, professional training, and research related to the optimal development of infants and their families): www.infant-parent.com.

International Cesarean Awareness Network (ICAN): www.ican-online.org.

International Childbirth Education Association: www.icea.org.

International Lactation Consultant Association (includes information on cosleeping and breastfeeding): www.ilca.org.

John Gottman Relationship Institute (information for researching and restoring couple relationships): http://www.gottman.com/48995/Parenting—BBH.html. www.gottman.com.

Kangaroo Mother Care Promotions (the work of Dr. Nils Bergman; promotions that provide a bibliography of skin-to-skin research): www.kangaroomothercare.com.

Alfie Kohn (author, speaker, and educator): www.alfiekohn.com.

La Leche League International (provides a network of mother-to-mother support for breastfeeding mothers): www.llli.org.

Lamaze International: www.lamaze.org.

Mamatoto Mother's Circle (general information about babywearing with "how-to" guides and videos): www.mamatotosb.com/.

Dr. Gabor Maté (physician and bestselling author, Dr. Maté specializes in ADD, mind-body wellness, adolescent mental health, and parenting): www.drgabormate.com.

Lynne McTaggart (researcher and investigative science and spirituality journalist): www.lynnemctaggart.com.

Mind Sight Institute (founded by Dr. Dan Siegel as an educational center devoted to promoting insight, compassion, and empathy in individuals, families, organizations, and communities): www.mindsightinstitute.com.

Mother-Baby Behavioral Sleep Laboratory at the University of Notre Dame (directed by Dr. James McKenna): www.nd.edu/~jmckenn1/lab.

Mothering **magazine articles** (a wide variety of articles that are related to many aspects of caring for a new baby): www.mothering.com/articles/new_baby/new_baby_main.html.

National Council on Family Relations (provides an educational forum for family researchers, educators, and practitioners to share in the development and dissemination of knowledge about families and family relationships, establishes professional standards, and works to promote family well-being): www.ncfr.org.

National Organization of Circumcision Information Resource Centers: www.nocirc.org.

Natural Child Project (founded by Jan Hunt): www.naturalchild.com.

Gordon Neufeld, PhD/Gordon Neufeld Institute (the Neufeld Institute's mission is to use developmental science to rejoin parents and teachers to their own natural intuition): http://neufeldinstitute.com/.

Nurturing Across Cultures (dedicated to babywearing and attachment parenting practices with information about the Rebozo carrier that originated in South America): http://nurturingacrosscultures.org/us/.

Organized Home (help with organizing your home and your life to achieve balance): www.organizedhome.com/.

Elizabeth Pantley (books, advice, links, and solutions about parenting): www.pantley.com/elizabeth/.

ParentFurther (information from the National Institute on Media and the Family for parents and other caregivers, organizations, and corporations to create better-quality media choices for families, so that we have healthier, less violent communities): www.parentfurther.com/media.

Parenting in the Workplace Institute (dedicated to promote, educate, and provide resources for successful implementation of parenting-in-the-workplace structures): www.parentingatwork.org.

Parenting Science (describes cutting-edge research news and practical, science-based tips about child development and child rearing): www.parentingscience.com.

Pathways to Family Wellness (website for the quarterly magazine *Pathways to Family Wellness*, which offers parents articles and resources to make informed healthcare choices for their families): www.pathwaystofamilywellness.org.

Playful Parenting (program designed by psychologist, author, and consultant Lawrence Cohen, PhD, on the world of play): www.playfulparenting.com.

Positive Discipline (author and speaker Jane Nelson's website): www.positivediscipline.com.

Project No Spank—Parents and Teachers Against Violence in Education (PTAVE): www.nospank.net.

Scream Free Parenting program (Hal Runkel's website on learning calm connections): www.screamfree.org.

Sears family website (provides information about nutrition, pregnancy, and childbirth): www.askdrsears.com.

Dr. Dan Siegel (information about mindfulness meditation and scientific research on the mind/brain connection): www.drdansiegel.com.

Simplicity Parenting (executive director, Kim John Payne; "using the extraordinary power of less to raise calmer, happier, and more secure kids"): www.simplicityparenting.com.

TBW (the Baby Wearer) (a resource for information on babywearing): www.thebabywearer.com.

Touch Research Institute (information about touch therapy): www6.miami.edu/touch-research.

UNICEF U.K. Baby Friendly Initiative (information on safe bedsharing): www.isisonline.org.uk/where_babies_sleep/parents_bed/.

United States Breastfeeding Committee (we recommend you do a search for the information on safe infant sleep): www.usbreastfeeding.org.

Waterbirth International (information about water births and how to find a water birth practitioner): www.waterbirth.org.

World Health Organization (providing information on infant feeding): http://www.who.int/nutrition/topics/infantfeeding_recommendation/en/

Notes

Introduction: Parents' Call to Arms

1. Weisfeld, *Principles of Human Adolescence*, 298.
2. Hartney, "US rates of incarceration."
3. Children's Defense Fund, *America's Cradle to Prison Pipeline Report*.
4. Adverse Childhood Experiences, www.cdc.gov/ace/findings.htm.
5. *Frontline,* "Medicating Kids."
6. Commission on Children at Risk, *Hardwired to Connect*, 3.
7. Perry et al., "Relationships between early experiences and long-term functioning."

Chapter One:
Charting a New Course

1. See Child Trends, www.childtrends.org/pages/statistics.
2. Walant, *Creating the Capacity for Attachment*, 8.
3. Fonagy et al., "Maternal representations of attachment during pregnancy."
4. Watson, *Psychological Care of Infant and Child*, 81–82.
5. Hartley, *Breaking the Silence*, 18.
6. Fonagy, "Maternal representations of attachment during pregnancy."
7. Childhelp, "National child abuse statistics."
8. Child Welfare Information Gateway, "Child abuse and neglect fatalities."
9. Child Welfare Information Gateway, "Protective factors for promoting healthy families."
10. Child Welfare Information Gateway, "Promoting healthy families in your community."
11. Walant, *Creating the Capacity for Attachment*, 8.
12. Dictionary.com, "Abuse."
13. Walant, *Creating the Capacity for Attachment*, 9.

14. Karr-Morse and Wiley, *Ghosts from the Nursery*, 37.

15. Siegel, *The Developing Mind*, 140–41.

16. Schore, "The experience-dependent maturation of a regulatory system."

17. Reiss et al., *The Relationship Code*, 49.

18. Begley, "The nature of nurturing."

19. McTaggart, *The Bond*, 24.

20. Ainsworth et al., *Patterns of Attachment*, 347–62.

21. Karen, *Becoming Attached*, 147–63.

22. Ainsworth et al., *Patterns of Attachment*, 347–62.

23. Karen, *Becoming Attached*, 159; Ainsworth et al., *Patterns of Attachment*, 347–62.

24. Karen, *Becoming Attached*, 159; Ainsworth et al., *Patterns of Attachment*, 347–62.

25. Karen, *Becoming Attached*, 159; Ainsworth et al., *Patterns of Attachment*, 347–62.

26. Schore, "The experience-dependent maturation of a regulatory system."

27. Montagu, *Learning Non-Aggression*, 7.

28. *Time*, "The Cornelians."

29. California Medical Association, Panel discussion.

30. Quoted in Miller, *For Your Own Good*, 5.

31. Freud, *The Schreber Case*.

Chapter Two:
PRINCIPLE 1: Prepare Yourself for Pregnancy, Birth, and Parenting

1. Feinberg et al., "Effects of family foundations on parents and children."

2. Declercq et al., "Executive summary."

3. Arms, *Immaculate Deception*, 25.

4. Declercq et al., "Executive summary."

5. Fonagy et al., "Maternal representations of attachment during pregnancy."

6. Chopra et al., *Magical Beginnings, Enchanted Lives*, 38.

7. DeCasper and Fifer, "Of human bonding."

8. Widström et al., "Gastric suction in healthy newborn infants."

9. Hodnett et al., "alternative versus conventional institutional settings for birth."

10. Coalition for Improving Maternity Services website.

11. O'Mara, *Having a Baby Naturally*, 102.

12. Enkin et al., *A Guide to Effective Care in Pregnancy and Childbirth*, 25.

13. Cleeton, "Attitudes and beliefs about childbirth among college students."

14. Tanzer, *Why Natural Childbirth?* 152.

15. Siddiqui and Hagglöf, "An exploration of prenatal attachment in Swedish expectant women."

16. Gaskin, "Understanding Birth and Sphincter Law."

17. Melender, "Experiences of fears associated with pregnancy and childbirth."

18. Rados, "FDA cautions against ultrasound 'keepsake' images."

19. Abramowicz, "Fetal thermal effects of diagnostic ultrasound."

20. Rados, "FDA cautions against ultrasound 'keepsake' images."

21. Abramowicz, "Ultrasound and autism."

22. Ibid.

23. Ibid.

24. Carter and Porges, "Neurobiology and the evolution of mammalian social behavior," 140.

25. Enkin et al., *A Guide to Effective Care in Pregnancy and Childbirth*, 177.

26. *Atlanta Journal Constitution*, "Georgia to end Medicaid payments for some early births."

27. Beilin et al., "Effect of labor epidural analgesia."

28. Klaus et al., *Mothering the Mother*, 4.

29. Doulas of North America, "What is a doula?"

30. Hodnett et al., "Alternative versus conventional institutional settings for birth."

31. Punger, "A physician's personal experience with a doula."

32. Klaus et al., *Mothering the Mother*, 33–51.

33. Arora et al., "Major factors influencing breastfeeding rates."

34. Tarkka et al., "What contributes to breastfeeding success after childbirth?" Midmer et al., "A randomized controlled trial of the influence of prenatal parenting education."

35. Arora et al., "Major factors influencing breastfeeding rates."

36. Siddiqui and Hagglöf, "An exploration of prenatal attachment in Swedish expectant women." *Journal of Reproductive and Infant Psychology.*]

37. Littman et al., "The decision to breastfeed."

38. Feinberg et al., "Effects of family foundations on parents and children."

39. Hendrix and Hunt, *Giving the Love That Heals*, xviii–xx.

40. American Academy of Pediatrics Task Force on Circumcision, "Circumcision policy statement."

41. Gottman and Gottman, *And Baby Makes Three*, 5–6.

Chapter Three:
PRINCIPLE 2: Feed with Love and Respect

1. Montagu, *Touching*, 70–74.

2. Brazelton and Cramer, *Earliest Relationship*, 55.

3. Mondloch et al., "Face perception during early infancy."

4. Uvnäs-Moberg and Eriksson, "Breastfeeding."

5. Lerman, "Epidemiology of acute diarrheal diseases in children"; Ford et al., "Breastfeeding and the risk of sudden infant death syndrome."

6. Dick, "The etiology of multiple sclerosis."

7. Alho, et al., "Risk factors for recurrent acute otitis media"; Davis, "Infant feeding and childhood cancer."

8. Young et al., "Type 2 diabetes mellitus in children."

9. Schwartzbaum et al., "An exploratory study of environmental and medical factors."

10. Lucas et al., "Breast milk and subsequent intelligence quotient in children born preterm."

11. Newcomb et al., "Lactation and a reduced risk of premenopausal breast cancer"; Freudenheim et al., "Exposure to breast milk in infancy and the risk of breast cancer."

12. Mezzacappa and Katkin, "Breastfeeding is associated with reduced perceived stress."

13. Montagu, *Touching*, 75.

14. Uvnäs-Moberg, "Short-term and long-term effects of oxytocin."

15. Ibid.

16. Newcomb et al., "Lactation and a reduced risk of premenopausal breast cancer."

17. Kendall-Tackett et al., "Depression, sleep quality, and maternal well-being."

18. Kendall-Tackett, *Depression in New Mothers*, 51.

19. Wiessinger et al., *The Womanly Art of Breastfeeding*, 358.

20. Artz, "Adopting a high-risk child."

21. Arora et al., "Major factors influencing breastfeeding rates."

22. McCann et al., "Food additives and hyperactive behavior."

23. World Health Organization, "Breastfeeding."

24. Neufeld and Maté, *Hold On to Your Kids*, 207.

Chapter Four:
PRINCIPLE 3: Responding with Sensitivity

1. Hendrix and Hunt, *Giving The Love that Heals*, 201.

2. De Wolff and van Ijzendoorn, "Sensitivity and attachment."

3. Isabella and Belsky, "Interactional synchrony and the origins of infant-mother attachment."

4. Zhou et al., "The relations of parental warmth."

5. Hendrix and Hunt, *Giving the Love That Heals*, 202.

6. Isabella and Belsky, "Interactional synchrony and the origins of infant-mother attachment."

7. Kendall-Tackett, *The Hidden Feelings of Motherhood*, 25.

8. Lester et al., "Developmental outcome as a function of the goodness of fit."

9. Ibid.

10. Concept originated by Isabelle Fox, PhD.

11. Schore, "The experience-dependent maturation of a regulatory system."

12. Gerhardt, *Why Love Matters*, 24–25.

13. Graham et al., "The effects of neonatal stress on brain development."

14. Field, "The effects of mothers' physical and emotional unavailability on emotion regulation."

15. Hariri et al., "Modulating emotional responses."

16. Sunderland, *The Science of Parenting*, 37.

17. Albers et al., "Maternal behavior predicts infant cortisol recovery."

18. Gerhardt, *Why Love Matters*, 78.

19. Hendrix and Hunt, *Giving the Love That Heals*, 201.

20. Zahn-Waxler et al., "Child rearing and children's prosocial initiations."

21. Gerhardt, *Why Love Matters*, 25.

22. Zhou et al., "The relations of parental warmth."

23. Sears, "Bonding with your newborn."

24. National Fatherhood Initiative, "Family structure, father closeness, and drug abuse."

25. Pollack, *Real Boys*, 83.

26. National Fatherhood Initiative, "Family structure, father closeness, and drug abuse."

27. Newberger, *The Men They Will Become*, 42.

CHAPTER FIVE: Principle 4: Use Nurturing Touch

1. Montagu, *Touching*, 97–99.

2. Ibid.

3. Perry and Szalavitz, *The Boy Who Was Raised as a Dog*, 235.

4. Montagu, *Touching*, 73.

5. Caplan, *To Touch Is to Live*, 54.

6. Heller, *The Vital Touch*, 119–20.

7. Ibid., 37.

8. Schanberg and Field, "Sensory deprivation stress and supplemental stimulation"; Gray et al., "Skin-to-skin contact is analgesic in healthy newborns"; St. James-Roberts et al., "Supplementary carrying compared with advice."

9. Gray et al., "Skin-to-skin contact is analgesic in healthy newborns."

10. Heller, *The Vital Touch*, 71.

11. Ruiz-Peláez et al., "Kangaroo mother care."

12. Ibid.

13. Schanberg and Field, "Sensory deprivation stress and supplemental stimulation."

14. Rey and Martinez, "Manejo racional del niño prematuro."

15. Conde-Agudelo et al., "Kangaroo mother care to reduce morbidity."

16. Saunder, "Co-bathing as a gentle solution for attachment difficulties."

17. Gordon and Adderly, *Brighter Baby*, 11.

18. McClure, *Infant Massage*, 13.

19. Mahal, "Massaging baby induces bonding."

20. Anisfeld et al., "Does infant carrying promote attachment?"

21. Heller, *The Vital Touch*, 199.

22. Littlefield, "Car seats, infant carriers, and swings."

23. Silver, "Slings and attachment parenting."

24. Hunziker and Barr, "Increased carrying reduces infant crying."

25. Heller, *The Vital Touch*, 199.

26. Caplan, *To Touch Is to Live*, 18–19.

Chapter Six:
PRINCIPLE 5: Ensure Safe Sleep, Physically and Emotionally

1. Sears and Sears, *Nighttime Parenting*, 16.

2. McKenna, *Sleeping with Your Baby*, 48–49.

3. Mosko et al., "Parent-infant cosleeping"; Mosko et al., "Infant arousals during mother-infant bed sharing."

4. Forbes et al., "The cosleeping habits of military children."

5. Witman-Flann, "Parent-child cosleeping."

6. Parker, "The greatest gifts we can give our children."

7. McKenna et al., "Infant-parent cosleeping in an evolutionary perspective."

8. McKenna, *Sleeping with Your Baby*, 48–49.

9. Barone, "Sleeping like a baby."

10. Ibid.

11. Yeh et al., "Injuries associated with cribs, playpens, and bassinets."

12. Fleming, "Where should babies sleep at night?"

13. Kimmel, "How the stats really stack up."

14. Fleming, "Where should babies sleep at night?"

15. McKenna, "An exclusive *Mothering* special report."

16. Fleming, "Where should babies sleep at night?"

17. Bleabey and Gessner, "Infant bed-sharing practices and associated risk factors."

18. Kendall-Tackett et al., "Mother-infant sleep locations and nighttime feeding behavior."

19. McKenna et al., "Infant-parent cosleeping in an evolutionary perspective."

20. McDonald, "Lullabies help children's language development."

21. McKenna, *Sleeping with Your Baby*, 52.

22. Sears and Sears, *The Attachment Parenting Book*, 90.

23. J. Gordon, "Changing the sleep pattern in the family bed."

24. Fleiss, "Pillow talk."

25. Sunderland, *The Science of Parenting*, 79.

26. Ibid., 80.

27. Narvaez et al., *Evolution, Early Experience and Human Development*, 459–60.

28. Parker, "The greatest gifts we can give our children."

29. American Academy of Pediatrics Task Force on Sudden Infant Death Syndrome, "SIDS and other sleep-related deaths."

30. Middlemiss et al., "Asynchrony of mother-infant hypothalamic-pituitary-adrenal axis activity."

Chapter Seven:
PRINCIPLE 6: Provide Consistent, Loving Care

1. U.S. Department of Labor, Bureau of Labor Statistics, Employment Characteristics of Families Summary.

2. Greenspan, *The Four-Thirds Solution*, 89–90.

3. Pert, *Molecules of Emotion*, 269.

4. Siegel, *The Developing Mind*, 32.

5. Belsky and Rovine, "Non-maternal care in the first year of life."

6. Sagi et al., "Shedding further light on the effects of various types and quality of early childcare."

7. Greenspan, *The Four-Thirds Solution*, 43.

8. Ibid., 5–6

9. Ibid.

10. Associated Press, "Study: Child aggression linked to hours in day care."

11. Magid and McKelvey, *High Risk*, 17.

12. Armour, "Day care's new frontier."

13. Phillips, Testimony before the U.S. Senate Committee.

14. Greenspan, *The Four-Thirds Solution*, 27–29 and 36–37.

15. Belsky and Rovine, "Non-maternal care in the first year of life."

16. Wallerstein et al., *The Unexpected Legacy of Divorce*, 216–17.

17. Amato and Rezac, "Contact with non-residential parents"; Emery, "Interparental conflict and the children of divorce and discord"; Hess and Camera, "Post-divorce family relationships"; Johnston et al., "Ongoing postdivorce conflict."

Chapter Eight:
PRINCIPLE 7: Practice Positive Discipline

1. Hendrix and Hunt, *Giving the Love That Heals*, 38.

2. Perry, "Childhood experience and the expression of genetic potential."

3. Neufeld and Maté, *Hold On to Your Kids*, 70.

4. Sunderland, *The Science of Parenting*, 133.

5. Bavolek and Keene, *Adult-Adolescent Parenting Inventory AAPI-2*, 6.

6. Patterson et al., "A developmental perspective in antisocial behavior."

7. Neufeld and Maté, *Hold On to Your Kids*, 71.

8. Straus, *Beating the Devil Out of Them*, 165.

9. Weiss et al., "Some consequences of early harsh discipline."

10. Thomas, "Aggressive behaviour outcomes for young children."

11. Patterson et al., "A developmental perspective in antisocial behavior"; Straus, *Beating the Devil Out of Them*, 165.

12. Gershoff, "Corporal punishment by parents."

13. American Academy of Pediatrics, "Guidance for effective discipline."

14. Straus, *Beating the Devil Out of Them*, 10.

15. Straus and Mouradian, "Impulsive corporal punishment by mothers."

16. Straus et al., "Spanking by parents."

17. Weiss et al., "Some consequences of early harsh discipline."

18. Straus, *Beating the Devil Out of Them*, 165.

19. American Academy of Pediatrics, "Guidance for effective discipline."

20. Hyland et al., "Beating and insulting children as a risk."

21. Sears and Sears, "Discipline and behavior."

22. Greven, *Spare the Child*, 48.

23. Zahn-Waxler et al., "Child rearing and children's prosocial initiations."

24. Kohn, *Unconditional Parenting*, 32.

25. Neufeld and Maté, *Hold On to Your Kids*, 72.

26. Center for Nonviolent Communication, "Nonviolent communication is . . ."

27. Ibid.

28. Eisenberg et al., "Prosocial development in childhood."

29. Eisenberg-Berg and Mussen, "Empathy and moral development in adolescence."

30. Baumrind, "Parental disciplinary patterns and social competence in children"; Maccoby and Martin, "Socialization in the context of the family."

31. Coombs and Landsverk, "Parenting styles and substance use."

32. Dornbusch et al., "The relation of parenting style to adolescent school performance"; Steinberg, Elman, et al., "Impact of parenting practices."

33. Steinberg, Elman, et al., "Impact of parenting practices."

34. Jackson et al., "Authoritative parenting, child competencies, and initiation of cigarette smoking."

35. Baumrind, "The influence of parenting style on adolescent competence and substance use"; Jackson and Foshee, "Violence-related behaviors of adolescents."

36. Baumrind, "Parental disciplinary patterns and social competence in children."

37. Neufeld and Maté, *Hold On to Your Kids*, 72.

38. Coloroso, *Kids Are Worth It*, 29.

39. Kohn, *Unconditional Parenting*, 1.

40. Coloroso, *Kids Are Worth It*, 29.

41. Lindgren, "Never Violence."

Chapter Nine:
PRINCIPLE 8: Strive for Balance in Your Personal and Family Life

1. Sidebotham and ALSPAC, "Culture, stress, and the parent-child relationship."

2. Goldstein et al., "Maternal characteristics and social support."

3. Sidebotham and ALSPAC, "Culture, stress, and the parent-child relationship."

4. Belsky, "The determinants of parenting"; Cox et al., "The transition to parenthood."

5. Belsky, *The Transition to Parenthood*, 12.

6. Ibid., 32.

7. Gottman Institute, "Bringing baby home."

8. Gottman and Gottman, *And Baby Makes Three*, 8.

9. Bringing Baby Home, "Research evaluation of the Bringing Baby Home program."

10. Belsky, "The determinants of parenting"; Cox et al., "The transition to parenthood."

11. Gottman and DeClaire, *Raising an Emotionally Intelligent Child*, 148–54.

12. Ibid., 139.

13. Wallerstein et al., *The Unexpected Legacy of Divorce*, 217.

14. Cox et al., "The transition to parenthood."

15. Belsky, "The determinants of parenting."

16. Lockard, "Back to the future."

17. Belsky, "The determinants of parenting."

18. Tarkka, "Predictors of maternal competence"; Sidebotham and ALSPAC, "Culture, stress, and the parent-child relationship."

19. Hanessian, "Chaos theory."

20. Kendall-Tackett, "Practical steps toward achieving more balance in your life."

21. Gordon, "The mommy marathon."

22. Sunderland, *The Science of Parenting*, 268.

23. Ibid., 260.

24. Sears and Sears, *The Attachment Parenting Book*, 118.

Chapter Ten:
Nurturing Children for a Compassionate World

1. Dalai Lama, "quotes."

2. Belsky et al., "Intergenerational transmission of warm-sensitive-stimulating parenting."

3. Grille, "Democracy begins at home."

4. Montagu, *Touching*, 88–89.

5. Pantley, *Gentle Baby Care*, 514–19.

6. National Institute on Media and the Family, "Families become MediaWise."

7. Ibid.

8. CSPCC, "Consumerism."

9. CCFC, "Baby Scam: Marketing to Infants & Toddlers."

References

Abramowicz, Jacques S. "Fetal thermal effects of diagnostic ultrasound." *Journal of Ultrasound Medicine* 27 (4) (2008): 541–59.

———. "Ultrasound and autism: Association, link, or coincidence?" *Journal of Ultrasound Medicine* 31 (2012): 1261–69.

Ainsworth, Mary D. Salter, and Silvia Bell, eds. "Some contemporary patterns of mother-infant attachment interaction in the feeding situation." In *Stimulation in Early Infancy*. London: Academic Press, 1969.

———, Mary C. Blehar, Everett Waters, and Sally Wall. *Patterns of Attachment: A Psychological Study of the Strange Situation*. New York: Lawrence Erlbaum Associates, 1978.

Albers, Esther M., J. Marianne Riksen-Walsrven, Fred C. Sweep, and Carolina de Weerth. "Maternal behavior predicts infant cortisol recovery from a mild everyday stressor." *Journal of Child Psychology and Psychiatry* 49 (1) (2008): 97–103.

Alho, Olli-Pekka, M. Koivu, M. Sorri, and P. Rantakallio. "Risk factors for recurrent acute otitis media and respiratory infection in infancy." *International Journal of Pediatric Otorhinolaryngology* 19 (1990): 151–61.

Amato, Paul R., and Sandra J. Rezac. "Contact with non-residential parents, interparental conflict, and children's behavior." *Journal of Family Issues* 15 (2) (1994): 191–207.

American Academy of Pediatrics. "Guidance for effective discipline." *Pediatrics* 101 (1998): 723–28.

American Academy of Pediatrics Task Force on Circumcision. "Circumcision policy statement." *Pediatrics* 103 (3) (1999): 686–93.

American Academy of Pediatrics Task Force on Sudden Infant Death Syndrome. "The changing concept of sudden infant death syndrome: Diagnostic coding shifts, controversies regarding the sleeping environment, and new variables to consider in reducing risk." *Pediatrics* 116 (2005): 1245–55.

American Academy of Pediatrics Task Force on Sudden Infant Death Syndrome. "SIDS and other sleep-related deaths: Expansion of recommendations for a safe infant sleeping environment." *Pediatrics* 128 (2011): 1030–39.

Anisfeld, Elizabeth, Virginia Casper, Molly Nozyce, and Nicholas Cunningham. "Does infant carrying promote attachment? An experimental study of the effects of increased physical contact on the development of attachment." *Child Development* 61 (5) (1990): 1617–27.

Armour, Stephanie. "Day care's new frontier: Your baby at your desk." *USA Today*, 2008. http://usatoday30.usatoday.com/money/workplace/2008-03-30-babies-at-work_N.htm.

Arms, Suzanne. *Immaculate Deception*. Berkeley, CA: Celestial Arts, 1996.

Arora, S., C. McJunkin, J. Wehrer, and P. Kuhn. "Major factors influencing breastfeeding rates: Mother's perception of father's attitude and milk supply." *Pediatrics* 106 (2000): E67.

Artz, Julie. "Adopting a high-risk child." *Attachment Parenting* 10 (5) (2007–8): 3.

Associated Press. 2001. "Study: Child aggression linked to hours in day care." www.themodernreligion.com/family/family-daycare.html.

Atlanta Journal Constitution. 2013. "Georgia to end Medicaid payments for some early births." www.ajc.com/ap/ap/georgia/ga-to-end-medicaid-payments-for-some-early-births/nW3T4/.

Ball, Helen, Sally Inch, and Marion Copeland. *The Benefits of Bedsharing*. DVD. Platypus Media, 2005. www.platypusmedia.com.

Barone, Miranda. "The influence of parenting style on adolescent competence and substance use." *Journal of Early Adolescence* 11 (1) (1991): 56–95.

———. "Mother-infant sleep behaviors in solitary and bedsharing conditions." (PhD Thesis. Claremont Graduate University, Claremont, CA, 2001).

———. "Sleeping like a baby: How bedsharing soothes infants." *Mothering* 114 (2002): 70–75.

Barker, Elliot. *The Critical Importance of Mothering*. Chicago: La Leche League International, 1989.

Baumrind, Diana. "Parental disciplinary patterns and social competence in children." *Youth and Society* 9 (1978): 239–76.

Bavolek, Stephen J., and R. G. Keene. *Adult-Adolescent Parenting Inventory AAPI-2: Administration and Development Handbook*. Asheville, NC: Family Development, 2001.

Begley, Sharon. "The nature of nurturing." *Newsweek*, March 27, 2000.

Beilin, Y., C. A. Bodian, J. Weiser, S. Hossain, I. Arnold, D. E. Feierman, G. Martin, and I. Holzman. "Effect of labor epidural analgesia with and without fentanyl on infant breast-feeding: A prospective, randomized, double-blind study." *Anesthesiology* 103 (6) (2005): 1211–17.

Belsky, Jay. "The determinants of parenting: A process model." *Child Development* 55 (1984): 83–96.

———. *The Transition to Parenthood*. New York: Dell Books, 1994.

————. "Quantity of nonmaternal care and boys' problem behavior/adjustment at ages 3 and 5: Exploring the mediating role of parenting." *Psychiatry: Interpersonal and Biological Processes* 62 (1999): 1–3.

Belsky, Jay and Michael J. Rovine. "Non-maternal care in the first year of life and the security of infant attachment." *Child Development* 59 (1) (1988): 157–67.

Belsky, Jay, Michael J. Rovine. Judith Sligo, Sara R. Jaffee, Lianne Woodward, and Phil A. Silva. "Intergenerational transmission of warm-sensitive-stimulating parenting: A prospective study of mothers and fathers of 3-year-olds." *Child Development* 76 (2) (2005): 384–96.

Blair, Peter S., Peter J. Fleming, Ian J. Smith, Martin W. Platt, Jeanine Young, Pam Nadin, P. J. Berry, and Jean Golding. "Babies sleeping with parents: Case-control study of factors influencing the risk of the sudden infant death syndrome." *British Medical Journal* 319 (7223) (1999): 1457–62.

Bleabey, Margaret H., and B. D. Gessner. "Infant bed-sharing practices and associated risk factors among births and infant deaths in Alaska." *Public Health Representative* 124 (4) (2009): 527–34.

Bond, James T., Ellen Galinsky, and E. Jeffrey Hill. *When Work Works: A Summary of Families and Work Institute Research Findings.* New York: Families and Work Institute, 2004. http://familiesandwork.org/3w/research/downloads/3wes.pdf.

Brazelton, T. Berry, and Bertrand G. Cramer. *Earliest Relationship: Parents, Infants, and the Drama of Early Attachment.* Reading, MA: Addison-Wesley, 1990.

Brazelton, T. Berry, and Stanley I. Greenspan. *The Irreducible Needs of Children.* Cambridge, MA: Perseus, 2000.

Bretherton, Inge. "The origins of attachment theory: John Bowlby and Mary Ainsworth." *Developmental Psychology* 28 (5) (1992): 759–75.

Bringing Baby Home. "Research evaluation of the Bringing Baby Home program." 2009. www.bbhonline.org/parenting-research/parenting-research.aspx.

California Medical Association. Panel discussion, section on Obstetrics and Gynecology, 78th Annual Session of the California Medical Association, Los Angeles, CA, May 8–11, 1949.

Canadian Society for the Prevention of Cruelty to Children (CSPCC). "Consumerism—the world's fastest growing religion: Corporations vs. parents." 1999. http://consumerism.ca/.

Caplan, Mariana. *To Touch Is to Live.* Prescott, AZ: Hohm Press, 2002.

Carter, C. Sue, and Stephen W. Porges. "Neurobiology and the evolution of mammalian social behavior." In *Evolution, Early Experience and Human Development*, edited by Darcia

Narvaez, Jaak Panksepp, Allan N. Schore, and Tracy R. Gleason. New York: Oxford Press, 2013.

Center for Nonviolent Communication. "Nonviolent communication is …" www.NonviolentCommunication.com.

Childhelp. "National child abuse statistics." 2005. www.childhelp.org/pages/statistics.

———. "Child abuse in America." 2013. www.childhelp.org/pages/statistics.

Child Welfare Information Gateway. "Promoting healthy families in your community." 2008a. www.childwelfare.gov/pubs/res_packet_2008/.

———. "Protective factors for promoting healthy families." 2008b. www.childwelfare.gov/.

———. "Child abuse and neglect fatalities: Statistics and interventions." 2010. www.childwelfare.gov/pubs/factsheets/fatality.cfm.

Children's Defense Fund. *America's Cradle to Prison Pipeline Report*. 2007. www.childrensdefense.org/child-research-data-publications/data/cradle-prison-pipeline -report-2007-full-highres.html.

Chopra, Deepak, David Simon, and Vicki Abrams. *Magical Beginnings, Enchanted Lives*. New York: Three Rivers Press, 2005.

Cleeton, Elaine R. "Attitudes and beliefs about childbirth among college students: Results of an educational intervention." *Birth: Issues in Perinatal Care* 28 (3) (2001): 192–201.

Coalition for Improving Maternity Services. "Ten steps of the mother-friendly childbirth initiative for mother-friendly hospitals, birth centers, and home birth services," 2007, www.birthnetwork.org/Resources/Documents/MFCI.pdf.

Coloroso, Barbara. *Kids Are Worth It! Giving Your Child the Gift of Inner Discipline*. New York: HarperCollins, 2002.

Commission on Children at Risk. *Hardwired to Connect: The New Scientific Case for Authoritative Communities*. New York, NY: Institute for American Values, 2003. www.americanvalues.org/ExSumm-print.pdf.

Conde-Agudelo, A., J. Diaz-Rossello, and J. Belizan. "Kangaroo mother care to reduce morbidity and mortality in low birthweight infants." *Cochrane Database of Systematic Reviews* 2 (2003), CD002771.

Coombs, R. H., and J. Landsverk. "Parenting styles and substance use during childhood and adolescence." *Journal of Marriage and the Family* 50 (2) (1988): 473–82.

Time. "The Cornelians." 1946. www.time.com/time/magazine/article/0,9171,855434,00.html.

Cox, M. J., B. Paley, C. C. Payne, and M. Burchinal. "The transition to parenthood: Marital conflict and withdrawal and parent-infant interactions." In *Conflict and Cohesion in*

Families: Causes and Consequences, edited by M. J. Cox and J. Brooks-Gunn. Mahwah, NJ: Lawrence Erlbaum, 1999.

Cummings, E. M., and A. Wilson. "Contexts of marital conflict and children's emotional security: Exploring the distinction between constructive and destructive conflict from the children's perspective." In *Conflict and Cohesion in Families: Causes and Consequences*, edited by M. J. Cox and J. Brooks-Gunn, 87–104. Mahwah, NJ: Lawrence Erlbaum, 1999.

Dalai Lama. "Quotes by His Holiness the Dalai lama," www.rudyh.org/dalai-lama-quotes-quotations.htm.

DaSilva, N. In press. "The AP Father." *Attachment Parenting: The Journal of API.*

Davis, M. K. "Infant feeding and childhood cancer." *Lancet* 13, 2 (8607) (1988): 365–68.

DeCasper, A. J., and W. P. Fifer. "Of human bonding: Newborns prefer their mother's voices." *Science* 208 (1980): 1174–76.

Declercq, E. R., C. Sakala, M. P. Corry, and S. Applebaum. "Executive summary." In *Listening to Mothers II: Report of the Second National Survey of Women's Childbearing Experiences*. New York: Childbirth Connection, 2006.

De Wolff, Marianne S., and Marinus H. van Ijzendoorn. "Sensitivity and attachment: A meta-analysis on parental antecedents of attachment." *Child Development* 68 (4) (1997): 571–91.

Dick, G. "The etiology of multiple sclerosis." *Proceedings of the Royal Society of Medicine* 69 (1976): 611–15.

Dornbusch, Sanford M., Philip L. Ritter, P. Herbert Leiderman, Donald F. Roberts, and Michael J. Fraleigh. "The relation of parenting style to adolescent school performance." *Child Development* 58 (5) (1987): 1244–57.

Dunham, Carroll. *Mamatoto*. New York, NY: Penguin Books, 1991.

Eisenberg, Nancy, R. Lennon, and K. Roth. "Prosocial development in childhood: A longitudinal study." *Developmental Psychology* 9 (6) (1983): 846–55.

Eisenberg-Berg, Nancy, and Paul Mussen. "Empathy and moral development in adolescence." *Developmental Psychology* 14 (2) (1978): 185–86.

Else-Quest, Nichole M., Janet Shibley Hyde, and Roseanne Clark. "Breastfeeding, bonding, and the mother-infant relationship." *Merrill-Palmer Quarterly* 49 (4) (2003): 495–517.

Emery, Robert E. "Interparental conflict and the children of divorce and discord." *Psychological Bulletin* 92 (2) (1982): 310–30.

Enkin, Murray, Marc Keirse, and I. Chalmers. *A Guide to Effective Care in Pregnancy and Childbirth*. New York: Oxford University Press, 1992.

Feinberg, Mark E., Damon E. Jones, Marni L. Kan, and Megan C. Goslin. "Effects of family foundations on parents and children: 3.5 years after baseline." *Journal of Family Psychology* 24 (5) (2010): 532–42.

Feldman, Ruth, Aron Weller, Arthur I. Eidelman, and Lea Sirota. "Comparison of skin-to-skin (kangaroo) and traditional care: Parenting outcomes and preterm infant development." *Pediatrics* 110 (1) (2002): 16–26.

Field, Tiffany M. "Infant massage." *Zero to Three* 14, 1993: 2.

———. "The effects of mothers' physical and emotional unavailability on emotion regulation." *Monographs of the Society for Research in Child Development* 59 (2–3) (1994): 208–27.

Fleiss, Paul. "Pillow talk: Helping your child get a good night's sleep." *Mothering* 96, 1999. Mother-2-Mother, www.mother-2-mother.com/pillowtalk.

Fleming, Peter. "Where should babies sleep at night?" *Mothering* 114: 68–69, 2002.

Fonagy, Peter, Howard Steele, and Miriam Steele. "Maternal representations of attachment during pregnancy predict the organization of infant-mother attachment at one year of age." *Child Development* 62 (5) (1991): 891–905.

Forbes, J. F., D. S. Weiss, and R. A. Folen. "The cosleeping habits of military children." *Military Medicine* 157 (1992): 196–200.

Ford, R. P., B. J. Taylor, E. A. Mitchell, S. A. Enright, A. W. Stewart, D. M. Becroft, R. Scragg, I. B. Hassall, D. M. Barry, and E. M. Allen. "Breastfeeding and the risk of sudden infant death syndrome." *International Journal of Epidemiology* 22 (1993): 885–90.

Fraiberg, Selma. *In Defense of Mothering: Every Child's Birthright.* New York: Basic Books, 1997.

Freud, Sigmund. *The Schreber Case.* New York: Penguin Books, 2003.

Freudenheim, Jo L., James R. Marshall, Saxon Graham, Rosemary Laughlin, John E. Vena, Elisa Bandera, Paola Muti, Mya Swanson, and Takuma Nemoto. "Exposure to breast milk in infancy and the risk of breast cancer." *Epidemiology* 5 (1994): 324–31.

Frontline, "Medicating Kids." on PBS, April 10, 2001.

Gaskin, Ina May. "Understanding birth and sphincter law." www.inamay.com/article/understanding-birth-and-sphincter-law.

Gerhardt, Sue. *Why Love Matters: How Affection Shapes a Baby's Brain.* New York: Brunner-Routledge, 2004.

Gershoff, Elizabeth T. "Corporal punishment by parents and associated child behaviors and experiences: A meta-analytic and theoretical review." *Psychological Bulletin* 128 (4) (2002): 539–79.

Goldstein, Lauren H., Marissa L. Diener, and Sarah C. Mangelsdorf. "Maternal characteristics and social support across the transition to motherhood: Association with maternal behavior." *Journal of Family Psychology* 10 (1) (1996): 60–72.

Gordon, Jay. "Changing the sleep pattern in the family bed." 2010. http://drjaygordon.com/attachment/sleeppattern.html.

Gordon, Jay and Brenda Adderly. *Brighter Baby: Boost Your Child's Intelligence, Health, and Happiness Through Infant Therapeutic Massage, the Mozart Effect, and More.* Washington, DC: Lifeline Press, 1999.

Gordon, Jay and Brenda Adderly, with Diane Reverand. *Preventing Autism: What You Can Do to Protect Your Children Before and After Birth.* Hoboken, NJ: John Wiley & Sons, 2013.

———. "The mommy marathon." *API News* 3 (2) (2000): 8–9.

Gordon, Macall. "Breaking the ties that bind." *API News* 4 (2001): 1.

Gottman, John M. *The Heart of Parenting.* New York: Simon and Schuster, 1997.

Gottman, John M., and Joan DeClaire. *Raising an Emotionally Intelligent Child.* New York: Simon and Schuster, 1997.

Gottman, John M., and Julie Schwartz Gottman. *And Baby Makes Three: The Six-Step Plan for Preserving Marital Intimacy and Rekindling Romance After Baby Arrives.* New York: Crown, 2007.

Gottman Institute. "Bringing baby home." www.gottman.com/51165/Bringing-Baby-Home.html.

Graham, Yolanda P., Christine Heim, Sherryl H. Goodman, Andrew H. Miller, and Charles B. Nemeroff. "The effects of neonatal stress on brain development: Implications for psychopathology." *Development and Psychopathology* 11 (3) (1999): 545–65.

Gray, L., L. Watt, and E. M. Blass. "Skin-to-skin contact is analgesic in healthy newborns." *Pediatrics* 105 (2000): e14.

Greenspan, Stanley I. *The Four-Thirds Solution: Solving the Child-Care Crisis in America Today.* Cambridge, MA: Perseus, 2001.

Greven, Phillip. *Spare the Child: The Religious Roots of Punishment and the Psychological Impact of Physical Abuse.* New York: Vintage Books, 1992.

Grille, Robin. "Democracy begins at home." *Empathic Parenting: Journal of the Canadian Society for the Prevention of Cruelty to Children* 26 (1) (2003): 11.

Hanessian, Lu. "Chaos theory." *Attachment Parenting:* 10 (1) (2007): 10–11.

Hariri, Ahmad R., Susan Y. Bookheimer, and John C. Mazziotta. "Modulating emotional responses: Effects of a neocortical network on the limbic system." *NeuroReport* 11 (1) (2000): 43–48.

Hartley, Mariette. *Breaking the Silence.* New York: Signet Books, 1990.

Hartney, Christopher. "US rates of incarceration: A global perspective." National Council on Crime and Delinquency, 2006. www.nccdglobal.org/sites/default/.../factsheet-us-incarceration.pdf.

Heller, Sharon. *The Vital Touch*. New York: Henry Holt, 1997.

Hendrix, Harville, and Helen Hunt. *Giving the Love That Heals: A Guide for Parents*. New York: Pocket Books, 1997.

Hess, R., and K. Camera. "Post-divorce family relationships as mediating factors in the consequences of divorce for children." *Journal of Social Issues* 35 (1979): 79–96.

Hodnett, E. D., S. Downe, and D. Walsh. "Alternative versus conventional institutional settings for birth." *Cochrane Database of Systematic Reviews* 10 (2012) 8, CD000012.

———, S. Gates, G. J. Hofmeyr, and C. Sakala. "Continuous support for women during childbirth." *Cochrane Database of Systematic Reviews* 10 (2012) CD003766.

Hunziker, Urs A., and Ronald G. Barr. "Increased carrying reduces infant crying: A randomized controlled trial." *Pediatrics* 77 (1986): 641–48.

Hyland, Michael E., Ahmed M. Alkhalaf, and Ben Whalley. "Beating and insulting children as a risk for adult cancer, cardiac disease and asthma." *Journal of Behavioral Medicine*, September, 2012.

Infant Massage USA n.d. "Frequently asked questions." http://babybuntings.massagetherapy.com/infant-massage-usa.

Isabella, Russell A., and Jay Belsky. "Interactional synchrony and the origins of infant-mother attachment: A replication study." *Child Development* 62 (2) (1991): 373–85.

Jackson, Christine, Donna J. Bee-Gates, and Lisa Henriksen. "Authoritative parenting, child competencies, and initiation of cigarette smoking." *Health Education Quarterly* 21 (1) (1994): 103–16.

———, and Vangie A. Foshee. "Violence-related behaviors of adolescents: Relations with responsive and demanding parenting." *Journal of Adolescent Research* 13 (3) (1988): 343–59.

Johnston, Janet R., M. Kline, and J. M. Tschann. "Ongoing postdivorce conflict: Effects on children of joint custody and frequent access." *American Journal of Orthopsychiatry* 59 (1989): 576–92.

Karen, Robert. *Becoming Attached*. New York: Warner Books, 1994.

Karp, Harvey. *The Happiest Baby on the Block: The New Way to Calm Crying and Help Your Newborn Baby Sleep Longer*. New York: Bantam Books, 2003.

Karras, Kaylene. "The ideal birth for the 'Naturally Birthing Challenged.'" *Attachment Parenting* 8 (2) (2005): 7.

Karr-Morse, Robin, and Meredith S. Wiley. *Ghosts from the Nursery*. New York: Atlantic Monthly Press, 1997.

Kendall-Tackett, Kathleen. *The Hidden Feelings of Motherhood*. Oakland, CA: New Harbinger, 2001.

———. *Depression in New Mothers*. New York: Hawthorn Press, 2003.

———. "Practical steps toward achieving more balance in your life." *Attachment Parenting* 10 (1) (2007): 14–15.

Kendall-Tackett, Kathleen, Z. Cong, and T. W. Hale. "Mother-infant sleep locations and nighttime feeding behavior." *Clinical Lactation* 1 (2010): 27–31.

———. "Depression, sleep quality, and maternal well-being in postpartum women with a history of sexual assault: A comparison of breastfeeding, mixed-feeding, and formula-feeding mothers." *Breastfeeding Medicine* 8 (1) (2013): 16–22.

Kimmel, Tina. "How the stats really stack up: Cosleeping is twice as safe." *Mothering* 114 (2002): 52–57.

Klaus, Marshall, John Kennell, and Phyllis Klaus. *Mothering the Mother*. Cambridge, MA: Perseus Books, 1993.

Kohn, Alfie. *Unconditional Parenting: Moving from Rewards and Punishment to Love and Reason*. New York: Atria Books, 2005.

Leboyer, Frederick. *Birth Without Violence*. New York: Alfred A. Knopf, 1984.

Lerman, Y. "Epidemiology of acute diarrheal diseases in children in a high standard of living settlement in Israel." *Pediatric Infectious Diseases Journal* 13 (1994): 116–22.

Lester, Barry, C. F. Zachariah Boukydis, C. T. Garcia-Coll, M. Peucker, M. M. McGrath, B. R. Vohr, F. Brem, and W. Oh. "Developmental outcome as a function of the goodness of fit between the infant's cry characteristics and the mother's perception of her infant's cry." *Pediatrics* 95 (4) (1995): 516–22.

Lindgren, Astrid. "Never Violence." Alliance for Transforming the Lives of Children, 1978. www.atlc.org/Resources/never_violence.php.

Littlefield, Timothy R., Kevin M. Kelly, Jacque L. Reiff, and Jeanne K. Pomatto. "Car seats, infant carriers, and swings: Their role in deformational plagiocephaly." *Journal of Prosthetics and Orthotics* 15 (3) (2003): 102–106.

Littman, Heidi, Sharon VanderBrug Medendorp, and Johanna Goldfarb. "The decision to breastfeed." *Clinical Pediatrics* 33 (1994): 214–19.

Lockard, L. "Back to the future: How early attachments shape your relationships." *Attachment Parenting* 10 (3) (2007a): 22.

———. "Mothering maven Martha Sears on balance." *Attachment Parenting* 10 (1) (2007b): 1–3.

Lucas, A., R. Morley, T. J. Cole, G. Lister, and C. Leeson-Payne. "Breast milk and subsequent intelligence quotient in children born preterm." *Lancet* 339 (8788) (1992): 261–62.

Maccoby, E. E., and J. A. Martin. "Socialization in the context of the family: Parent-child interaction." In *Handbook of Child Psychology*, vol. 4, *Socialization, Personality, and Social Development*, edited by P. H. Mussen and E. M. Hetherington, 1–101. Hoboken, NJ: John Wiley & Sons, 1983.

Magid, Ken, and Carol McKelvey. *High Risk: Children Without a Conscience*. New York, NY: Bantam Books, 1987.

Mahal, Jennifer K. "Mass aging baby induces bonding." *San Diego Union-Tribune*, May 3, 2008.

McCann, Donna, Angelina Barrett, Alison Cooper, Debbie Crumpler, Lindy Dalen, Kate Grimshaw, Elizabeth Kitchin, Kris Lok, Lucy Porteous, Emily Prince, Edmund Sonuga-Barke, John O. Warner, and Jim Stevenson. "Food additives and hyperactive behaviour in 3-year-old and 8/9-year-old children in the community: A randomised, double-blinded, placebo-controlled trial." *Lancet* 370 (9598) (2007): 1560–67.

McClure, Vimala. *Infant Massage: A Handbook for Loving Parents*. New York: Bantam Books, 2000.

McDonald, Timothy. "Lullabies help children's language development: Study." ABC News, 2007. www.abc.net.au/news/2007-12-07/lullabies-help-childrens-language-development-study/980958.

McKenna, James. "Babies need their mothers beside them!" *World Health* 49 (1996): 14–16.

———. "An exclusive *Mothering* special report." *Mothering* 114 (2002): 8.

———. *Sleeping with Your Baby: A Parent's Guide to Cosleeping*, Washington, DC: Platypus Media, 2007.

McKenna, Jamie, E. B. Thoman, T. F. Anders, A. Sadeyh, V. L. Schechtman, and S. F. Glotzbach. "Infant-parent cosleeping in an evolutionary perspective: Implications for understanding infant sleep development and the sudden infant death syndrome." *American Sleep Disorders Association and Sleep Research Society* 16 (1993): 263–82.

McTaggart, Lynne. *The Bond: How to Fix Your Falling-Down World*. New York: Simon and Schuster, 2011.

Melender, Hanna-Leena. "Experiences of fears associated with pregnancy and childbirth: A study of 329 pregnant women." *Birth: Issues in Perinatal Care* 29 (2) (2002): 101–11.

Mezzacappa, Elizabeth S., and Edward S. Katkin. "Breastfeeding is associated with reduced perceived stress and negative mood in mothers." *Health Psychology* 21 (2) (2002): 187–91.

Middlemiss, Wendy, Douglas A. Granger, Wendy A. Goldberg, and Laura Nathans. "Asynchrony of mother-infant hypothalamic-pituitary-adrenal axis activity following extinction of infant crying responses induced during the transition to sleep." *Early Human Development* 88 (4) (2012): 227–32.

Midmer, D., L. Wilson, and S. Cummings. "A randomized controlled trial of the influence of prenatal parenting education on postpartum anxiety and marital adjustment." *Family Medicine* 27 (1995): 200–205.

Miller, Alice. *For Your Own Good: Hidden Cruelty in Child-Rearing and the Roots of Violence.* New York: Farrar, Straus, and Giroux, 1990.

Mondloch, Catherine J., T. L. Lewis, D. R. Budreau, D. Maurer, J. L. Dannemiller, B. R. Stephens, and K. A. Kleiner-Gathercoal. "Face perception during early infancy." *Psychological Science* 10 (5) (1999): 419–22.

Montagu, Ashley. *Learning Non-Aggression: The Experience of Non-Literate Societies.* London: Oxford University Press, 1978.

———. *Touching.* New York: Harper and Row, 1986.

Mosko, Sarah, James McKenna, M. Dickel, and L. Hunt. "Parent-infant cosleeping: The appropriate context for the study of infant sleep and implications for sudden infant death syndrome (SIDS) research." *Journal of Behavioral Medicine* 16 (6) (1993): 589–607.

———, Christopher Richard, and James McKenna. "Infant arousals during mother-infant bed sharing: Implications for infant sleep and sudden infant death syndrome research." *Pediatrics* 100 (5) (1997): 841–50.

Nachmias, Melissa, Megan Gunnar, R. Hornik-Parritz, K. Buss, and S. Mangelsdorf. "Behavioral inhibition and stress reactivity: The moderating role of attachment security." *Child Development* 67 (2) (1996): 508–22.

Narvaez, Darcia, Jaak Panksepp, Allan Schore, and Tracy Gleason, eds. *Evolution, Early Experience and Human Development: From Research to Practice.* New York: Oxford. University Press, 2013.

National Fatherhood Initiative. "Family structure, father closeness, and drug abuse." www.docstoc.com/docs/26786066/Family-Structure_-Father-Closeness_-and-Drug-Abuse.

National Institute of Child Health and Human Development. "Does amount of time in child care predict socioemotional adjustment?" *Child Development* 74 (2003): 976–1005.

National Institute on Media and the Family. "Fact sheet: Children and advertising." www.parentfurther.com/technology-media/facts/facts_childadv.shtml.

———. "Families become MediaWise." www.search-institute.org/hc-hy/become-mediawise-national-institute-media-and-family.

Neufeld, Gordon, and Gabor Maté. *Hold On to Your Kids: Why Parents Need to Matter More Than Peers.* New York: Ballantine Books, 2006.

Newberger, Eli. *The Men They Will Become: The Nature and Nurture of Male Character.* Cambridge, MA: Perseus Books, 1999.

Newcomb, Polly A., Barry E. Storer, Matthew P. Longnecker, Robert Mittendorf, E. Robert Greenberg, Richard W. Clapp, Kenneth P. Burke, Walter C. Willett, and Brian MacMahon. "Lactation and a reduced risk of premenopausal breast cancer." *New England Journal of Medicine* 330 (2) (1994): 81–87.

Northrup, Christiane, MD. *Mother-Daughter Wisdom: Understanding the Crucial Link Between Mothers, Daughters, and Health.* New York: Bantam, 2006.

———. *Women's Bodies, Women's Wisdom: Creating Physical and Emotional Health and Healing.* Rev. ed. New York: Bantam, 2010.

———. *The Wisdom of Menopause: Creating Physical and Emotional Health During the Change.* Rev. ed. New York: Bantam, 2012.

O'Mara, Peggy. *Having a Baby Naturally.* New York: Atria Books, 2003.

Palmer, Linda F. "The chemistry of attachment." *Attachment Parenting* 9 (2004).

Pantley, Elizabeth. *Gentle Baby Care.* New York: McGraw-Hill, 2003.

Parker, Lysa. "The greatest gifts we can give our children: An interview with Dr. Jim McKenna." *Attachment Parenting* 8 (1) (2005): 1–5.

———. "Happy being blue." *Attachment Parenting* 9 (1) (2006): 1–3.

Patterson, G. R., Barbara D. DeBaryshe, and Elizabeth Ramsey. "A developmental perspective in antisocial behavior." *American Psychologist* 44 (2) (1989): 329–35.

Payne, Kim John. *Simplicity Parenting.* New York: Ballantine Books.

Perry, Bruce. "Childhood experience and the expression of genetic potential: What childhood neglect tells us about nature and nurture." *Brain and Mind* 3 (2002): 79–100.

———, M. Brown-O'Connor, D. Runyan, G. Walter, J. Rubenstein. "Relationships between early experiences and long-term functioning: The role of affect development in adjudicated adolescent males." Feb. 2, 2002. www.childtrauma.org/apsac_rel_between_early_exp.htm.

———, and Maia Szalavitz. *The Boy Who Was Raised as a Dog.* New York: Basic Books.

Pert, Candace B. *Molecules of Emotion.* New York, NY: Scribner, 2006.

Phillips, D. Testimony before the U.S. Senate Committee on Labor and Human Resources. March 1, 1995.

Pollack, William. *Real Boys: Rescuing Our Sons from the Myths of Boyhood*. New York: Owl Books, 1999.

Punger, Denise. "A physician's personal experience with a doula." *Attachment Parenting*, New Baby Issue 3, 2005.

Rados, Carlos. "FDA cautions against ultrasound 'keepsake' images." *FDA Consumer*, 2013. https://secure.sdms.org/pdf/FDAKeepsake.pdf.

Reiss, David, Jenae M. Neiderhiser, E. Mavis Hetherington, and Robert Plomin. *The Relationship Code: Deciphering Genetic and Social Influences on Adolescent Development*. Cambridge, MA: Harvard University Press, 2000.

Rey, E., and H. Martínez, eds. "Manejo racional del niño prematuro"[Rational management of the premature infant]. In *Curso de medicina fetal y neonatal*, 137–51. Bogotá, Colombia: Universidad Nacional, 1983.

Ruiz-Peláez, Juan G., Nathalie Charpak, and Lius G. Cuervo. "Kangaroo mother care: An example to follow from developing countries." *British Medical Journal* 329 (7475) (2004): 1179–81.

Sagi, A., N. Koren-Karie, M. Gini, Y. Ziv, and T. Joels. "Shedding further light on the effects of various types and quality of early childcare on infant-mother attachment relationship: The Haifa Study of early child care." *Child Development* 73 (4) (2002): 1166–87.

Saunder, S. "Co-bathing as a gentle solution for attachment difficulties." *British Journal of Midwifery* 1 (11) (1998): 716–19.

Scelfo, Julie. "The risks of parenting while plugged in." *New York Times*, June 10, 2010. www.nytimes.com/2010/06/10/garden/10childtech.html?pagewanted=all&_r=0.

Schanberg, Saul M., and Tiffany M. Field. "Sensory deprivation stress and supplemental stimulation in the rat pup and preterm human neonate." *Child Development* 58 (6) (1987): 1431–47.

Schore, Allan N. "The experience-dependent maturation of a regulatory system in the orbital prefrontal cortex and the origin of developmental psychopathology." *Development and Psychopathology* 8 (1996): 59–87.

———. *Affect Dysregulation and Disorders of the Self*. New York: W. W. Norton, 2003.

Schwartzbaum, Judith A., Stephen L. George, Charles B. Pratt, and Bertha Davis. "An exploratory study of environmental and medical factors potentially related to childhood cancer." *Medical and Pediatric Oncology* 19 (2) (1991): 115–21.

Sears, William. "Bonding with your newborn." *Attachment Parenting*, New Baby Issue 2, 2004.

Sears, William, and Martha Sears. *Nighttime Parenting*. Chicago (1999): La Leche League International.

———. *The Attachment Parenting Book*. New York: Little, Brown, 2001.

———. "Discipline and behavior: Spanking." Ask Dr Sears, www.askdrsears.com/search/node/Discipline%20and%20behavior%3A%20Spanking.

Segal, Jeanne. "Creating Secure Attachment." Help Guide, 2013. http://www.helpguide.org/video/attachment_sd.htm.

Shaffer, David R. *Developmental Psychology: Childhood and Adolescence*. Pacific Grove, CA: Brookes/Cole, 1999.

Shaw, Benjamin A., Neal Krause, Linda M. Chatters, Cathleen M. Connell, and Berit Ingersoll-Dayton. "Emotional support from parents early in life, aging, and health." *Psychology and Aging* 19 (1) (2004): 4–12.

Siddiqui, B., and M. E. Hagglöf. "An exploration of prenatal attachment in Swedish expectant women." *Journal of Reproductive and Infant Psychology* 17 (4) (1999): 369–80.

Sidebotham, P., and the Avon Longitudinal Study of Parents and Children (ALSPAC). "Culture, stress, and the parent-child relationship: A qualitative study of parents' perceptions." *Child: Care, Health, and Development* 27 (6) (2001): 469–85.

Siegel, Daniel. *The Developing Mind: How Relationships and the Brain Interact to Shape Who We Are*. New York: Guilford Press, 1999.

Siegel, Daniel, and Mary Hartzell. *Parenting from the Inside Out*. New York, NY: Tarcher, 2004.

Silver, Amy. "Interview with Reedy and P. J. Hickey." *Attachment Parenting* 7 (2) (2004a): 1.

———. "Slings and attachment parenting." *Attachment Parenting* 7 (2) (2004b): 2.

Stein, M. T., and J. D. Call. "Extraordinary changes in behavior in an infant after a brief separation." *Journal of Developmental and Behavioral Pediatrics* 22 (2001): 11–12.

Steinberg, Laurence, Julie D. Elmen, and Nina S. Mounts. "Impact of parenting practices on adolescent achievement: Authoritative parenting, psychosocial maturity, and academic success among adolescents." *Child Development* 60 (6) (1989): 1424–36.

———, Susie D. Lamborn, S. M. Dornbusch, and N. Darling. "Impact of parenting practices on adolescent achievement: Authoritative parenting, school involvement, and encouragement to succeed." *Child Development* 63 (5) (1992) : 1266–81.

Stewart, David, and Lee Stewart. "Childrearing, the roots of violence, and the principles of peace." *NAPSAC News* 10 (2) (1985): 15.

St. James-Roberts, Ian, Jane Hurry, J. Bowyer, and R. G. Barr. "Supplementary carrying compared with advice to increase responsive parenting as interventions to prevent persistent infant crying." *Pediatrics* 95 (3) (1995): 381–88.

Straus, Murray A. *Beating the Devil Out of Them: Corporal Punishment in American Families.* New York: Lexington Books, 1994.

———, and Vera E. Mouradian. "Impulsive corporal punishment by mothers and antisocial behavior and impulsiveness of children." *Behavioral Sciences and the Law* 16 (3) (1998): 353–74.

———, D. B. Sugarman, and J. Giles-Sims. "Spanking by parents and subsequent antisocial behavior of children." *Archives of Pediatric and Adolescent Medicine* 151 (1997): 761–67.

Sunderland, Margot. *The Science of Parenting.* New York, NY: DK, 2006.

Tanzer, Deborah. *Why Natural Childbirth?* Garden City, NY: Doubleday, 1972.

Tarkka, Marja-Terttu. "Predictors of maternal competence by first-time mothers when the child is 8 months old: Issues and innovations in nursing practice." *Journal of Advanced Nursing* 41 (3) (2002): 233–40.

Tarkka, Marja-Terttu, Marita Paunonen, and Pekka Laippala. "What contributes to breastfeeding success after childbirth in a maternity ward in Finland?" *Birth: Issues in Perinatal Care* 25 (1998): 175–81.

Thomas, Eleanor M. "Aggressive behaviour outcomes for young children: Change in parenting environment predicts change in behaviour." Statistics Canada Catalogue no. 89-599-MIE. 2004. Available at www5.statcan.gc.ca/bsolc/olc-cel/olc-cel?catno=89-599-MIE2004001&lang=eng.

UNICEF. "The ten steps to successful breastfeeding." Baby Friendly Hospital Initiative, 2008. www.babyfriendlyusa.org/.

U.S. Department of Labor, Bureau of Labor Statistics. *Women in the Labor Force: A Databook.* Washington, DC: U.S. Government Printing Office, 2005.

———. Employment Characteristics of Families Summary, 2012. www.bls.gov/news.release/famee.nr0.htm.

Uvnäs-Moberg, Kerstin. *The Oxytocin Factor.* Translated by Roberta Francis. Cambridge, MA: Da Capo Press, 2003.

———. "Short-term and long-term effects of oxytocin released by suckling and of skin-to-skin contact with mothers and infants." In *Evolution, Early Experience and Human Development*, edited D. Narvaez, J. Panksepp, A. N. Schore, and T. R. Gleason. New York: Oxford University Press, 2013.

Uvnäs-Moberg, Kerstin, and M. Eriksson. "Breastfeeding: Physiological, endocrine, and behavioural adaptations caused by oxytocin and local neurogenic activity in the nipple and mammary gland." *Acta Paediatrica* 85 (1996): 525–30.

Walant, Karen B. *Creating the Capacity for Attachment: Treating Addictions and the Alienated Self.* Northvale, NJ: Jason Aronson, 1995.

Wallerstein, Judith, Julia M. Lewis, and Sandra Blakeslee. *The Unexpected Legacy of Divorce: A 25-Year Landmark Study.* New York: Hyperion, 2000.

Watson, John B. *Psychological Care of Infant and Child.* New York: W. W. Norton, 1928.

Weisfeld, G. E. *Principles of Human Adolescence.* New York: Basic Books, 1999.

Weiss, Bahr, Kenneth A. Dodge, J. E. Bates, and G. S. Pettit. "Some consequences of early harsh discipline: Child aggression and maladaptive social information processing style." *Child Development* 63 (6) (1992): 1321–35.

DONA International n.d. "What is a doula?" website, www.dona.org/mothers.

Widström, A. M., A. B. Ransjo-Arvidson, K. Christensson, A. S. Matthiesen, J. Winberg, and K. Uvnäs-Moberg. "Gastric suction in healthy newborn infants: Effects on circulation and developing feeding behaviour." *Acta Paediatrica Scandinavica* 76 (1987): 566–72.

Wiessinger, Diane, Diana West, and Teresa Pitman. *The Womanly Art of Breastfeeding.* New York: Ballantine Books, 2010.

Witman-Flann, L. "Parent-child cosleeping: The impact on family relationships." (PhD dissertation, Pacific Graduate School of Psychology, CA, 1991).

———. "Global strategy for infant and young child feeding." 2002. www.who.int/nutrition/topics/global_strategy/en/.

World Health Organization n.d. "Breastfeeding." http://search.who.int/search?q=breast feeding&ie=utf8&site=who&client=_en&proxystylesheet=_en&output=xml_no_dtd&oe=utf8&getfields=doctype.

Yeh, Elaine S., L. M. Rochette, L. B. McKenzie, and G. A. Smith. "Injuries associated with cribs, playpens, and bassinets among young children in the US, 1990–2008." *Pediatrics* 127 (3) (2011): 479–86.

Young, T. K., P. J. Martens, S. P. Taback, E. A. Sellers, H. J. Dean, M. Cheang, and B. Flette. "Type 2 diabetes mellitus in children: Prenatal and early infancy risk factors among native Canadians." *Archives of Pediatric and Adolescent Medicine* 156 (7) (2002): 651–55.

Zahn-Waxler, Carolyn, Marian Radke-Yarrow, and Robert A. King. "Child rearing and children's prosocial initiations toward victims of distress." *Child Development* 50 (2) (1979): 319–30.

Zhou, Qing, Nancy Eisenberg, Sandra H. Losoya, Richard A. Fabes, Mark Reiser, Ivanna K. Guthrie, Bridget C. Murphy, Amanda J. Cumberland, and Stephanie A. Shepard. "The relations of parental warmth and positive expressiveness to children's empathy-related responding and social functioning: A longitudinal study." *Child Development* 73 (3) (2002): 893–915.

Index

About Attachment Parenting International

Attachment Parenting International (API) is a 501(c)3 nonprofit grassroots organization that offers parents and professionals education about attachment parenting and support through local support groups with trained facilitators, publications, research information, e-newsletters, website information, and online forums. API also functions as a clearinghouse of information on all aspects of child and family-related topics and engages in advocacy work on behalf of children and parents.

The mission of API is to support all parents in raising secure, joyful, and empathetic children in order to strengthen families and create a more compassionate world. Through education, support, advocacy, and research, our principal goal is to heighten global awareness of the profound significance of secure attachment—not only to invest in our children's bright futures but also to reduce and ultimately prevent emotional and physical mistreatment of children, addiction, crime, behavioral disorders, mental illness, and other outcomes of early unhealthy attachment.

nurturing children for a compassionate world

The Training You've Been Waiting for is Here!

Be One of the First Trained in the Only Attachment Parenting Curriculum Ever Created Based on the Award-Winning Book- Attached at the Heart!

If you are interested in expanding your knowledge of attachment parenting, learning cutting-edge research that supports the *Eight Principles of Parenting* and teaching parents these new concepts, this training is for you! We welcome mental health professionals, childbirth educators, doulas, La Leche League Leaders, child development specialists pediatricians, nurses, family law attorneys, social workers, and anyone who works with children and families.

Our two-day training will enhance your professional skills and knowledge about child and neurological development. You will learn the fundamentals of positive parenting with new strategies you can teach the parents you serve.

Please join us in spreading the message of attachment parenting to help all parents raise connected and compassionate children.

Lysa and Barbara
Cofounders, Attachment Parenting International

Check out current trainings and apply at:
www.attachmentparenting.org/parented.php

You will learn:
- ♥ The basics of attachment theory
- ♥ Why attachment is critically important for the family and society
- ♥ Attachment parenting as defined by API
- ♥ Cultural myths about parenting
- ♥ The myths about AP
- ♥ Hands on strategies and activities for teaching the parents you serve
- ♥ And much more!

Training includes:
- ♡ Ten step-by-step lesson plans, complete with downloadable materials, music, videos, activities, parenting tips, and parent handouts
- ♡ Two full days of training with an option for CEUs
- ♡ Training in using the **Adult-Adolescent Parenting Inventory (AAPI-2)**
- ♡ On-site healthy lunch is included for two days

DON'T MISS OUT!

Contact us to schedule
training in your area:

training@attachmentparenting.org

attachment
parenting
INTERNATIONAL

nurturing children for a compassionate world

About the Authors

Barbara Nicholson received a master's degree in education from Stephen F. Austin State University and a bachelor's degree in education from North Texas State University, with learning disabilities certification from Texas Women's University. Professionally she has taught children with learning disabilities and has been a La Leche League International support group facilitator for more than twenty-five years, educating and helping mothers with breastfeeding. In 1994, Barbara cofounded Attachment Parenting International (API), a nonprofit parent education organization, where she served as president of the board of directors for fifteen years. As API cofounder, she has given talks and conducted parenting workshops all over the country and internationally on attachment-parenting issues. She is the mother of four grown sons and lives with her husband in Nashville, Tennessee.

Lysa Parker received her bachelor's degree in education and her master's degree in human development and family studies from the University of Alabama. She earned her designation of Certified Family Life Educator (CFLE) from the National Council on Family Relations in 2004. As cofounder of Attachment Parenting International (API), she served as the executive director for thirteen years, focusing on program development, public relations, and fund-raising. Before her involvement with API, she worked as a special education teacher helping children with multiple handicaps and learning difficulties. She is married and is the mother of two grown sons and a stepdaughter and is the grandmother of three. Currently Lysa is a writer, speaker, and parenting consultant in private practice at www.parentslifeline.com.

Made in the
USA
Lexington, KY

55669904R00186